IMAGES OF

Cultural Responses to Psychoanalysis

Images of Freud

CULTURAL RESPONSES TO PSYCHOANALYSIS

Barry Richards

J. M. DENT & SONS LTD
LONDON

First published 1989
©Barry Richards, 1989

This book is set in $10\frac{1}{2}$/$11\frac{1}{2}$pt Baskerville

Made in Great Britain by
Butler & Tanner Ltd, Frome and London for
J. M. Dent & Sons Ltd
91 Clapham High Street, London SW4 7TA

British Library Cataloguing in Publication Data

Richards, Barry
    Images of Freud: cultural responses to
psychoanalysis.
    1. Psychoanalysis. Social aspects
    I. Title
    150.19'5

ISBN 0-460-02490-6

CONTENTS

PREFACE

This is a book about ideas in psychology, and about the social and moral meanings that such ideas can have outside of psychology, in the wider culture. Ideas are not just ideas; they serve to initiate, organize, justify and reproduce action. So in reading and writing about ideas we can make some input to practical considerations about social conduct.

This book is mainly about what can happen to ideas at a particular kind of location in culture, namely at those points where the esoteric ideas of an elaborate theory are drawn into the polyphonic chaos of thinking that comprises an intellectual culture in the widest sense. Specifically, I trace some of the mutations undergone by psychoanalytic ideas as they have been received and passed on in various fields of psychology, and have thus been funnelled out into our everyday thinking about ourselves. Chaotic though this thinking is, it also reflects the persistent influence of certain basic values or preconceptions, which are active throughout our intellectual culture.

These values are, broadly speaking, those of utilitarianism and of romanticism. Though in many ways divergent, these two outlooks are joined in opposition to a vision of the tragic separateness yet interdependence of human lives. Such a vision is the deepest contribution psychoanalysis has to make to contemporary thought, but is often obscured by more superficial or wishful readings of Freud, which play up other elements in the psychoanalytic tradition. At the heart of these readings, when they are themselves viewed psychoanalytically, there is a degree of incapacity to accept the most difficult fact which early in life we are required to learn. This is that other people exist, with needs and desires which inevitably restrict our freedom, not least because we need others – indeed we are in a way constituted by them.

Although, therefore, the empirical focus of the book is quite narrow – on a few chapters in the history of psychological thought – there is a broader intention at work here, and a larger objective: to identify the denial of the other as a significant force in the unconscious dimensions of theoretical and moral choice.

This has been a difficult book to write, for a number of reasons at least some of which are linked to the basic aims of my undertaking. Firstly, I have attempted to write both for those with some specialist knowledge of the topics concerned, and also for the 'general reader', or at least for some of those who may be covered by that term. I hope, for example, that some students and teachers of psychology and the social sciences will find here a useful addition to their reading on general psychological theory, one giving a different perspective on psychoanalysis to that offered by many other sources they are likely to read. On the other hand, some psychotherapists and other welfare professionals who are well versed in the theories I discuss may find something new in my attempt to locate those theories in philosophical and moral contexts. And for readers who may be familiar with the general issues raised here in social and cultural analysis, there is I hope some interest in the specific analyses I make of the cultural and political significance of psychological ideas.

Those familiar with the work of Philip Rieff may quickly orient themselves to some of my main concerns, since without the framework set by his essays on Freud and culture[1] I could not have defined the project of this book. I am also following in a direction indicated partly by the writings of Christopher Lasch and others on the psychoanalytic study of culture and the history of ideas, and partly by British traditions of psychoanalytic theorizing. (Of course, those with whom I think I am in substantial agreement on some matters may not themselves hold the same view.)

Inevitably I will have failed to write equally appropriately at all times for all intended readers. Parts of the book may be obscure to some, while other parts will seem commonplace. I must hope everyone will feel that in the end, and overall, there is enough stimulus here for new thought.

Listing some of the different potential readers of the book highlights another of its aims, and difficulties. It is an attempt at an interdisciplinary work, at a bringing together of psychoanalysis, philosophy, social and cultural theory, and the history of ideas. Interdisciplinary work around psychoanalysis is now a growing area of study, and I have no doubt about its importance, but it is one where it is easy for ambition to outstrip ability. No one can claim total competence in the area; in my own case an original training in academic and then clinical psychology provided much relevant experience for it, and my doctoral research, primarily in occupational sociology and the sociology of knowledge, was an initial exploration of the social meanings of psychology. At various times I have been attracted towards, and in some cases involved in, the ideas and work which are criticized here. A long period of teaching, to both undergraduates and practitioners, has given me some opportunity to reflect on the interesting changes that ideas undergo as they circulate in classroom discussions, in textbooks and in students' written work. Lastly, my involvement in the journal *Free Associations* has provided an important and facilitating context for an interdisciplinary approach. I hope to be developing here an adequate strategy for work in this area.

As if this were not enough, there is a third difficulty, again due to the attempt to bridge between or combine different elements. This book is intended as a contribution both to the academic study of psychology in its social context, and to ongoing debates about the nature of contemporary culture, as seen through some uses of psychology. While all academic work in the social sciences, even the most self-consciously 'objective', is also necessarily some kind of implicit contribution to such debates, there is a tension between the aims of scholarly research and those of partisan argumentation. Works of cultural critique which attempt to combine the two risk being found over-polemical by one group of readers, and excessively academic or specialized by another. Nonetheless, it seems to me that the understanding of the history of psychology can be enhanced by an approach which has an explicit moral delivery, and conversely that a moral critique of some aspects of contemporary culture is strengthened if it can be based upon detailed historical and textual research.

Finally, I have found it difficult at times to keep going at the negative task of criticism. A few years ago this might have been no problem. I was introduced to psychological and social theory at a time (the late 1960s) when the negative work of criticizing others was widely regarded as the most important and constructive thing to do. All advances and new insights seemed to require, or even to consist of, detailed refutations and condemnations of what already existed. However necessary or useful such negativity may have been at that time, in the late 1980s things are very different. A persistent preoccupation with the critique of others seems at best an inadequate, impoverished approach to intellectual work, and at worst an expression of the critic's own sourness of mind. And yet it is arguably always one task of intellectuals to think and write about what seem to them to be falsehoods, to try to understand and oppose them. The problem is how to combine that task in the right proportions with more constructive, generous and conciliatory theorizing.

So this book addresses readers at different levels and in different disciplines; it does so with more than one aim, and with some internal tensions. The justification for such an ambitiously integrative project is that the need for more work that is interdisciplinary and critical is very great, and no less so in books for a wider readership than in works of more specialized theory. As I shall be arguing, many of the apparently 'straightforward' introductions to psychoanalytic ideas in psychology books present particularly narrow views of it, and sometimes very inaccurate ones. And there is certainly a case for students of any subject to be introduced to material in ways which take on board from the beginning its social and moral meanings. There is also a case for bringing together between the covers of one book some of the concerns and preoccupations of the psychoanalytically influenced practitioner, of the social scientist, and of the politically minded intellectual. In this attempt to do so there will be found, I hope, a broad introduction to psychoanalytic thinking, a study in the history of ideas, and a contribution to some of the current debates about politics and culture.

ACKNOWLEDGMENTS

I am very much indebted to a number of people who have read and commented on drafts of parts of this book, or discussed some of its contents and its problems with me: Philip Boys, Karl Figlio, Christoph Hering, Paul Hoggett, Russell Keat, Rosalind Leigh, Michael Rustin, Amal Treacher, Anna Witham, and Robert Young. In a general and deep way, my colleagues on the editorial board of *Free Associations* have provided a base and a space for the work of which this is a part. My colleagues in the Department of Sociology at North East London Polytechnic have provided space for writing in a very concrete way, by relieving me of a substantial amount of teaching during the academic year 1987–88. I am grateful to Kay Edge for help with the index. Jocelyn Burton has been as supportive and flexible an editor as one could wish for, and the book owes its existence to her initiative in looking for a work on the contemporary significance of psychoanalytic ideas. In a different way, the book owes its existence to Janet Richards. I do hope it does some justice to those who have helped it along.

1

INTRODUCTION: FREUD IN CULTURE

The Consumption of Psychoanalysis

In societies where the consumption of goods is a prominent feature of life, it is not only material goods which are consumed. As many social critics have long observed, a consumerist spirit tends to invade all spheres of life, permeating our experiences of relationships with people as well as with manufactured things.

There are many facets to this development, and it is wrong to be one-sidedly doleful about it. However we are subject to a lot of propaganda, mainly through advertising, about the benefits of consumption and its promises of happiness, so that it has been necessary for social theory to focus on the limits of consumption as a way of life, and on the lies it sometimes involves. Whether it is carried on reclusively or ostentatiously, consumption is generally an individualized activity, corrosive of communal bonds. It serves to promote hedonism above altruism, and to emphasize market values rather than moral values. It encourages a dominative, destructive approach to the world and its resources, which are seen to exist only in order to be consumed, used up.

Our ways of understanding ourselves can also be affected by the prevailing ethos of consumption. Psychological theories and techniques of psychological therapy can be promoted and consumed in ways that are often close to the marketing and consumption of consumer goods. This has happened, to some extent, to the therapeutic techniques offered by psychoanalysis. The popular image of psychoanalysis as a luxury appurtenance for wealthy neurotics, while not a true picture of its overall standing, does point towards one aspect of its absorption into consumer culture. In this book, the focus is not on the consumption of psychoanalytic therapies but on the consumption of psychoanalytic ideas, on some of the ways in which those ideas have been understood and responded to.

These responses to psychoanalysis are shaped by philosophical outlooks which themselves have deep affinities with consumer culture – the philosophies of utilitarianism and romanticism. Freud is seen (whether approvingly or not) as having restated some of the basic principles of one or the other of these philosophies. Yet while it is true that psychoanalysis itself was indeed shaped to some degree by these powerful intellectual traditions, it has also developed as a challenge to them. This element of challenge is lost in the images of Freud and his theory which predominate in our culture. So our intellectual culture consumes Freud, by assimilating his ideas to psychological theories rooted in our experience of ourselves as consumers, and thereby also consuming him in the sense of destroying the most original and fruitful parts of his work.

The Fluctuating Fortunes of Psychoanalysis

Recently the reading public has had to cope with a great many books about Freud. Beginning in the mid-1970s, and continuing through the 1980s, publishers' lists – outside of the specialist pyschoanalytic press have been swelling with titles about psychoanalysis and its founder. Fifty years after his death, knowledge of and interest in Freud and psychoanalysis have been growing, on various fronts.

In the case of Britain, there has for example been a very considerable increase in the practice of psychoanalytic psychotherapy. This has been mainly in the private and voluntary sectors,[1] though the influence of psychoanalytic thinking upon many professionals in the statutory health and welfare services is growing.

After enjoying a position of considerable influence in the inter-war and immediate post-war periods,[2] psychoanalysis was to some extent overshadowed by the rise of applied behaviourism in the 1950s and 1960s. It was often marginalized, and sometimes rejected, by those coming into the 'caring' professions which were growing within the then expanding welfare state. Later on, though, this decline was reversed, mainly in the wake of the social and intellectual changes of the 1960s, and as a *consequence* of these wider cultural developments rather than as a change begun in the field of welfare practice.

In the broader cultural context, beyond professional helping, the fortunes of psychoanalysis have fluctuated in a similar fashion. Up until and during World War II, psychoanalytic ideas circulated relatively freely amongst academic psychologists and social scientists, and by a variety of different routes exercised an important influence – though often heavily filtered – in some spheres of everyday life. Then, however, a reaction against psychoanalysis occurred. The social sciences narrowed their conceptions of what constituted proper knowledge, and psychoanalysis was often seen as beyond the pale. As a clinical, interpretive practice, psychoanalysis was indeed beyond the limits of the scientific method when that was defined only in terms of observational and quantitative approaches. Outside of academia, too, sceptical and cynical reactions to psychoanalysis became dominant, and the negative image of Freud, with which some later chapters of this book will be concerned, took shape. Banalized, fifth-hand accounts of Freud's alleged theory of sex came to be the most common knowledge about psychoanalysis.

However, in the late 1960s, a number of developments challenged the dominance of many established paradigms, in both the academic and practice settings. The idea that science was the business of making objective, value-free statements about the world (broadly speaking, the 'positivist' conception of science) came under attack from different directions. The concept of all knowledge as socially constructed became axiomatic in many areas of sociological research and theory. A related concern with the political values embedded in different forms of knowledge was introduced by the Marxist schools of thought which were coming to prominence. Psychoanalysis was not at the centre of these developments, but it was a beneficiary of them.[3] Once the restrictive canons of positivism and the naive belief in objectivity were discredited, the case for ignoring psychoanalysis – on the grounds that it was not objective science – was fatally weakened.

Alongside these changes in philosophical climate, there was emergent in the culture of the 'Sixties' an emphasis on personal experience and on subjectivity. There was little that was intrinsically new in this; at one level it was a restatement of some of the characteristic concerns of romanticism[4] with individuality and the inner world. However, these nineteenth-century concerns were being reactivated in a late twentieth-century world which was accustomed both to technological triumph and to proliferating welfare provision. In this context the old concerns fed new demands, for techniques and services to help in the exploration of the inner world.

In the 1960s these demands began a period of explosive growth. Again, psychoanalysis was not in the vanguard of this development; that role fell mostly to the humanistic psychologies, of which more later. However, a new cultural space had been opened up for personal therapy of all sorts, and along with many other schools and techniques psychoanalysis has benefited from this. The behavioural therapies (those aiming at changing *outward* behaviours, without reference to inner states) had been moving towards dominance in many areas of professional practice in the mental health field, but they were unable by definition to meet the surging demand for guided tours of inner worlds.[5]

There have also been some positive reasons for the rising fortunes of psychoanalysis, some specific factors which – in addition to the broad changes of context just described – have worked to place psychoanalysis, rather than some other theory or practice, on a number of contemporary agendas. Feminism led the way in its attempt to use psychoanalysis to throw light on the social construction of gender identities. From this starting point there has grown a large body of work which has drawn upon psychoanalysis for its particular value in studies of sexuality and subjectivity in culture, for example in film studies.

In addition, in the aftermath of the failure of 1968 to lead to social revolution, some political radicals turned to psychoanalysis either as a replacement for or a modification of their revolutionary aspirations. Increasing numbers of people, too, find their way to psychoanalysis after an engagement with some other form of therapeutic work, whether as patient or practitioner, has proved unsatisfying: psychoanalysis is seen as offering greater depth, and a fuller confrontation with the complexity and the negativity of mental life. For therapeutic as well as intellectual purposes, we need a way of thinking that clearly focuses upon the forces of destructiveness and irrationality which seem to predominate in the world.

This picture of the changing fortunes of psychoanalysis must be contrasted with the scenarios sketched out by writers such as Hans Eysenck and Ernest Gellner.[6] There never has been anything as powerful and monolithic as a 'Freudian empire', as Eysenck terms it, nor can we now speak in the past tense of the impact of psychoanalysis, after its alleged 'decline and fall'. Gellner's reference to the psychoanalytic 'movement' may be a little more accurate, since in some ways psychoanalysis does have the characteristics of a social movement, but his suggestion in the opening chapter of his book that psychoanalysis constitutes an intellectual and moral revolution of 'enormous' and 'global' proportions, equivalent to Christianity, is a polemical fancy.

Gellner's bitter portrayal of psychoanalysis as a quasi-religious cult contrasts with the fundamentally appreciative reading of psychoanalysis offered here, not only in its hostility but also in the nothing-but style of his assessment. Psychoanalysis is actually an enormously complex and many-sided phenomenon. In its internal structure of concepts and techniques, and in its external effects upon the wider culture, psychoanalysis has a multiplicity of meanings. It is, amongst other things, a potential source of insight into some of the most pressing problems of our time – not least the threat of nuclear war, racism, and the search for community – and there is a widening awareness of this potential.

Yet although the recent growth of sympathetic interest in psychoanalysis may partly explain the appearance of yet another book on Freud,[7] it does not provide a justification for it. That must be given in the book's aims and content.

Freud in Psychology

At the centre of this book is an attempt to trace the ways in which Freudian ideas have been received and understood in various fields of work, and to draw out a common pattern in the receptions of psychoanalysis. The three fields to be considered are academic psychology, humanistic psychology, and the theories of the radical left. The intention is to look at how psychoanalysis has been understood by writers in these areas, as a means of exploring the general response of contemporary culture to the messages brought by Freud and his successors. The choice of these particular areas rests on the belief that they are of especial importance in the transmission of psychoanalytic ideas into the wider culture.

Official Knowledge and Academic Psychology

Psychoanalysis is widely, and appropriately, thought of as being part of psychology. Psychology today is in some ways a quite clearly defined institution: it is a recognized academic discipline, and entry into the various branches of applied, professional psychology is usually through that discipline. This is not to say that it is necessarily intellectually coherent, which it is not; nor that many activities involving broadly 'psychological' matters (not the least of which is psychotherapy) do not go on largely outside the purview of official psychology. There is nonetheless a powerful institution of official psychology, and many people inside and outside this institution believe that within it can be found the most authoritative statements about psychoanalysis.

The problem here is that although psychoanalysis is, in broad and commonsense terms, part of psychology, it is not part of *official* psychology. The professional practice of psychoanalysis has, for a number of historical reasons, proceeded largely separately from academically based psychology, and many authorities on psychoanalysis are not psychologists. This is partly because official psychology has sought to exclude psychoanalysis from its domain, using the philosophical arguments about its allegedly unscientific nature. Positivism survived the onslaught of the Sixties (though not without some modifications), and thus the active exclusion of psychoanalysis is still a force to be reckoned with.

The separation of psychoanalysis from official psychology is also, however, due to the ties between psychoanalysis and medicine, from which official psychology has often been concerned to disentangle itself. These ties are weak in Britain, where non-medical people have always been able to became psychoanalysts, but are still strong – albeit controversial– in the United States. They exist mainly because psychoanalysis has developed, especially in its early days, as a therapy for the emotionally distressed, and has therefore been closely linked to psychiatry, which is historically a branch of medicine.

So close have the links between psychoanalysis and medical psychiatry seemed to some observers that it is not unusual to find psychoanalysis pejoratively described as a version of the 'medical model'. This is the now much-criticized application of a medical conception of disease process to the conceptualization of mental disorder, so that emotional distress is seen as a physiologically based condition requiring medical supervision. Psychoanalysis in

6

fact has very little necessarily in common with 'medical models' in psychiatry, but as we shall see the facts about psychoanalysis are not always prominent in many responses to it. Also, there have in any case been enough people inside psychoanalysis ready to don the mantle of medical authority for this characterization of psychoanalysis to have some credibility.

Nevertheless, despite the widespread perception of its links with medicine, psychoanalysis is still seen by a lay public unconcerned with the finer points of disciplinary demarcations as a part of psychology. Official psychology is likely to be regarded by many lay persons as a source of reliable information about psycho-analysis, and so official psychology is arguably the most important medium through which psychoanalytic ideas are transmitted into the wider culture. Whatever conceptions or misconceptions we may find there about psychoanalysis should therefore tell us a great deal about what 'Freud' is seen to stand for, and about how our culture is seeking to accommodate him. At the intellectual heart of official psychology is the content of approved psychology courses, especially at degree level. Accordingly the research on which Chapter 4 is based consisted of a study of the representations of psychoanalysis found in some of the undergraduate textbooks of fundamental psychology currently or recently in use in Britain. (Many of these texts are American, and so here as elsewhere in the book the conclusions drawn probably have some validity not only in Britain but throughout the Anglophone world.)

Therapeutic Services and Humanistic Psychology

Psychoanalytic ideas are a complex tangle of theory, based upon a highly specialized practice found only in metropolitan centres. As such, they must appear in the general culture of the intel-ligentsia (for example, in book reviews in the 'quality' papers) in simplified and probably modified ways. A fortiori, their percolation into the commonsense culture of the whole society (for example, in the problem pages of the 'tabloid' press) will involve a substantial reworking of their content. Psychoanalysis is not unique in this respect; advocates of many complex sets of ideas may have cause to complain about the metamorphoses the ideas undergo in the process of becoming common knowledge.

Notwithstanding the fame and notoriety attached to the name 'Freud', and despite the recent growth of interest in psycho-analysis, the reading and thinking public outside of the specialist psychoanalytic community has had very little direct contact with the literature of psychoanalysis, much of which is formidably technical. One of the reasons for this is that official psychology, instead of being a duct through which psychoanalytic theory might have flowed outwards to a larger audience, is itself remote from psychoanalysis.

Another reason is related to the very small scale of psychoanalytic practice. Psychoanalytic therapy[8] is an intensive and expensive affair which cannot be available to more than a small minority of those who might be able to benefit from it. Many psychoanalytic practitioners are aware of this inherent constraint upon the social value of their work, and seek to overcome it by working as supervisors and consultants to a wide range of other practitioners – social workers, GPs, health visitors, teachers and so on – in diverse health, welfare and educational settings. Through such work, the practical insights that psychoanalysis may be able to offer into states of emotional distress and interpersonal conflict can be deployed beyond the consulting room. The Tavistock Centre in London has always had this 'missionary' project as one of its central aims.[9]

However this project cannot multiply the resources of psychoanalytic expertise in such a way that they would then be sufficient to meet directly the demand for therapeutic services. Even prior to its most recent growth, demand had been expanding throughout this century, and has been met by a very large number of techniques, cults, salesmen and saviours. The notion that we live in a 'therapeutic' society has become an important focus for sociological theory;[10] the importance of therapeutic techniques and terminologies in the establishment of personal identities and in the smooth running of organizations has been frequently observed. The delivery of therapeutic help is a major problem for service planners, who must try to ensure the provision of adequate services in the area of what is now often known generically as 'counselling'. The direct contribution of psychoanalytic work to this area is a relatively small one, and though now growing significantly in Britain, as noted earlier, it is still a minor presence compared with the sum of non-psychoanalytic approaches. (And in the US, where psychoanalysis formerly enjoyed a relatively stronger position, it is now in relative decline.) Chief amongst these non-psychoanalytic approaches now are the 'humanistic' psychologies, which since the 1960s have become established as the most influential paradigms in a number of different areas, for example in many fields of counselling, in education, and in many occupational training contexts.

It is therefore often through the ideas and techniques of one sort or another of humanistic psychology that people become acquainted with the idea of self-exploration, and with some of the turmoil of their inner worlds. For reasons that will be discussed in Chapter 5, humanistic psychology is a powerfully attractive force in contemporary culture, and it has touched the lives of millions who have little or no contact with academic psychology. Much of what is now thought by many people about *other* approaches to psychology is therefore strongly influenced by the views propounded by the humanistic schools.

A study of how psychoanalysis is portrayed in the writings of the leading figures in humanistic psychology promises therefore to be an important way of looking at how psychoanalytic ideas are being transmitted across, and perhaps transmuted within, the wider culture. The results of this study are presented in Chapter 5. It is argued there that in an important sense the humanistic approach is based upon psychoanalytic understanding. Many humanistic psychologists disavow this lineage,[11] and so whereas academic psychology is generally remote from psychoanalysis, the humanistic portrayal of psychoanalysis is – though closer to its subject – often more hostile.

Political Change and Radical Psychology

The third area chosen for the study of the transmission of psycho-analytic ideas is the less clearly defined one of 'radical psychology'. Again the Sixties are an important point of reference here, specifically the revolutionary movements of 1968 and the changes in intellectual life associated with them. In retrospect, the element of grandiose iconoclasm in those movements can more easily be seen. The inadequacy or in some cases falsity of many of the 'critical' perspectives and 'radical' theories that were enunciated has since become apparent – for example the profound re-evaluation of 'anti-psychiatry' and other movements in the field of mental health. Before the 1970s were out it was clear to many erstwhile supporters of these movements that psychiatry is a complex institution, and that hospitalization and drugs are sometimes of invaluable help. As Peter Sedgwick put it, mental illness *is* illness.

Yet there could be no return to a naive positivism, to the different falsities that held sway before the critical storm of '68'. Sedgwick's *Psycho-Politics* is an eloquent example of the new positions reached by a critique of the critiques.[12] This is not to say that *all* was changed, and that no older ideas from the mainstream were still tenable – that would be to reintroduce the self-important belief of the '68' generation that they marked a fundamental turning point in history. But it is to point out that many present-day debates and developments in social thought, and in thinking about the relations between individual and society, have the positions represented by '68' as one of their reference points, if only implicitly.

For the attempt to be made here to assess something of the place of psychoanalytic ideas in our intellectual culture, therefore, the consideration of how those ideas have been refracted through the lens of '68' is an important undertaking. To do so systematically, however, would have been too large and spreading a project to encompass here, involving the pursuit of at least two divergent lines of thought. In one, psychoanalysis is vigorously rejected, as the epitome of bourgeois ideology. Freud is seen as the arch-reactionary, the patriarchal priest of biologism and apologist for 'Victorian' repressiveness.[13] The intellectual content of this first, completely hostile, line is minimal. Also, with the fading political presence of this and other more simplistic doctrines of the ultra-left, its present-day influence is not very significant. Much of its critique of Freud has been absorbed back into the crude positivism from whence it came – e.g. the dismissal of Freud's ideas as based upon a narrow sample of 'middle-class' patients.

In the other line of thought, Freud is partially rehabilitated as a critic of that same repressiveness, albeit a reluctant and sometimes unknowing one. This approach originates in the Freudo-Marxism of the 1920s, and continues in a number of different directions, including some types of neo-Marxism, critical theory, and feminism. Though often no less revolutionary in its political vision than the first, the second line has included some theoretical work which is scholarly and original. It continues to have a productive influence upon interdisciplinary studies of psychoanalysis, and to be an important medium for the transmission of psychoanalytic ideas to the wider public, especially to those members of the intelligentsia whose outlook was crucially formed by the oppositional spirit of '68' and many of whom now occupy positions of influence in education, welfare and the media. It is therefore this more positive approach to psychoanalysis by politically radical writers of the post-1968 period which is the subject of Chapter 6.

The Pursuit of Happiness: Psychological Utilitarianism

Much of this book, therefore, is a study in the cultural history of ideas; specifically, in the recent history of psychoanalytic ideas as they have become established – and in the process changed – in our intellectual culture. Yet it is not a comprehensive and systematic study of the fate of those ideas and the forces which have worked upon them, even within the areas chosen for study.[14] My aim has been to combine adequate but not exhaustive scholarship with some partisan contributions to current thinking and debate.

One of my concerns is with the action upon psychoanalytic ideas of some utilitarian assumptions which hold sway in many areas of intellectual life and commonsense understanding. My contention is that in the cultural transmission of psychoanalytic ideas these assumptions will enter into the popular reformulations of those ideas, and result in rewritten versions of them which somehow conform with the prevailing utilitarian outlook.

The kind of utilitarianism referred to here is *psychological* utilitarianism, the doctrine that individuals are fundamentally motivated by the need to maximize their pleasures and minimize their pains, and that accordingly their mental lives are organized around the calculation of the costs and benefits of different courses of action. This basic psychological theory is frequently associated with, but not logically tied to, the *ethical* utilitarianism which states that the greatest good is that which secures the greatest happiness of the greatest number, the largest overall surplus of pleasure over pain. Jeremy Bentham, the founder in the nineteenth century of utilitarianism as a major school of philosophy, was both a psychological and ethical utilitarian, as is B. F. Skinner, whose theory of behaviourism is the most direct and influential heir in contemporary psychology to Benthamite utilitarianism. However, most psychological thinking is not concerned with questions of social ethics, and so remains within the scope of *psychological* utilitarianism only.

We can trace the influence of this utilitarianism upon the reception of psychoanalytic ideas, in an observable process of change in the content of those ideas. In the course of their cultural diffusion the concepts of psychoanalysis are redefined to bring them into increasing conformity with the tenets of psychological utilitarianism. This is a difficult area, owing to the complexity and multivalence of Freud's own ideas, let alone of the many divergent post-Freudian developments in psychoanalysis. It is certainly possible to find in Freud, and in many post-Freudians, statements which clearly express the utilitarian belief that we all pursue happiness in a calculating way (qualified by the observation that we do not always calculate in a rational fashion). However in Chapter 2 I set out a reading of psychoanalysis which owes little to utilitarian notions, and which to a considerable extent may be posed against them. This non-utilitarian, tragic conception of the human condition is as inherent in Freud's work as any utilitarian position, and more importantly it is much closer than utilitarianism to the values and perspectives of the most important present-day developments within psychoanalysis.

It may be wondered why this process, by which a different and in some ways opposing set of ideas is absorbed into the stream of utilitarian thought, is worth studying. There may of course always be reasons of scholarship, of the pursuit of knowledge for its own sake, for studying any process of influence and change in the history of ideas, but here I am invoking considerations of a more partisan kind, concerned with the relationships between psychological theory on the one hand and morality and politics on the other.

There is no one-to-one relationship between psychological theories and moral positions or political ideologies. The moral outlooks and political sympathies of contemporary psychologists are probably, in many countries, skewed generally in left-liberal and social-democratic directions. This is basically because most psychologists are, whether as human scientists or welfare professionals, very much a part of the broad modern tradition of humane, rational interventionism which has been expressed in such politics. Nonetheless, individual psychologists can be found across the political spectrum, and their theoretical affiliation is no guide to where they will be found. There are behaviourists and psychoanalysts, experimentalists and therapists of right, left and centre. Moreover, the socio-economic restructuring and political rethinking of recent years has in any case brought into question the adequacy of the conventional categories of 'right' and 'left' for describing our main political choices. The social forces and ideologies underpinning these categories are currently fragmenting and recomposing, and one-dimensional descriptions of political positions are now very obviously inadequate.

But even then, we can still point out that psychological theories are part of our cultural stock of ideas, and are therefore necessarily implicated in the conflicts and debates amongst those ideas. We can further observe that there may be some general relationships between the assumptions made in a psychological theory, and an explicit set of moral and political assumptions. Most importantly, the presence of utilitarian preconceptions at the heart of a psychological description ties that description in to utilitarian conceptions of morality and politics.

Those conceptions entail a serious impoverishment of moral sensibility and political vision. Two related features of the utilitarian outlook may be noted in this connection. Firstly, it is an individualistic philosophy, in the sense of taking the individual as the basic unit of analysis and as an original and irreducible entity. The individual's fundamental needs and desires are taken as given; the individual is an absolute agent, and is the only locus of social action. This is 'individualism' in the philosophical sense, as an epistemological or ontological principle (i.e. as a statement of what can be known, or of what exists), and is to be distinguished from 'individualism' in the more everyday and often pejorative sense of pursuing self-interest. Philosophical individualism (sometimes called 'methodological individualism', since it is about how to approach the study of social life) may be used to provide a rationalization for an ethic of self-interest, but it may also be espoused alongside a collectivistic political doctrine.

However, all forms of individualism have common roots in market society (see Chapter 7), and all are opposed by more social and relational understandings of the individual and of social processes. The latter approaches do not necessarily reject the principle that individuals, once grown, are responsible for their conduct and even to some degree for their fate, but they stress the basic constitution of individual subjectivity in relations with others, the social mediation of all desires, and the effectivity of various *group* processes. The position taken here is that some such relational conception of individuality is necessary both for an adequate understanding of individuals and for the development of practical, political approaches to contemporary social problems of conflict and disorder.

Secondly, psychological utilitarianism is essentially a doctrine of hedonism: pleasure and pain are the determinants of action. Pleasure and pain might be defined very widely, to include for example pleasure in the happiness of others. Yet still the role of moral feelings, such as concern for others and a sense of civic responsibility, is necessarily seen as secondary, derivative and marginal. An amoralizing streak is relentlessly at work in the utilitarian mind.

Opposed to this are conceptions of emotional development such as that drawn from psychoanalysis and outlined in Chapter 2, according to which the growth of a moral capacity must be recognized as central to the development of subjectivity, and the vicissitudes of moral feeling to be a key consideration for political theory and strategy.

The importance of psychological utilitarianism, and the reason why its influence on psychological theories is worth studying, is then that it makes particular sorts of input to moral and political discourse, taken here to be disabling ones. Our ideas about politics and society come from all sorts of different sources, but of particular importance amongst these are the dominant conceptions of our psychological nature. Many questions of policy (for example, about tax structure and about welfare provision) are decided by appeal to one view or another about what people are basically like (for example whether we do or do not need tax incentives to work harder, or whether our personal initiative can be undermined by guaranteed welfare benefits). The ideological affiliations of psychological theories are not merely a topic of academic interest, but are of practical importance in so far as they help to shape the political outlooks of the many people who are in contact with them. Hence the concern here to identify utilitarian readings of psychoanalysis and to oppose them with a more relational and moral conception of the individual.

The influence of psychological utilitarianism upon academic psychology's rendering of psychoanalysis (described in Chapter 4) is to be expected, given the historical strength of behaviourism in official psychology. The hypothesis that a similar influence can be found at work in the humanistic and radical traditions of psychology may be more surprising, since these traditions are often represented as offering fundamental alternatives to official psychology and its sterile philosophical base, and as owing more to romantic expressivism than to the rational cost-benefit accounting of Bentham. What Chapter 5 reports is that in humanistic psychology the official, utilitarian reading of Freud found in academic psychology is taken as the genuine article, and that Freud is then criticized for having done the sums wrongly. Freud saw the benefits of repression as outweighing its costs; this, say the humanists, is an error based on his mistaken belief that nothing but evil lurked in the repressed unconscious. In their critique, as in the version of psychoanalysis which they attack, there predominate individualistic and hedonistic concerns with happiness and pleasure.

Something similar can be seen to have taken place in radical psychology (Chapter 6). While methodological individualism is rejected here, the preoccupation with individual happiness persists. Freud is again accused of having got the cost-benefit analysis wrong, this time because he erroneously believed the benefits of repression to be necessary for civilization, rather than for particular social orders. In a different social order, the costs of repression to individuals, which Freud had believed to be inevitable, need not all be paid – so implies much of the radical appropriation of psychoanalysis. Here, as in humanistic psychology, the relational and moral vision of psychological nature which can be derived from Freud is neglected.

The Pursuit of Happiness: Romantic Transcendence

While utilitarianism remains an important reference point in all three areas studied, in the discourses of humanistic and radical psychology an overlapping but separable theme emerges and claims priority. Hedonic maximization, or happiness, is for utilitarianism the ultimate goal and value of life, but there is no level of happiness regarded as a necessary minimum: we simply get the most we can, whatever that might be for the particular and general circumstances we find ourselves in. There is, however, another kind of concern with happiness, which owes less to utilitarianism than to the philosophical tradition which is often seen as bearing one of the most important refusals of the calculating spirit of utilitarianism, namely romanticism.

In this second kind of concern with happiness, what counts is the absolute level of satisfaction achieved, rather than the relative amounts of pleasure and pain. There is also a strong preoccupation with particular qualities of experience as necessary for the attainment of happiness, rather than with some general, abstract total of happiness. Above all, the qualities of freedom, self-expression, and unity with nature are seen as the necessary and possible conditions of happiness.

These three conditions are often closely related together. The 'freedom' invoked is from internal as well as external constraints; it is in large part the freedom to express oneself, which results in a harmonious fusion with nature since this is our natural, true condition. In conditions of unfreedom, we are unable to realize ourselves and so remain alienated from nature. On this view, happiness is not merely an individual, selfish goal; it is a moral and spiritual imperative. Happiness and truth are one. In this romantic ideal, happiness is not to be found in the small adjustments of prosaic utilitarianism, the halfpence of difference between income and outgoings, or pleasures and pains. It is to be found by breaking through into a new realm of experience, by transcending the ordinary limitations of life.

This liberatory impulse may be given either an internal or external emphasis – that is, the shackles to be cast off may be seen either as primarily psychological and self-inflicted, or as primarily social and imposed by others. Ultimately, the former emphasis usually reduces to the latter, in that self-enslavement is seen as being due to our succumbing to some social pressure towards untruth and alienation. There is an important difference, though, in whether the remedy for this condition is seen as lying primarily in the social domain or as being – despite the ultimately social causation of our malaise – accessible to *individual* action. Broadly speaking, we find humanistic psychology tending towards the belief in individuals' capacity to redeem themselves by acts of will, while in radical psychology there is an insistence upon social and collective modes of action as the only effective cure.

These two bodies of thought share, however, the belief in a transcendent condition of happiness and its pursuit through a rejection of the actually existing ordinariness of life. Whether unhappiness is attributed to failures to 'self-actualize', as by the humanists, or to capitalist or patriarchal social relations, as in much radical psychology, it is contrasted with an extraordinary realm of possibility.

In the world of the humanists' self-actualized person, or of the society which has undergone a revolutionary transformation unhappiness exists, but at a secondary level. It is an episodic and contingent condition, recognized as an inevitable part of life but contained and surrounded by positive experience. In the basic ground of their being, people in these scenarios are not vulnerable to limitless pain, nor do they suffer a sense of conflict or loss in the depths of their souls. Life is not to be endured, but celebrated. The party need not be disturbed by chronic illness or death, since these too can become special sources of emotional enrichment,[15] or occasions for the excellence of post-revolutionary welfare services to manifest itself.

Happiness and Justice

The orientation of radical psychology towards social, collective transformation does, though, distinguish it sharply from much humanistic psychology in one important respect. For the political radical, happiness is indivisible, in the sense that for one to have it, all must have it. No-one can rest content while a loved one is in distress, and through the extension of modified familial sentiment to unknown peoples, which is the great moral strength of socialist radicalism, no-one can be happy while any others are known to suffer. A sense of individual well-being is necessarily vitiated by all the hungry, ill and abandoned individuals in the world. The characteristic failure of humanistic psychology to register this potential dimension or our relatedness to others is its greatest weakness, and gives to its rhetoric of 'human potential' a feel of moral emptiness.

But what of the politicized forms of psychological theory, and specifically of the politicized readings of psychoanalysis to be discussed in this book? The vision of universal social justice as a precondition for individual happiness may not always be so straightforward, nor so worthy, as might first be thought. It may for some of those proclaiming it have a hidden significance.

This point has for long been made by critics of revolutionary militancy, especially of the militants of '68'. Just recently, in the summer of 1988, there has been a considerable output, on television and in the press, of retrospective and reflective comment on May 1968, and a renewed scrutiny of the deeper meanings of the impulses that took many people 'on to the streets' at that time. Antony King, for example,[16] suggests that the events of May '68 were basically a 'revolt against the human condition', rather than an uprising against specific, changeable conditions attributable to the malign forces of capitalism and imperialism. He suggests that the anti-war protesters had no really sincere concern for the Vietnamese people, but used the US involvement in Vietnam as a cover for the expression of their yearnings, not for a different social order but for an unattainable escape from the pains of life.

In Chapter 6 there is an exploration of the idea that the left's appropriation of psychoanalysis has *in part* expressed such a 'revolt against the human condition'. It will be argued that there is a tendency to see justice not merely as a necessary precondition for happiness but as a *sufficient* condition for it, an implicit belief that the arrival of justice throughout the world would automatically entail the departure of unhappiness. Hidden in and animating the demand for social justice can be the demand for happiness: happiness for all, perhaps, ostensibly, but happiness conceived of in such a way as to betray that its basic meaning here is the happiness – transcendent, extraordinary happiness – of the individual making the demand.

This critique of radical programmes is not meant to be an exhaustive analysis of their psychological and moral meanings, nor a simple endorsement of views such as that of King, who writes of '68' at a dangerous level of generality. There are whole complexes of contradictory feelings around and supporting the more sophisticated radical readings of Freud, and only one dimension of these feelings is focused on here. This selectivity is tied to the hope that a clearer understanding of the more obscure and irrational sources of political idealism can help to strengthen the forces of rational protest. These forces are probably now more in need of strengthening than they were twenty years ago, however critical we may be, with hindsight, about the impulse of '68'.

In the late 1980s some of the main political and cultural forms taken by the demand for absolute happiness are of a different kind, less easily tempered with authentic demands for justice. For example in the US there is the power of 'born again' religiosity, with its apocalyptic promise of deliverance, and the growth of 'New Age' spirituality with its gentler paths to harmony. The latter is matched by many similar developments in Britain (e.g. in the expanding number of spiritual and therapeutic cults), though these cohere less here as an identifiable social phenomenon. Britain's fascist movement remains in recession, but elsewhere in Europe the fascist pursuit of happiness in a pure and ordered world seems again to be gathering force.

In sum, the romantic search for happiness, for deliverance to another order of being in which all the unhappiness characteristic of the actually existing world is left behind, can take a variety of forms, both in psychological theory and in political ideology. The quest for happiness needs to be distinguished from the struggle for social justice. Justice may be attainable while happiness is not, and when the need for happiness predominates then it may be difficult to pursue a struggle for justice in an effective way.

Tragedy and Endurance

The view of the human condition as an intrinsically unhappy one is at the centre of Freud's challenge to utilitarian and romantic philosophies. It is famously expressed in Freud's comment that the aim of psychoanalysis is to return the patient from the condition of neurotic misery to that of common unhappiness. In this kind of perspective, one version of which is outlined in Chapter 2, our lives are seen as inevitably grounded in tragedy, which has several sources in the biosocial limits and pressures of our existence. Our total helplessness as babies, modified later into the dependence and impotence of the child, is a material and social fact with the most profound implications for our psychological development. However successfully we might move on to an experience of adult autonomy and potency, we are left with a permanent capacity for terror at the prospect of abandonment, and a deep readiness for feelings of frustration and belittlement.

Also, we never fully give up the infantile illusions of omnipotence and of exclusive possession of another, which are at the start of life the only psychological means at the baby's disposal for coping with the brute fact of its vulnerability. Given adequate care, the infant begins to develop more realistic ways of confronting the world. It takes into its emergent self its experiences of those who care for it and so constructs itself as a person using, so to speak, bits of the persons whom it loves. However, the early illusions are never fully given up, and remain within us. They may become dominant again in times of difficulty, when the actual intractability of the world becomes intolerable. Even when submerged beneath more mature outlooks, they persistently bring a quality of disappointment to our experiences of the real world. They are the main source of the pursuit of happiness, of those fundamentally untroubled states of mind which we imagine can exist, perhaps even that we once knew. When the condition of happiness is seen in the context of our inner worlds and their development, then in a sense we *did* once know it, and indeed still do – it is the ultimate means we have of insulating ourselves from life in the real world, by pretending that we have it, or that it is within our reach.

Furthermore, we have to struggle throughout life with the destructiveness which – for whatever reasons – is an integral part of our psychological make-up. Sometimes it is self-directed, and when it is not we are left guiltily preoccupied with fears of its expression and their consequences. In many popular understandings of Freud, he is seen as important primarily for having drawn attention to the guilt we feel about our sexual impulses, but it is guilt about destructiveness which – in the overall development of the Freudian tradition – emerges as the more fundamental discomfort. Actually, the sexual and aggressive components of psychic striving are anyway typically interwoven – the boy's Oedipal crime, for example, is both to desire his mother *and* to wish to strike down his chief rival for her love.

The part which aggressivity plays in emotional development is complex, since it is arguably a necessary element in the process of self-differentiation as well as a major source of hatred and despair. Moreover, the context in which it plays this part is equally complex, involving not just sexuality but the whole field of relations with others of which the sexual is just one dimension, albeit a crucial one. Most fundamentally, the greatest tragedy with which we must contend is that our relations with others necessarily involve *loss*. People leave, die or are taken away; or they are left behind or rejected. All these losses, and those impersonal ones of place or possession, of health and vigour, are painful not only in themselves but also in what they re-evoke in our minds of the feelings aroused by earlier losses.

The clinical evidence suggests that those fortunate enough to come through childhood without experiencing actual, major loss may have an advantage in later life in that their internal worlds are less ravaged, their expectations less catastrophic than those of others whose early lives were outwardly blighted by death or separation. But no amount of good fortune or successful care can enable us to evade the basic experience of loss, which is written into the core developmental process of separating from parents, of psychological differentiation, and of giving up the infantile illusions of possession and control. So we are all subject to the inward blight of felt loss; as Chapter 2 will describe, loss is *constitutive* of the developing self.

In this psychoanalytic understanding of the darkness of the soul, the themes of loss and guilt become at times fused, since one may feel (without, often, any rational justification) that one has brought the loss upon oneself through one's aggression towards the person who has gone away, or died.[17] Also, many experiences not obviously connected with loss make more sense when they are understood as being mediated through the existential frame of loss – for example the undertow of anxiety in positive, gainful experiences of change and moving on.

Freud reflected upon the different responses we make to our tragic situation, and saw these as basically of two kinds. There are evasive responses, and resigned ones. In the former, we seek somehow to evade or transcend the reality of our inner and outer worlds and the burdens of pain which we have to carry in them. We pursue diverting consolations, or imagine that we have forgotten our fears, and become happy. In the latter, we make continual attempts to confront our tragedy, to acknowledge and harness our infantile wishes, and to moderate our aggression. It is in his advocacy of this form of modern stoicism that Freud made his most powerful contribution to moral theory, as Philip Rieff has made clear in his momentous analysis of the cultural significance of Freud.[18] In this spirit of clear-sighted resignation to our tragic condition, we aim to integrate and contain within a rationally led self the panic and rage which are the legacy of our early development. Psychoanalytic therapy is the model for and the most systematic form of this approach to life, but the resignation which Freud enjoined upon us is not basically a therapeutic technique: it is a philosophy of life. To live successfully is to endure the disappointment, guilt and fear which are ineradicably within us.

The Freudian philosophy of endurance has not, at least not outside psychoanalysis, found a ready audience. I will be describing some of the ways in which it has been rejected, either explicitly or by ignoring it and deriving a different philosophy from Freud. The focus of this study is on psychological thought, and specifically on how psychoanalysis has been received in three contemporary areas of thinking about mental life, but the issues are wide ones, extending into many areas of philosophy and social thought. What we find in the areas studied is that there are very narrow limits of endurance; there is very little willingness or capacity to live with the kind of self-knowledge towards which Freud pointed. Culturally we do not appear to find the notion of life as endurance a very tenable one, and there are accordingly – as will be seen – severe limits on the extent to which a voice insisting on this notion will be heard, let alone understood.

Two provisos should be made at the outset of this exploration of Freudian stoicism and its refusal in contemporary culture. Firstly, the philosophical and diagnosic critique of happiness to be offered is a critique of a tendency in contemporary thought, of a utilitarian belief in happiness or of a craving for an extraordinary, transcendent state of release and harmony. It is not an attack upon the everyday aspirations of ordinary people to lead contented and satisfying lives, within limits that they may regret but accept. Nor is it a form of intellectual lugubriousness, a denial that *any* sense of well-being is possible, or that experiences of delight or fulfilment may be frequent in many lives, often against the odds.

Secondly, it must be noted that there is a continuing difficulty in distinguishing resignation to the unavoidable from resignation to the possibly avoidable. What are the proper, necessary limits of endurance? While we might fairly easily agree that apartheid and Ethiopian famine are not things which just had or have to be endured, rather than acted against, the distinction becomes harder to make when we consider, say, some of the differentials of income in British society. Psychoanalysis probably has little that is fundamentally new to say about the problems of making such social judgments (though psychoanalytic insights into envy and greed may help to sharpen understanding of our feelings about differences of wealth). But such problems cannot be ignored, and in trying to make a case for Freudian endurance as a basic principle of a psychologically sophisticated morality, we must continually guard against the tendency – also Freudian – to slip towards a political quietism.

Cities and Markets

What has been said so far has probably done little to convey what is attractive about psychoanalysis, except perhaps to those of unusually melancholic temperament. A simple insistence upon the tragedy of human life would not have made Freud an original thinker, and would not have generated the elaborate concepts of psychoanalytic theory. Nor would it have brought new perspectives to some areas of social science in the way that psychoanalysis has done. The question of why and how psychoanalysis has achieved such popularity and influence as it has is an enormously complex one, on which much scholarly effort has been expended.

To some extent, its emergence and development is part of the story of the history of modern psychology, all the founding schools of which crystallized during the same period in the decades spanning the turn of the century. So some questions about psychoanalysis are questions about the way in which twentieth-century societies have produced 'psychology' as a specialized form of knowledge and set of techniques. Answers to these questions lie largely the study of the military, industrial, commercial and cultural uses of psychological expertise. Beyond this general analysis, though, are questions about the *particular* forms of psychology that we now have. What has psychoanalysis had to offer that distinguishes it from other forms of therapy and other psychological theories?

In Chapter 3 one kind of answer to this question is outlined, as a contribution to the historical understanding of psychoanalysis. It is suggested that the peculiar appeal of psychoanalysis has rested partly in its attempt to *integrate* experience, to find structures of meaning within which even the most bizarre and trivial elements of experience may be located, and so be found to belong to a meaningful whole. This is a very familiar conception of the nature of psychoanalytic therapy; what has been remarked upon less often, and what is stressed here, is the significance of this task in the particular social context in which psychoanalysis developed. This was, and still largely is, the context of the modern metropolitan city.

There is abundant testimony, both literary and social-scientific, to the *fragmented* quality of everyday experience in the modern city environment. That the metropolis presents some kind of assault on the integrity of experience is one of the most common clichés of contemporary life. Obviously we must beware of such received wisdom, but a strong case remains for positing some connection here between cultural experience and the nature of the psychoanalytic approach. In the kaleidoscopic nonsense of modern urban existence, to heal is to put together, to make sense and coherence out of the disconnected bits of experience. Healing integration was offered by many other approaches as well as psychoanalysis, but the Freudian strategy had, in free association, a particularly appropriate and effective method for constructing matrices of meaning from the raw material of experience. And unlike the holistic syntheses promised by contemporaneous cults, it was intended – at least by Freud – to remain truthful to the conflictual core of experience. Its goal was to manage tensions, not to transcend them.

Exactly why the new urban, and especially metropolitan, environments were experienced as so fragmenting of subjectivity is another very large and complex question, involving major problems in social and economic history. Again, just one aspect will be singled out for discussion here, because of its particular relevance to the cultural transmission of psychoanalytic ideas. An important theme in sociological theory has been the social and cultural impact of market relations, as these have come in the capitalist era to dominate economic life and arguably much else besides.

Some varieties of Marxist theory have been particularly eloquent on the tendency of market relations to corrode the affective and moral ties between people, and between individuals and institutions, on which the cohesion of communities depends. While there may be ethical restraints on how business in the marketplace is conducted, market transactions are in essence amoral. What counts is exchange or money value, an abstract quantitative dimension along which specific human qualities and values cannot be measured. Furthermore, the increasing mobility and malleability demanded of labour in competitive capitalist economies help to create a social environment characterized by uncertainty and a sense of the constantly provisional, while the important role of advertising guarantees that we are surrounded with a dense flux of imagery. The major cities of the advanced capitalist economies are the places where these destabilizing pressures are most intense.

It is not only the coherence of communities which has been impaired in this historical process, but the coherence of experience. Some early commentaries on the incoherence of the new urban experience, at the frontiers of market society, are discussed in Chapter 3. The historical opportunity for the integrative healing of psychoanalysis was therefore produced, at least in part, by the disintegrative impact of market forces upon social and psychic organization.

These are highly generalized remarks, and as such are vulnerable to being qualified or falsified in specific empirical contexts. Still, any work concerned with the history of psychoanalytic ideas or

techniques should take some account of this tradition of sociological theorizing, and should consider to what extent the historical
context of psychoanalysis is necessarily that of market society.
Here, where the main focus is upon the transmission and transformation of psychoanalytic ideas, the question that arises is
whether market forces may in some way have determined the
particular transformations that the ideas can be seen to undergo.
In Chapter 7, the utilitarian and romantic reworkings of psychoanalysis described in Chapters 4–6 are considered as intellectual
expressions of market relations, and thereby of the culture of
consumption. The tenacious recovery of illusion, the persistent
rebuilding of ideals of happiness in the shadow of the Freudian
critique of happiness, are important present-day examples of individualistic ideologies which are rooted in market society and the
social relations of consumption. Even within the explicitly anti-
market ideologies of the radical left, the appropriation of psychoanalysis can be understood as embodying the same imperatives
towards individual happiness. The cultural assimilation of Freud
is yet another instance of consumption, of ideas being rethought
in order to incorporate them into consumer culture and its intolerance of pain.

In analysing this assimilation I am attempting not only to
identify the ideological locations of the ideas studied, but also to
reach towards a more psychologically interpretive assessment of
where they come from. In other words there is a *diagnostic* element
in my critique of the banalizations and inversions of Freud, a
suggestion that they reflect the influence of a pathological kind of
mental functioning which is barely able to recognize the existence
and the needs of other people. If these ways of thinking are
expressions of market relations, there is a case for pursuing the
psychoanalytic diagnostic inquiry into those relations themselves,
into the material exchanges between people which are usually
taken to constitute a 'market'. This could both deepen our understanding of the reasons for the particular mutations which we
can see psychoanalytic ideas as undergoing, and also provide an
illustration of the possibilities for using psychoanalytic insights in
the study of social processes.

As we survey attempts to fix the psychological characteristics of
exchange relations, the notion of the 'market' as a constant objective reality becomes, however, more and more elusive. This turns
our attention towards *ideologies* of the market. Why are ideologies

and critiques of 'the market' such a powerful force in political debate, when the market itself is so hard to define? Chapter 7 pursues this question through the analysis of a set of ideas about 'the market', rather than persisting in a psychoanalytic investigation of 'the market' as actual social relations. The particular ideas chosen for analysis are those of the 'neo-liberal', strongly pro-market philosophy, because of their influence on the present-day political climate. These ideas, when considered psychoanalytically, are seen to bear the stamp of the same kind of psychopathology as those forms of psychological thinking evident in the consumption of Freud.

What we find in the neo-liberal eulogy of the market is that the limits of endurance are rapidly reached. The reasons for this are similar to those found in the responses to Freud. The facts of our dependence on others, of their dependence on us, of the inevitable component of guilt in human relationships, and of the renunciation inherent in all responsible human striving, cannot be endured by the neo-liberal mind, any more than they can by the psychologist connoisseurs of happiness.

Yet market relations, however they might be defined, will not go away, and there may in any case be positive reasons for not wanting them to. A central problem in politics is that of how best to manage them, and to what ends. In the concluding chapter, I contend that psychoanalytic thought can make an important contribution to this problem, by helping to distinguish between the illusory and the realistic elements in visions of social change. For what it is worth, the 'Freudian' credentials of this project, that is the authority it can claim in Freud's own writings, are very good indeed.

Psychoanalysis and Interdisciplinary Studies

This book is about ideas and their uses. For the reader of such a book, a host of questions about the origins, validity and status of the arguments it contains – in short about the authority of the book – are raised from the moment the title is glimpsed on a shelf. Arguably, nearly all books raise such questions, since they nearly all have authors. The implicit authority exercised over the reader by the author of fiction, for example, has been discussed in literary criticism. In the case of a non-fictional book about ideas, the authorial voice usually has explicit claim to authority: it is seeking to enlighten or instruct.

For a book such as this which is in large part about psychoanalytic ideas, and particularly about some of the vicissitudes in culture of psychoanalytic ideas, the question of authority is an especially troubling one. What is its claim to authority? It is worth spending a short while looking at some of the problems involved in answering this question. I am assuming that authority can be a real quality of writing or speech, based on knowledge, reason, experience and emotional resonance, and that it is not – as for example Jane Gallop[19] has put it – a 'phallic illusion'.

For books about the clinical *practice* of psychoanalysis, things are less complicated: a clear and necessary condition for the capacity to speak authoritatively is to have experience of doing it – that is, the clinical experience of working as a psychoanalyst or psychoanalytic psychotherapist. Some people in the psychoanalytic world may hold the view that the experience of such practice is a necessary condition for the authority to make almost any kind of statement about psychoanalysis, on the grounds that clinical experience is the source of all psychoanalytic thinking. The relationship between on the one hand clinical psychoanalysis, and on the other psychoanalytic theory and its possible applications outside of the clinical situation, is a quite contentious matter. Just a few points will be made here with the aim of clarifying the basis of this author's claim to authority.

The relationships between ideas and practices are very complex. Ideas are ultimately derived from practices – this is the basic truth in materialist theories of knowledge. Our ideas about the world derive, in general, from our social, material being in the world, from the particular pressures, demands and limitations of the social practices in which we engage. These are quite different for an academic than they are for a therapist, and the difference is often reflected in the contrasting ways that academics and therapists think and talk about psychoanalysis. As an academic I am routinely concerned with presenting formal specifications of sets of ideas, and with whether students have understood these ideas, and can compare them with others. If I were a therapist, I might make explicit use of theoretical concepts only when something about a particular patient suggested one of them to me. It would be a concrete specification, which I would be trying to link to other things I thought I knew about that particular patient, rather than to other parts of a conceptual system and to the general body of evidence bearing upon it.

My social practice as an academic, therefore, predisposes me towards a certain kind of approach to psychoanalytic theory, a formal, schematizing and not very concrete approach. This may well be a problem, in that knowledge needs to be concrete as well as abstract, particular as well as general, but it is unavoidable. For academic teaching purposes it is necessary to some extent to deal with things in formal and generalized ways; moreover such teaching is normally to undergraduates and other students who are not likely to have any experience of psychoanalytic therapy. The original, richest and most powerful source of evidence for and illustrations of psychoanalytic concepts is the clinical literature. But such examples are not easily taken out of their context and presented to an audience unfamiliar with the clinical situation. Examples from everyday life are easier to use, but then the link with the practical grounding of the theory may be lost.

It could be concluded from this line of thought that psycho-analytic theory cannot satisfactorily be pursued in academic settings, and some recent developments in psychoanalytic writing, notably the later work of Wilfred Bion, do seem designed to render this task impossible, in their refusal to submit to systematic exposition. It would then be a short further step to the position that psychoanalytic theory cannot satisfactorily be used outside of the clinical setting, e.g. in attempts to research or to theorize about social processes. However, while the difficulties of using psychoanalytic ideas in academic teaching or research should not be minimized, such attempts cannot be ruled out of court. In the final analysis, the conceptual apparatus of psychoanalysis is intellectual public property.

Although ideas are generated in particular practices, once for-mulated and published they then have a certain life of their own. This is for a number of reasons. Different areas of social practice, despite their differences, belong to the same social totality at the same point in history and as such are likely to have certain features in common. Attempts to explain phenomena in one area may therefore on occasion, with suitable caution, legitimately be taken up in another. Social thought would not get very far without this kind of generalization. The states of mind and modes of relating found in psychoanalytic therapy must occur elsewhere – if they did not, psychoanalysis would be a useless curio. And practising therapists may not be the best people to consider the role of unconscious processes in conjunction with other factors in non-clinical settings, unless they also have competences in other bodies of knowledge, and some kind of interdisciplinary, synthesizing flair.

Moreover, psychoanalytic methods and theories themselves will, as cultural phenomena, partake of concerns and assumptions found elsewhere in the culture. In this sense to apply psycho-analytic concepts to other areas of social life is, to some extent, merely to return with the ideas from whence they came. Of course they have in the meantime been heavily modified or refined in psychoanalytic clinical experience; a major example here would be the great complexity and systematicity brought to the notion of the unconscious by psychoanalysis. The point is, though, that clinical practice is not the absolute *fons et origo* of psychoanalytic theory; it is rather a creative exercise upon and a particular elaboration of a mass of independently existing cultural experience and ideas. It is the necessary site for the generation of the theory, but not the entire material for it.

Psychoanalytic ideas therefore emerge from traditions of thought in the wider culture; they are culturally embedded and thereby partially autonomous from clinical practice. A further point is that not only do they come from wider traditions, they are also under pressure to return to them, and they are contributions to the further development of those traditions. This will be a central concern of this book: the ways in which ideas are re-absorbed back into existing traditions of thought, sometimes obliterating the modifications or refinements which they may have undergone in a particular practice.

For example, there has been much criticism of certain post-Freudian developments in psychoanalysis, especially of ego-psychology and of the 'neo-Freudians', which has sought to dem-onstrate this process of re-absorption. It has been argued that the genuinely new elements of understanding introduced by Freud – mainly in the theory of sexuality and the conception of psychic conflict – have been whittled away in the interests of blunting Freud's disturbing impact upon rationalistic liberal ideologies. Some of these criticisms help to underpin, or are echoed by, my arguments here. Freud certainly came from, and remained within, the liberal tradition of social thought, but it is doubtful whether that tradition (or, indeed, the socialist tradition and its alternative route to happiness) could remain intact if the full significance of psychoanalytic understanding were confronted. I shall be describing various attempts to preserve the pre-Freudian traditions by presenting Freudian ideas in particular ways.

Thus psychoanalytic ideas are inevitably part of the cultural whole and its conflicts, and their study is an intrinsically interdisciplinary project. They are used on all sides (e.g. by antisocialist liberals and by radical socialists) in debates about the futures of the traditions (e.g. liberal individualism) to which they are related. Sometimes, the invocation of the *clinical* dimension of psychoanalysis is an effective way of refuting an attempt to misrepresent psychoanalytic theory and obscure its new contributions. Good clinicians should more than anyone be aware of the depth and complexity of the theoretical formulations, and be able to speak to these from their clinical experience.

Certainly, too, a clinical sensibility is an essential component of the interdisciplinary approach – where for example there is the intention of using psychoanalytic ideas to help throw some light on a particular social phenomenon, or of making some psychoanalytic observations on the psychological significance of certain ideas. Interpreting theoretical texts in this way is not the same as making sense of an individual person in therapy, but it is a para-clinical activity, and as such it is open to challenge on the grounds of clinical accuracy.

But the primary purpose here is to trace particular kinds of transformations which psychoanalytic ideas have undergone in the wider culture, and to suggest why they have occurred, and what significance they may have beyond the history of psychology. In this domain of public debate about the social meaning of psychoanalysis and its impact, clinical practice has no guaranteed authority, and certainly no exclusive right to speak.

Images of the Father

There is a case then for an interdisciplinary exploration of psychoanalytic ideas and their fate in the twentieth century. We must now face a major problem for a prospective author on Freud. At many levels of our intellectual culture, from secondary school syllabus to the ruminations of professors, there is a powerful, condensed image of 'Freud' and 'psychoanalysis': the two words are fused together at the centre of a repetitive pattern of associations and connotations. To attempt to write about 'Freud', or even on any related subject caught within this pattern of received meanings, is to invoke the many strong feelings associated with them. These are predominantly negative and rebellious ones.

For a variety of reasons, some of which it is one task of this book to explore, 'Freud' and 'psychoanalysis' have become emblematic of an outmoded or corrupt authority which must be rejected. To stand in defence of 'Freud' is to stand also against this strong current of contemporary feeling and to invite upon oneself some of the same scorn. The rejection of Freud is symptomatic of a wider crisis of authority, but it has some very specific features of its own. Freud has become an international scandal. Not only is he an unwanted father figure, he is also a shameful figure, a dirty old man whose grotesque preoccupations only the gullible could mistake for a rational theory. He is the father who brings incest to the family, and blames the children for it.

In those areas of intellectual life where Freud and psychoanalysis are more deeply known, the predominance of scornful hostility is replaced by more complex and generally more positive attitudes. Sometimes these remain quite ambivalent, as in some of the feminist, Lacanian-influenced writing on psychoanalysis. There the corpus of Freud's work is a body which is endlessly examined, both in admiration and in anger. And even where attitudes are not ambivalent, but more thoroughly positive, then a different difficulty for the author presents itself, in that there are different schools of positive valuation of Freud, which do not agree with each other.

Differentiated conceptions of what Freud and psychoanalysis are – or should be – about, command powerful feelings amongst their adherents. A rendering of Freud which seems to contradict or ignore that favoured by a differently oriented reader may then be set aside. This book is not directly concerned with such internal divergences within contemporary psychoanalysis, and in outlining a broadly 'Freudian' philosophy in the next chapter I hope to work from a wide basis of agreement amongst the different schools of psychoanalysis. There is a limit to this ambition, since no position is above or beyond the theoretical issues of the day, but one can at least try to alienate no more readers than is unavoidable.

Theoretical dogmatism is unattractive and unhelpful, and there is no doubt that it exists in the psychoanalytic world, both towards non-psychoanalytic ideas and – probably more – in the attitudes of some schools towards each other. But on the other hand, theoretical commitment can also be extremely fruitful; one might say that the whole history of psychoanalysis is an illustration of this. Without the generally single-minded pursuit of unconscious phenomena shown by psychoanalytic workers, we would not be in a position to enrich interdisciplinary work with the fruits of their labours.

It will not be easy to pick our way around and between the culturally dominant negative images of 'Freud' and the subcultural allegiances to different 'Freuds'; nor to maintain active respect for the clinical dimension of psychoanalytic thinking while attempting to plant psychoanalytic ideas within an interdisciplinary framework. Whether all this is done successfully here, the reader may want to judge later on. The claim to authority of his book, and its justification, rest mainly on the extent to which these problems are adequately confronted.

Summary of Following Chapters

Chapter 2 outlines a reading of Freud as a theorist of tragedy who sought to extend the limits of our endurance of unhappiness.

Chapter 3 adds to this a conception of Freud's analytic method as an attempt to combat the disintegrative tendencies in modern experience.

Chapter 4 assesses the very different, desiccated reading of Freud found in academic psychology.

Chapter 5 finds a similar 'Freud' in humanistic psychology, this time as fall guy for the transcendental promises of the humanists.

Chapter 6 considers the different but similar transcendence sought by the politically radical, and ambivalent, followers of Freud.

Chapter 7 traces the common ideological origins of many of these receptions of Freud, and finds that the capacity to endure our condition is as limited in some political thought as in psychology.

Chapter 8 discusses some of the political and cultural implications of the limits of endurance revealed by the reflections in the Freudian mirror.

The Tragedy
of the Individual

2

THE FIRST DUTY

A Kind of Resignation

> To tolerate life remains, after all, the first duty of all living
> beings. Illusion becomes valueless if it makes this harder for us
> ... If you want to endure life, prepare yourself for death.[1]

In this much-quoted and eloquent passage, Freud succinctly presents three of the basic principles of his psychological theory and
his world-view. These form the core of a tragic vision of life. Firstly,
life is something which has to be endured; it is inherently painful
and difficult. Secondly, we are unlikely to find an escape from
pain in illusion, though we may well try; beliefs that happiness is
just around the corner, or already upon us, may by virtue of their
unreality create more difficulty and suffering for us, at least in the
long run. And thirdly, it is in confrontation with death that we
are closest to the fundamentals of life.

There are many accounts of Freud and of psychoanalysis in
which these principles do not appear, or are at most seen as
secondary to the main body of psychoanalytic theory. There is an
occlusion of Freud the tragedian, of a major and persistent theme
in psychoanalytic thought. In Freudian tragedy there is no saving
catharsis, no redemptive finale; things will continue as they are –
painful, incomplete, and in tension. Clear-thinking and dignified
resignation is the most we can aspire to, though this is far more
than most of us can achieve.

This is by no means the same as a desperate survivalism, a let's-get-through-the-day, or let's-get-through-the-war mentality. Christopher Lasch has delineated such strategies of the 'minimal self',[2] and shown them to be quite different from the ideal of mature endurance posited by psychoanalysis. Many of our present-day preoccupations with 'survival', argues Lasch, stem from an incapacity to endure the pains of living, an unwillingness to bear the costs and uncertainties of relationships. Hopes are cancelled, and deeper emotional investments are withdrawn from others and from a social future. Survivalists look only to themselves, and to the present, or at best to the preservation of our bare collective existence, rather than to the moral and social content of our relationships. In contrast the capacity to endure, which psycho-analysis counsels us to develop, is necessary for the preservation of certain kinds of hope, and for a constructive involvement in the public domain. It involves a recognition that the affective and expressive rewards which relations with others can bring are not without cost, and that if we wish to sustain certain ideals (e.g. of democratic participation) then we have to bear those costs of disappointment, conflict, and loss.

The active, engaged quality of this endurance also distinguishes it from classical stoicism. The stoic claimed to be essentially untouched by misfortune and tragedy, valuing only inward, vir-tuous accord with the cosmos. Everything in the world is ordained by an omnipotent power, so anyway nothing can be prevented or changed. The psychoanalytic version of stoicism is a different philosophy, in at least two respects.

Firstly, it neither advocates, nor sees as possible, a complete detachment from the pains of life. Psychoanalytic therapy seeks to create or strengthen within the individual a capacity for the analysis of emotional life, so that an individual may be able to understand something of the sources and nature of his or her feelings. In a sense, this is certainly a capacity for 'detachment' about one's emotions. The aim though is not to re-locate the whole subjectivity of the individual in this 'detached' space, far above the struggle of life. It is rather to try to create possibilities for new patterns of feeling to develop. By introducing some self-understanding, the grip of established patterns of feeling on sub-jectivity may be weakened. Possessing a capacity for some detached analysis of oneself is not the same as inhabiting a space outside of emotional response (indeed, psychoanalysis sees such detachment as a pathological condition, a symptom of a schizoid state of mind).

Secondly psychoanalysis does not regard all of the distress in life as inevitable – it could not exist as it does if this were its philosophy, since its evolution as a therapeutic technique would not have made sense. A therapy of any sort entails a belief in the possibility of change, of melioration, perhaps even of prevention. Some of the clinical literature of psychoanalysis testifies to a quite resilient therapeutic optimism, a belief that even the most profound of mental disturbances may yield a little to skilled and steadfast effort, and that such effort is often worth while. The reduction of self-inflicted distress is sometimes one of the most obvious benefits to issue from psychoanalytic treatment. And while many inner conflicts and anxieties may be regarded as ineradicable, for reasons to be discussed, one general aim of psychoanalysis is to modify the ways in which both these internal pains, and the blows inflicted on us from without, are experienced and managed. The capacity to reflect upon experience cannot dull the pain of, for example, a bereavement, but it may extend the ability to withstand it, and may help to prevent an inner reserve of guilt from converting the grief into a clinical depression. So the 'resignation' which is the therapeutic aim and philosophic ideal of psychoanalysis is of a particular sort; it enjoins us to be resigned to our condition, but not necessarily to our fate.

The Lost Empire

What then is so difficult about our condition, that demands so much endurance? From the writings of Freud himself, and especially from some of the popular understandings of Freud, we might derive the idea that the problem is sex. A gap between the amount of sexual gratification which individuals want or need, and that which can be allowed them by society, is sometimes taken to be the core of the Freudian tragedy.

There are two major variations on this theme. In one, our sexual wishes are seen as insatiable, while the demands of civilization for restraint are irreducible. The gap is therefore wide and profound. This was close to Freud's own view. In the other, the gap is seen as wide but not as absolutely unbridgeable. Satisfaction is in principle possible, and with different social arrangements it could become a reality. It is specific forms of society, not civilization per se, which make life tragic. This, broadly speaking, is the point of

35

view developed by a number of 'neo-Freudian' writers, and taken up in the Freudo-Marxist tradition. There is also some warrant in Freud's work for this view; in his earlier writing especially he can envisage some scope for a relaxation of constraint.[3] But no conceptualization which turns around a notion of sexuality (least of all around an untheoretical idea of 'sex') is at all adequate to define the burdens we carry as these have been theorized in the development of the psychoanalytic tradition.

Even the most basic or derivative accounts of Freudian theory usually acknowledge that Freud decisively widened the concept of sexuality to include more or less the whole range of pleasurable bodily experience. This was a profound and complex theoretical step, which both threw a new light on emotional development and also threw up a range of new questions and problems about the nature of motive and desire. It was both an extension of the notion of sexuality beyond genital and reproductive meanings *and* an assimilation of other bodily pleasures to the matrix of genital sexuality. It facilitated the identification of both sexuality in the infant, and of the infantile elements in adult sexuality.

Sexuality in the Freudian sense is thus a momentous concept. It reaches towards an encompassing definition of all our feelings about others, because these have their origins in early bodily experiences between infant and caretaker. However the equally Freudian concepts of ego-development and sublimation[4] require that the whole field of relations with others is not equated with the sexual – that would be to slip into the reductionism of which psychoanalysis is often accused.

Moreover, much of the post-Freudian development of psycho-analytic theory has pushed the theorization of relations with others beyond the point at which even the most extended concept of sexuality can continue to address them. For some surveys of this development, readers can consult a number of recent works.[5] What follows is a distillation of my own understanding of the most important principles established by a number of the different schools of post-Freudian thought, given a particular emphasis relevant to this context, and without detailed theoretical elab-oration.

Partly for its brevity, this account may seem unsatisfactory to many of those committed to particular post-Freudian schools, although such dissatisfaction is more likely to spring from the deep philosophical differences which exist within psychoanalysis notwithstanding the claim usually and plausibly made by all that they are following lines of inquiry initiated by Freud himself. Distinctive and specialized though the psychoanalytic tradition may be, especially in Britain where it has not been part of the cultural mainstream, it nonetheless accommodates some major divergences of outlook and style.

For instance, both Lacanian psychoanalysis in France, and in a different way some contemporary thinking which takes the writings of the British analyst Wilfred Bion as its key texts,[6] have mounted a challenge to the kind of investigative rationalism which has hitherto informed most of the psychoanalytic enterprise, seeing instead the work of analysis in linguistic–poetical terms. This philosophical issue is not of immediate relevance here; nor is the overlapping argument between the proponents of psychoanalysis as a form of actual–historical investigation and those who prefer to see it as an exercise in the construction of personal meanings and narratives.[7] The tenor of my own rendering of Freud is more in sympathy with an understanding of psychoanalysis as a logical and systematic empirical discipline, rather than as a process of semantic deconstruction or poetic revelation. All these kinds of approaches are however compatible with an appreciation of the tragedy inherent in our emotional development and mature psychic organization.

Rather crudely speaking, there are two major sources of this tragedy: loss and destructiveness. Both are unavoidable facts of experience; we need not be concerned here with metapsychological debates about the ultimate sources of human aggression, a question on which there are differing views within psychoanalysis. The sufficient point in this context is that aggressivity is present consistently, deeply and early enough in life for it to be considered ineradicable and universal (though varying in strength between individuals). About the inevitability of loss as an impingement from the external world upon psychic life, there can be no argument, except perhaps with an advocate of such Zen-psychotic detachment from the things and people of the world that their disappearance is of no significance. However, the psychoanalytic focus on loss is, as with aggression, on its *intrapsychic* rather than reactive origins, that is with experiences of loss as intrinsic to the developmental process and as welling up from within the individual, rather than as reactions to external events.

The first and most fundamental loss might not appear, to a

commonsense observer, to be a loss at all. Nothing has visibly changed; the baby is still being looked after by its mother, who is no less devoted to it. The loss is of a state of mind, rather than of an external object. (This term is often used in psychoanalysis to refer to a person or image of a person. The point of this questionable usage is not to equate persons with impersonal objects but to convey that the persons are being considered in the context of the mental life of one particular individual, a *subject* for whom others are the *objects* of relationships.) What has been lost is the sense of oneness, of fusion, of merger with the maternal environment and thereby with all that matters in the world.

Such a condition of oceanic oneness has been posited by psychologists of various persuasions, and is not a discovery of psychoanalysis. What the psychoanalytic literature has done, though, is to provide abundant evidence for the existence of such a state (mainly as a survival in the mental lives of adults), and to attach great importance to specific aspects of this primal state of mind and its persistence in the unconscious. Above all, the role of *omnipotence* has been stressed: in recognizing no subjectivity or agency other than its own the baby is being omnipotent. This is a mad and domineering state of mind; the psychoanalytic picture of infantile bliss is a good deal less sympathetic than others, which may be more likely to find here the grounding of love, or of mystical wisdom.

Certainly while in this state the baby may, in some non-omnipotent part of its mind, be learning of love, since it will if lucky be receiving a more intensive love than ever again. But in the state of fusion itself, no learning of any kind is possible, since there is nothing to learn. There are no differences between thought and reality, wish and fulfilment, self and other. The only 'wisdom' to be found here is that of fools, or tyrants. This mental condition, to which psychoanalysis applies the term 'narcissism', may perhaps issue spontaneously from our bio-psychological make-up (the hypothesis of a 'primary narcissism'), or it may always have been a more active construction by the neonatal mind. Whichever, it is put to use, and powerfully reproduced for its usefulness, in protecting the baby from the terrors to which it is disposed.[8]

For in reality, in its physical existence the baby is anything but omnipotent. It is completely helpless, and remains so for a very long time. Feelings of omnipotence are phantasies which our infantile minds produce, protective illusions which can stand in the place of the overwhelming anxieties to which we would be subject if the full helplessness of our condition were borne in upon us as infants. We can abandon these imperial illusions only to the extent that we can face the world without them, having been convinced that it is a sufficiently benign place for our weakness not to be catastrophic, and having gained some faith in our growing powers of independent functioning. The British psychoanalyst Donald Winnicott is well known for his descriptions[9] of the process by which the mother can make this dis-illusionment possible, by the empathic provision of a reliably benign environment and by modulating the baby's experience, providing the world in 'small doses', so that its illusions of omnipotence may be sustained when necessary to protect against intolerable anxiety.

Nonetheless, and despite the increasing rewards from reality-orientation as the infant's competences grow, the process of dis-illusionment involves a most profound loss. It is an expulsion from Paradise, entailing the setting aside of the psychic reality which the infant had created in its escape from outer reality. The helplessness and the anger which it produces may be evoked by all subsequent experiences of loss, and a sense of dispossession is placed at the centre of subjectivity. For one can become a distinctive, functioning human subject only through emerging, dispossessed, from the narcissistic matrix of early experience; the process of individuation involves positive acquisitions and enrichments of the psyche, but its premise is the negation of infantile omnipotence.

One of its results is the capacity to mourn, to confront and recover from loss. As Freud showed in his essay on 'Mourning and melancholia', mourning can be carried through only when the lost object is firmly experienced as an object, i.e. as other than the self. A regressive narcissistic identification with the object may be made in an attempt to preserve it, and so avoid the pain of mourning.

We are slow learners, and reluctant mourners. A stable dis-illusionment sets in only through many bruising encounters with the other-ness of external reality. Even then, omnipotent phantasy continues to inform our thoughts and feelings. In the Oedipal crisis, the child's wish to displace the same-sex parent is in part a regression to early omnipotence as an escape from the conflicts and complexities of family life involving differentiated persons. Life is much simpler and better if all one's feelings can be contained within one perfectly secure symbiotic relationship, with the other-ness of the world a mere backdrop (as echoed also in the sublime state of falling in love). On the long haul through childhood and adolescence, the craving for fusion with an idealized other, so obliterating its other-ness, is perpetually reappearing, albeit in increasingly displaced or symbolized forms.

Much of the clinical effort of psychoanalysts in recent decades has been directed towards rooting out this craving in adult patients, often very successful and apparently mature adults. Sophisticated intellectual understanding of and practical competence in the external world (as in the form of scientific expertise, or business acumen) can co-exist with an inner life dominated by omnipotent phantasy. In fact this is to some extent the case from the beginning of life, since there is now wide agreement that the infant is cognitively quite sophisticated, and quite able in some ways to register the separate existence of other people.

If development proceeds well, however, the reserves of omnipotence and idealization are put to good use. The French psychoanalyst Janine Chasseguet-Smirgel[10] has paid particular attention to the ways in which our constant attempts to recover absolute contentment give rise to our 'most sublime achievements', as well as 'the most baleful errors'. The dream of perfection is not entirely given up, she argues, but, as the 'ego ideal', is projected on to objects which we then identify with. The choice of such objects is infinite; professional identities, lovers, social movements may be frequent and important cases.

Depending on the demands of these ideal objects, we may then commit ourselves to constructive and creative work in the attempt to be worthy of and to merge with them. This work could end only if perfection were achieved; if we remain aware of our imperfections, we will be led to the constant renewal of effort and achievement. A particularly sophisticated outcome is that the desire for truth and learning should in this way become infused with narcissistic ambition, so that the desire for perfection is turned against itself by being committed to explore and accept the real world of imperfection. As Thomas Mann put it, writing about the moral project of psychoanalysis, 'the stern love of truth characteristic of the [nineteenth] century ... combated idealism out of love for the ideal.'[11]

It is not only the total dependence of infancy that leaves us with the wishful, defensive tendency towards illusion, though that may be the ultimate source of the most profound illusions. The dependence of the child, less total in a physical sense but often no less intense psychologically, means that growing up is in one main respect a whole series of experiences of needing other people. Correspondingly the illusion that other people do not exist as such, or that one does not need them, has constantly to be renewed and elaborated, for deployment at those moments when, or in those parts of the mind where, the fact of dependence – with its risk of abandonment or disappointment – cannot be tolerated. And to some degree, the feelings of smallness, incompetence and weakness live on in all of us, as do the illusory means of blotting these out.

For the older child and adolescent, emotional development means more than the giving up of an illusory empire. There is a *real* loss of parents, of people to provide physical care, a social base and (even if only implicitly) moral example. In the later, adolescent stages of what is often called 'identity formation', it is especially clear that the psychological differentiation and emotional consolidation of the individual can proceed only on the basis of a renunciation of much that has hitherto been valued in the timeless security of home.

Of course, this is something of an ideal picture, and there is greater tragedy in the many lives where dependence is never properly matched by provision, and where the struggle to separate cannot be fought out in relation to a *valued* object. Unlike popular wisdom, psychoanalytic theory predicts that emotional deprivation may lead to greater illusion, rather than to a hard realism, because the necessary benignity in the real world – necessary for the demotion of illusion in the inner world – has been absent. This is a complex question, involving an appreciation of different layers of the personality; a worldly cynicism may be symptomatic of inner phantasies of perfection. Again, Lasch has described many of the paradoxical cultural manifestations of the refusal to give up narcissistic phantasy.

The main point here is that however good the external provision, loss and renunciation are the sine qua non of psychological development and of realistic engagement with the world. Freud said as much, though in a language which stressed specific sexual renunciations; it has been the work of post-Freudian theory to expand Freud's own preliminary explorations of narcissism into a framework for understanding development. Within this framework, sexuality may re-enter as the most common and potent expression, as the literal embodiment, of the omnipotent wish and of the terror against which it defends, and as the primary field

41

within which the struggle between illusion and renunciation is played out. The renunciation we have to make is in a sense, as Freud maintained, of pleasure, but it is – in its most basic form – the pleasure of omnipotent control rather than the pleasure of sexual discharge. Sexual feeling can play a complex, many-sided role in the internal scenario where omnipotence confronts otherness.

The tragedy of the individual begins, then, with the fact that individuation entails separation and loss. Subjectivity is grounded either in an illusory clinging to omnipotence, or in resignation to the loss of omnipotence, and to one's vulnerable separateness in a world where many things are out of one's control. In particular, uncontrollable losses of valued people and things in the external world have to be contended with. These losses vary enormously in degree, but any such loss – or the prospect of it – can re-open the basic narcissistic wound, or reactivate the yearning for cosmic oneness.

This picture of narcissistic fusion as the state to which we regressively tend as the ultimate sanctuary in life, and as the source of illusions of happiness, must be qualified. There is another, contrary tendency at work, based on fear of the loss of selfhood which merger with the other brings. For some psychoanalytically influenced writers, especially in the recent feminist tradition (see also Chapter 6), this fear is more damaging that the omnipotent impulse. From this point of view, the human tragedy is seen to reside in our rejection of our psychic beginnings in intimate union with the mother, rather than in the costs of going beyond those beginnings. However, recognition of the fear of fusion, and of its constricting and impoverishing effects, does not require us to reconsider the primary significance attached to omnipotence. The fear of fusion is strongest where the state of omnipotence exerts such a powerful hold on the mind that no compromise with reality is possible. Where no gradual weakening of omnipotent phantasy and its subordination to reality can take place, the only route out of infantile dependence is into a rigid pseudo-independence, based not on the renunciation of omnipotence and fusion but on the denial that they ever existed.

Such a resolution is, like the classical neurotic symptom, both a denial and an expression of the impulse it seeks to deny. It tends to assimilate *all* relationships of dependency to the model of absolute, infantile dependency, and so rejects all forms of dependency in favour of a mythically free-standing subject. This is omnipotence in a different guise, a narcissistic self-sufficiency based not on the incorporation of the other but on a cancelling of all need and feeling for the other.

The two modes of illusion – narcissistic fusion and narcissistic pseudo-independence – have been seen by a number of influential writers as, respectively, characteristically female and male. This is too schematic an analysis, but in any case we need not go here into this debate about gender and psychopathology. The main point is that both modes arise from the incapacity to endure the anxiety which the loss of infantile omnipotence entails.

The movement towards authentic differentiation, in which this anxiety is confronted, is assisted by the aggressivity which inheres in the psyche. The physical and emotional attacks which babies and children launch on their parents are usually – amongst other things – an important part of the process of separating out, by testing the consequences of primitive self-assertion. However, paeans to 'adaptive' or 'healthy' aggression, reassuring though they may be, can provide an account of only the lesser part of the role of aggression in everyday mental life. Aggression has many other meanings, which analytic study has shown to be connected with feelings of persecution, envy, rivalry and guilt. We are aggressive pre-emptively, in retaliation, and in greed; and although we may be socialized well enough to moderate the outward expressions of this aggression, we are still deeply troubled by our feelings of rage and hatred.

As in much psychoanalytic investigation, what is ostensibly done between people, and what some *other* person's actual motives may be, are of little relevance; the focus is upon what the individual in question takes others to mean, and with what feelings he or she responds. This is all a function of inner phantasy life as well as of the actuality of external situations. So the promptings of aggression to which we are subject are of great importance, even if they are largely unconscious and plainly irrational, and even if they do not result in much overtly aggressive behaviour.

It is a major achievement of the Kleinian school of psycho-analysis to have explored and established the role of aggression in phantasy life and in emotional development. Again the starting point is Freud, in whose later work there is a very complex understanding of the interweaving of sexual and aggressive strivings. Freud's anti-utopianism became, as Martin Kalin has shown, increasingly linked to his theories of aggression and guilt. In the Kleinian conception of development the crucial process in the whole formation of personality is the struggle with aggression, which has to be acknowledged and contained.[12] In the best outcome, aggressive urges are fully integrated into the self and there is consequently a capacity to restrain and sublimate them, and a concern for the damage they might do to others. This resolution was termed by Klein the 'depressive position', because the experience of depression is seen to rest on the capacity for guilt and concern about the consequences of one's destructiveness. With this concern comes the wish for reparation, the impulse to make good the damage, the unconscious basis of many of our constructive dealings with the world. The alternative to this benign development is the persistence of 'splitting', a primitive mental process by which the experiential world, both subject and object, is split into two, one good and one bad. A pure, idealized relation with a good object can thus be preserved, in phantasy, since all aggression is split or hived off into another phantasy relation between a different part of the subject and a bad object, about which no guilt need be felt.

Health and maturity are thus moral achievements, and in a manner reminiscent of some religious traditions they are seen as founded on a recognition of the inner mixture of evil with love, and of the need for continual inner struggle. The tendency to disown and project aggressive impulses is a recurrent one, due to the great costs, in guilt and tension, which their integration incurs. This then is the other major dimension of tragedy inherent in subjectivity: it is constituted by guilt. Differentiated selfhood is an ongoing moral achievement, a struggle to own and control the destructive impulse. With this formulation, Kleinian theory transforms Freud's anthropological fable of the roots of society in guilt about a parricidal crime[13] into an empirical, developmental account of how guilt is central to our social relations.

This has been a simplified and highly schematic account of some basic psychological principles, which should not be taken as anything other than an abstract and condensed statement made in the context of a particular study. The reasons for the particular emphasis upon the omnipotent rejection of the other will become clear in later chapters, though this emphasis is also to be found in much contemporary psychoanalytic theorizing.

My account bears a particular local stamp of the British schools of psychoanalysis, though stopping short of the 'post-Kleinian' work of the later Bion *et al.* From other positions in the psychoanalytic tradition rather different accounts of the tragedy of the psyche would be constructed. From the later Freudian metapsychology with its dualism of life and death forces, a number of grand pictures of an inevitably conflictful dynamic underlying history have been developed,[14] although these are almost purely speculative. And Lacanian theory with its emphasis on the lack and absence at the centre of subjectivity might appear to be another analysis in the same tragic spirit, although there are reasons for thinking this not to be so. From the position taken in this chapter, our personal subjectivity is seen as constituted by others and by our recognition of their otherness, whilst also being at least potentially an authentic selfhood. This understanding of the contradictions of selfhood, of the possibilities for (indeed the need for) a self that can define and struggle with itself in the midst of otherness, is absent in Lacanian thought. There the impossibility of restoring narcissistic oneness (of satisfying 'desire') is taken to mean the impossibility of establishing any kind of stable satisfactions in one's relationships with the world. To be differentiated is to be fragmented, and to be separate from the other is to be lost to oneself. (See also Chapter 6.)

These differences are not to be glossed over; the account given here has, despite its brevity, some specific features with which the analysis in the following chapters must stand or fall. However, as Freud's own formulation quoted at the beginning of this chapter suggests, there is a strong case for seeing the psychoanalytic tradition overall as a meditation on, and specification of, the tragedy of the individual. All else, it tells us, is illusion – either an impediment to or flight from the 'first duty', which is to acknowledge and endure our tragedy. The most basic, persistent illusion is that other people do not exist, and that the individual can omnipotently avoid the pains of life which flow inevitably from our investments in and conflicts with other people, and from our biological vulnerability. To endure life is to endure the existence of others – which is also to endure oneself as a separate, conflicted individual.

The Others Inside

And Goethe might well have given some such heading to his autobiography as 'My strength has its roots in my relation to my mother.'[15]

What, though, is to replace the basic illusion? How and from where does the baby begin to assemble a differentiated self, mindful of its own limits and cognizant of the existence of others? The answer towards which psychoanalytic theory has moved may seem to be a paradoxical one: it is from other people that we derive the raw materials for the sense of our separateness and difference from others. Psychoanalysis belongs in that broad tradition of psychological theorizing, perhaps most often associated with the social-psychological theory of symbolic interactionism, that asserts the *intersubjective* nature of individuality. (In other ways, psycho-analytic theory differs sharply from symbolic interactionism, as will be noted in the next chapter.)

We are, then, made of other people, receiving into ourselves elements of personal being which are handed on and worked over from one parental undertaking to the next. The social historian's conception of a living tradition, continually reproduced in every-day life at the same time as it is modified and even transformed by changes of context, is a close parallel to the reproduction of selves as understood psychoanalytically. The unique interaction in each parental couple of two different family histories, and the speed of social changes, mean that the lines of psychic inheritance, the continuity of traditions of feeling, may be so complex as to appear broken or untraceable. Nonetheless the conclusion to which psychoanalytic thinking points is that the basic constituents of self are derived from the matrix of affect which our early caregivers provide for us. Other schools of thought may assert something similar; the distinctive contributions of psychoanalysis are in the very complex description it can develop of the ways in which this happens, and in its account of the internal world which is thereby built up in the emerging subject.

The theoretical language of psychoanalysis has a rich and unsettled vocabulary for describing the means by which the outside, including above all aspects of other persons, is taken in. Three terms in particular are in wide and sometimes overlapping usage: internalization, introjection, and identification. A fourth term, incorporation, is often discussed in relation to these, and is usually taken to refer to a primitive devouring of the other, characteristic of the greedy infant's relation to the breast. Where the intention of this relation is completely to possess the object, or to destroy it, then incorporation is best thought of as an omnipotent mode of relating to the world, by destroying its otherness. Where, however, the intention is understood as being to 'appropriate the object's qualities',[16] rather than to possess the total object itself, incorporation begins to shade into the work of differentiation and self-development denoted by the other terms. It can then be seen more positively as a corporeally rooted model for the other more sophisticated processes, in the way that the experience of the physical boundary of the body is seen as the model for the appreciation of the boundary of the self.

Internalization is the broadest and most loosely used of the terms, most frequently being used to refer to all or any aspects of the process of taking in, of somehow adding to the internal world some representation of part of the external world.

Introjection and identification are not always sharply distinguished from each other; common to the leading definitions of both is the idea that here is 'not simply one psychical mechanism amongst others, but the operation itself whereby the human subject is constituted',[17] through the appropriation of the object's qualities. We take in our representations of others; we install them in our inner worlds, and use them to map out and to fill in the developing contours of the self.

The process of introjection creates 'introjects', representations of objects which become part of the psychic apparatus, participating in relationships with other introjects and so creating the ongoing inner scenarios which are the medium through which we experience and respond to the external world. In the early days of psychoanalytic theorizing there were two divergent ways of understanding introjection. One, beginning with Ferenczi (who introduced the term), saw introjection mainly as a defensive process whereby the image of a threatening object is taken in in order to control either it or an impulse with which it is associated.[18] This is a regressive manoeuvre, with more than a hint of omnipotence; once inside, the object can be subject to control in the phantasy life of the individual. Like all defences, though, this cannot really be successful; the object becomes lodged in the psyche as a bad, persecuting presence. The other understanding, stemming from Freud's own formulation,[19] saw introjection as an expression of the pleasure principle, and again as a defensive and omnipotent technique. Splitting is involved here: all those objects that are the sources of pleasure are taken in, while all experiences of unpleasure are projected out.

In the later development of the theory, this divergence has been largely overcome. Introjection is seen as a process involving both good and bad objects, and as an essential part of emotional life with positive as well as defensive, regressively omnipotent functions. Particularly in Kleinian theory, the relative strength of good and bad introjects is a crucial factor in the development of personality, with the basis of mental health seen as residing in the firm intro-jection of a good primary object (the 'good breast', as the Kleinians partly metaphorically describe it). The ego coheres around this good introject, which will function throughout life to provide the individual with a sense of inner goodness, safety and resource-fulness. A complex interchange is at work between introjection, projection, reintrojection and so on, such that on the one side feelings arising within the infant, and on the other aspects of the mother's care and presence, are constantly being located and relocated either inside or outside the experienced boundary of the self.

This kind of interchange continues throughout life, but quite early in development it will have laid down some basic deposits in the internal world. Optimally, these will be organized around fundamentally good internal objects, which will give the strength needed to set aside infantile omnipotence and to confront the guilt aroused by aggressive phantasy. Bad objects – the internal representations of unloving or attacking parents (whether they are *actually* so, or are perceived to be so under the influence of projected aggression) – will be acknowledged but subordinate to the good.

The earlier theoretical divergence remains of significance, however, in that the emphasis which Ferenczi gave to the concept has had particular influence outside of psychoanalysis, in some of those partial, mediated appropriations of psychoanalytic ideas which will be examined later. There has been an influential strand of theorizing in social psychology and personality theory according to which anything that has been taken in from the outside is likely to be a malign presence within the self. Examples of this thinking, and a discussion of its significance, will be given later.

A similar dualism, of healthy and pathological types of process, occurs in the theory of identification. There are identifications whose effect is to enrich or extend the self, and there are defensive or regressive identifications. For example, in the latter category a person may identify with another who is desired but is unattainable, or who was loved and is dead. As Freud described this, 'object-choice has regressed to identification'.[20] In the absence of the desired relation with the external object, the individual resorts to what may be imagined as a cannibalistic device, or as a sort of psychic cloning: trying to mould the self to the features of the object representation, sometimes with a marked degree of outward behavioural mimicry, as well as with an internal sense of identity. The best-known form of defensive identification is probably 'identification with the aggressor', as described by Anna Freud.[21] In fear of attack (whether the threat is real or phantasied), the child identifies with the putative attacker.

By contrast, in developmentally healthy identifications the object of identification does not replace the subject's own ego but is assimilated into it, extending its repertoire and resources. The optimal condition for this sort of identification to occur is reciprocated love, as with the introjection of the good object. On the Kleinian view, there is no difference between identification and introjection: the former is seen as the result of the latter. Others, e.g. Laplanche and Pontalis, and Meissner,[22] see identification as a somewhat different, more sophisticated process, further removed from the oral, corporeal prototype of ingestion.

For many people their first and perhaps only contact with the concept of identification in psychoanalytic theory is in the context of the theory of the Oedipus complex, as the process by which the complex is resolved. The boy renounces his incestuous wish, but is able to reclaim it – albeit in displaced and deferred form – through his identification with his father. Again it is significant that popular renderings of this most notorious part of Freudian theory have tended to see this identification entirely as a defensive process, as an identification with the aggressor threatening castration, or at best as a calculative bid for future gratification. The component of *loving* identification with the father, who is assimilated into the ego and superego structures of the child as a valued, protective figure, is absent or underplayed, as admittedly it is in Freud's own writings.

What these popularizations ignore is that in much of the post-

Freudian development of psychoanalytic theory more attention is paid, in various ways, to the loved and admired paternal introject. This is part of the general movement of the theory towards the conceptualization of emotional development as a moral enterprise rather than as a series of utilitarian adjustments. If identification with parental authority is made in love as much as or more than in fear, then we can see how identificatory processes may provide the core of a good self, as well as being – in a different form – the means for the installation of a harsh, punitive superego. As we shall see in more detail later, an exclusive preoccupation with the taking in of bad objects makes it impossible to conceive of how a benign superego, or indeed any goodness within the ego, might develop.

In more recent years the concept of identification has been decisively widened, though not without much confusion, by the development of the notion of 'projective identification'. There is no agreed definition of this term,[23] but as the name implies it usually refers to some process in which both projection and identification are involved. Projection is the process by which some unacceptable feeling is imagined to belong to someone (or something) in the outside world. In its narrowest meaning, it is a simple phantasy of evacuation, the aim of which is to rid the subject of all contact with the rejected feeling, and which has no effect, in the external world, on the person who is the target of the projection. (As always, this defence does not work properly, since people or things in the outside world are now perceived as threatening embodiments of whatever it is that the subject wishes to reject.) In projective identification, as the term is now used particularly by some Kleinians,[24] the projection is combined with an element of the subject's continuing active involvement with the projected material. The subject *identifies with* the part of the other into which an aspect of the self has been projected. Furthermore there is some implication that the person into whom the feeling has been projected makes some response to the projection. Projective identification is thus the basis for empathy and for powerful emotional communication.

Thus projective identification is a term referring to an unconscious phantasy but with an interactive dimension. It is an attempt by the individual to get some other person to act out or to contain some intolerable feeling. In its widest usage, it is seen as a crucial aspect of early development: the baby projects its intolerable feelings into its mother, partly as a hostile attack, but it also identifies with what has been projected, and with how the mother responds. If the mother can contain and modulate the projected material, so that it becomes less threatening, the baby may then introject both the detoxified feelings and the mother's capacity for detoxifying them. If, however, the mother allows the baby's projections to amplify her own anxieties, and is unable to contain the bad feelings, then the baby will have much less opportunity to learn how to live with its own fears and rages. Thus the concept of projective identification, when applied in this context to describe the function of maternal containment, suggests that not only the specific contents of a bounded self but also the very capacity to become a reasonably integrated individual is something which we must take in from outside.

This is an area of particular controversy amongst present-day analysts. However, beneath all the theoretical disputes which have been glossed over in this chapter we can confidently hold on to the characterization of psychoanalysis as making two propositions about personal character: that in its emergence from primitive illusion it is constituted by pain, and by the internalization of others. In Freud's famous statement that the aim of psychoanalysis is to transform 'hysterical misery into common unhappiness',[25] the unhappiness he spoke of is that of the disenchanted person who has learnt of the depth of his connections to others.

As a whole then the psychoanalytic discourse of internalization is a complex elaboration of the proposition that we are made of other people. This proposition has been given far more emphasis and elaboration in post-Freudian theory than it received in Freud's own work. However as the quote at the beginning of this section suggests, he anticipated this development. His observation on Goethe is interesting because of the relative neglect in Freud's work of the importance of the mother, and because it is his purpose here to suggest that the mother's contribution to her son's development is to confirm him in his narcissism, by making him her 'undisputed darling'. This points to the paradox that although internalization and intersubjectivity are the negation of narcissism, the earliest internalizations of others (which are not only of the mother) take place under the auspices of omnipotent illusion.

It is a great strength of psychoanalysis that it can formulate and explore such contradictory aspects of our emotional lives. We are both intersubjectively created and sustained yet also capable of feeling ourselves to be terrifyingly alone.[26] While more commonsensical psychologies might have some explanation of this in terms of the simple fact of our bodily vulnerabilities and mortality, psychoanalysis can add to this an understanding of intersubjectivity as the path away from narcissistic fusion, which is the only state of absolute togetherness and security we ever know.

3

PSYCHOANALYSIS IN REVERSE: FREUD AND MODERNITY

Free and Determined

Psychoanalytic theory and techniques have changed almost totally since the days of Freud's early work, and continue to do so. One of the few things about the practice of psychoanalysis which has remained unchanged from its early days to the present is what is known as the 'fundamental rule'. This is the instruction given to analysands at the beginning of their psychoanalysis that they must speak about whatever comes into their minds, however trivial, irrelevant or unpleasant it seems. This is the *only* instruction given; no agenda is provided for the analysand. The fundamental rule is an injunction not only to be honest with the analyst, but also to be honest with oneself, and to face whatever there is to be faced in one's mind. The rule is about *speaking* freely, and there is no explicit instruction to *think* freely, but the rule is intended to encourage the analysand to let thoughts and images and feelings present themselves to conscious experience. If the analysand can stick to the rule, and minimize censorship of what is spoken, there may grow a capacity to minimize censorship of what is thought. Thus the aim of free association, according to one recent writer on the subject,[1] is nothing more than simply to extend itself; the process has no specific aim outside of itself.

The associative process is greatly assisted by the nature of the analytic situation, in which the analysand is for at least fifty minutes per day freed from the necessity of using thought to accomplish tasks in the external world, with the focusing and narrowing of thought which that usually entails. The tasks of psychoanalysis are in the internal world. So one thing the psycho-analytic method does is to study the flow of thoughts when there is no agenda set by the external world for them to follow, when they are therefore likely to lead to and follow each other in ways determined more by the person's internal agendas. This is what is meant by 'free association' – it is not free in the sense of being without determinants, but it is free (or largely so) from externally imposed determinants and from conscious direction, and it is subject to minimal unconscious restriction.[2]

The analysand's speech and thought during the analytic session may then consist in significant part of the tracing out of complex networks of words and images, each one leading to another or others. The work of the analyst, of course, is to try to interpret this flow of material, to suggest to the analysand what certain sequences of images and ideas may mean, to find the threads of meaning which link together what may initially appear to be disconnected thoughts and feelings. Over the years of an analysis, through a long and in essence cooperative effort, analyst and analysand try to generate frameworks of meaning, within which diverse aspects of the analysand's life experience may be situated. Through this excavation of unconscious meaning, significance may be found in many apparently trivial or accidental experiences and actions. Thus the meaningfulness of *conscious* experience can be recomposed and enlarged.

This is a familiar conception of the nature of psychoanalytic work. A number of observers have noted Freud's commitment to meaning, and some have seen it as in part a product of his Jewishness, that is as a secularized expression of the Judaic mystical belief in the meaningful connectedness of things.[3] Others, as noted in Chapter 2, have suggested that psychoanalysis is *basically* a semantic activity, an exercise in the creative production of meaning rather than an empirical investigation. Again, there is no need to pose such a hermeneutic account of psychoanalysis against all claims that it is concerned with establishing causes, or with a verifiable reality. We can see psychoanalysis as both a practice of producing meaning, and an investigation of what is causing what in someone's internal world. The latter implies the former.[4]

This meaning-generating work of free association is what the 'fundamental rule' is about; it is the basis of clinical psychoanalysis.

If then we explore the social meanings of free association, we are likely to find something of importance to the understanding of the social meanings of psychoanalysis as a whole. This chapter aims to do this by looking historically at the emergence of free association as a specific technique, and asking some questions about why it emerged when it did and in the way that it did. The basic question is this: what is the *social* meaning of the psychoanalytic project of recovering *personal* meaning through associations and their interpretation? Answers to such a question should tell us something about what kind of enterprise psychoanalysis is, socially speaking, both in its emergent phase and today.

To begin with it may be helpful to say a few more words about, and to clarify further, one potential misconception about free association, already noted above. Free association is not in fact free. It is internally determined, by the person's internal conflicts and anxieties. Laplanche and Pontalis note[5] that the conscious suspension of censorship which it requires will result in the workings of deeper, unconscious censorship coming more into view. Thus the technique of free association does not involve breaking out of all psychic inhibitions into a realm of spontaneity and freedom. It is not an exercise in psychic liberation. When, however, the production of associations is combined with the consistent analytic effort to understand why they have been produced – that is, when free association is the basis of clinical technique – then it can become an exercise in self-understanding. As Leo Bellak[6] puts it, there needs to be an oscillation between regression and critical cognitive functioning, that is between associative and interpretive functions.

In theoretical and historical writing about psychoanalysis, free association has received remarkably little attention, considering its importance to the whole enterprise, compared to the concepts of the unconscious, infantile sexuality, repression and so on. However, scattered in the literature there are a number of suggestions as to where it came from, that is, as to what sources Freud was drawing upon during the long period (from about 1892 to 1910) when he was clarifying the technique and establishing it at the centre of psychoanalytic practice. Freud himself is not a great deal of use to us here since he did not write very much about his antecedents and about influences upon him. It is anyway unlikely that he was fully aware of them, since specialist work in the history of ideas is often required to trace an intellectual lineage. The main suggestions to be found concerning the roots of free association are the following.

The Shouting of the Market

Firstly it must in some way be linked to the long-established philosophical interest in association as a basic principle of mental functioning. This goes back to Plato and Aristotle, though it is most developed in the works of English philosophers from the seventeenth to nineteenth centuries. Associationism, as formulated by David Hartley and James Mill, is the doctrine that the complex activities of the mind are built up from simple elements. On this view the task of psychology is to find the laws of association by which elementary sensations and ideas are combined together to produce complex mental states. Freud was not close to this tradition (he had translated a volume of John Stuart Mill's essays in 1880 but these dealt mainly with social questions),[7] but he was very familiar with the work of the early German psychologist Wilhelm Wundt, in whose theories the composition of experience from basic elements is a strong theme. Wundt's experiments were a model for those of Bleuler and Jung – in whose hands, Freud thought, they then became fruitful.[8] It is not difficult to see a broad affinity between the associationist conception of the chaining together of mental elements, and the psychoanalytic procedure of constructing chains of association.

On the whole, however, psychoanalysis is not thought of as a derivative of associationism, and with good reason. Both offer general theories of mental life, but while associationism is primarily an epistemology, the focus of psychoanalysis is primarily upon the organization of affects. Moreover the elements being combined are seen very differently, being perceptually and logically simple for associationism while being already in some ways whole and complex for psychoanalysis.

The main influence upon psychology of associationism, at least in its pure English forms, has been in the development of theories of a reductionist nature. By this I mean theories which seek to reduce the complexity of psychological functioning to a few simple laws, and which try in their empirical work to isolate the elementary particles of human experience or action. Classical behaviourism is the most important of the reductionist, atomizing outcomes of associationism. Along with Gestalt psychology, psychoanalysis can be seen as part of the reaction against the reductionist tendency, and as an attempt to provide a more holistic alternative, notwithstanding popular conceptions of psycho-analysis as biologically 'reductive' in its alleged attempt to reduce everything to sex. So associationism has both a positive and a negative relation to psychoanalysis.

This relation with associationism is of particular significance here because of the strong links between associationism and psychological utilitarianism. The utilitarian calculus can really only work with a picture of mental life as something to which arithmetic can be applied, i.e. as a combination of discrete elements which are substitutable for each other. Indeed we might say that psychological utilitarianism is one form of associationism; hedonism is one principle by which mental elements may be linked together. Both philosophies formed part of the outlooks of Bentham and of James and John Stuart Mill, and classical behaviourism is both utilitarian and associationist.

It would, though, be wrong to speak of a simple conflict between reductive associationism and the various forms of dynamic and holistic psychology. This is because in the nineteenth and early twentieth centuries there were a number of attempts to combine associationist principles with holistic emphases on the total organ-ization of mental life. We can note here the position taken by John Stuart Mill on 'Complex Ideas' (which were seen as generated by but not reducible to series of simple ideas), and especially the work of the British philosopher F. H. Bradley, and that of the nineteenth-century German philosopher Johann Herbart, who is often cited as an important influence on Freud.[9] The influence of Herbart goes some way to explain the apparently contradictory relationship of psychoanalysis to associationism. Freud absorbed something of the associationist approach to the study of mental processes (e.g. he was much influenced by Meynert, the source of the concept of projection, and an associationist[10]), but did so partly via a German preoccupation with the whole individual which was opposed to the English associationists' concentration on elementary processes.

That preoccupation was particularly evident and developed in the second major philosophical tradition to which free associ-ation can be related, namely romanticism, the diverse range of movements in early nineteenth-century thinking and art which valued nature, feeling, imagination and wholeness, and posed them against the spiritual impoverishment of the new industrial, rational–scientific order. It is plausible to see the associative technique, with its use of a kind of creative activity as a healing procedure, and its discovery of the uniqueness of the individual in the patterns of association, as a part of the romantic rejection of the technical and the standardized in favour of subjective meaning.

This conception of free association is supported by considering one of the specific sources to which Freud himself attributed free association. This was a short article by the German writer Ludwig Boerne (published in 1823 and again in 1862), 'The art of becoming a writer in three days'. Boerne recommended writing down everything that came into the mind for three days. Freud as an adolescent read Boerne closely, and subsequently admitted that this article was probably a cryptomnesic, hidden influence on his formulation of free association. Boerne was a political reformer rather than a romantic poet, but this short essay is of a very romantic temper, as in one passage where Boerne claims that 'Whoever listens to the voice of his heart rises above the shouting of the market.'[11]

Psychoanalysis as a whole, particularly in its basic concept of the unconscious and its emphasis on sexuality and affect, is generally recognized by friends and foes to be substantially indebted to romanticism.[12] Fritz Wittels emphasizes that Freud's rejection of mechanistic, Cartesian science, in favour of the pursuit of meaning, was inspired by Goethe and the organicist, holistic concerns of 'Naturphilosophie'. Iago Galdston stresses the influence on Freud via Fliess of romantic medicine and its concern with the interrelatedness of all phenomena. Lancelot Whyte documents the extensive prefiguration of Freudian discourse by numerous romantic writers. At the same time, however, psychoanalysis reworked the concerns of those writers. In the psychoanalytic, clinical development of free association, the romantic notion of the unconscious as a link with nature and a source of cosmic connectedness is replaced by a conception of it as a matrix of *personal* meaning and biographical connections.

Harry Trosman argues that Freud blended romanticism with classicism, with philosophical emphases on rationality, abstraction and universals. While this portrays Freud rather too neatly as the grand synthesizer of Western thought, it is common to many influential systems of ideas that their appeal rests partly on their capacity to offer resolutions of long-standing intellectual or cultural contradictions. Freud, as a committed rationalist[13] whose work was to establish the irrationality of much human behaviour, could be seen to have offered such a resolution.

These larger issues concerning the basic philosophical status of psychoanalysis as a whole need not be gone into any further here. At this point it is relevant to note just that the technique of free association can be thought of as owing something to associationism, and also as an accommodation made by rational inquiry to claims for the importance in human affairs of the imaginative and the irrational. In these two ways psychoanalysis as a whole can be seen as influenced by, respectively, utilitarianism and romanticism. It is thus linked in its origins to the two philosophical traditions which have shaped much of its cultural reception. In the critique of its reception in the following chapters it will not therefore be argued that things have been read into it which are simply not there. The position is rather that in the course of the transmission of Freudian ideas into the wider culture, some minor or discarded themes in the psychoanalytic tradition have been pushed to the front while those aspects of the ideas which diverge from the dominant intellectual traditions have been occluded. Thereby the challenges which psychoanalysis can pose to prevailing theories of society and of self have not been widely taken up.

This location of psychoanalysis in the history of ideas corresponds, to a degree, to Gellner's characterization of Freud as offering a Nietzschean reassertion of blood and guts to counter the passionless vision of Enlightenment psychology. (Only to a degree, because Gellner misses Freud's commitment to Enlightenment rationality.) It also corresponds, somewhat more closely, to Foucault's view (still ultimately hostile to Freud, though more temperate than Gellner and more able to grasp that psychoanalysis is a synthesis of some contradictory elements) that psychoanalysis represents the establishment of an administrative, rational, 'normalizing' power in the domain of sexuality.[14] And it corresponds still more closely to the notion that psychoanalysis is a statement on behalf of affective need and non-rational desire in an age when instrumental relationships and rationalized organization were coming to dominate human affairs.[15] This latter, neo-romantic sort of view combines a sympathetic position towards psychoanalysis with a powerful account of the social context of its emergence. It does, however, like some versions of Lacanian theory, tend to celebrate psychoanalysis (or rather some version of it) as the voice of disorder in an age of repressive order. As the next sextion will argue, I want here to commend psychoanalysis more for its role in the production of order in an age of oppressive disorder.

The Psychohistory of Modernity

With these points about the intellectual lineage of free association in mind, we can turn to consider its origins in more social and material terms. I will present a case for seeing its emergence partly as a response to the simultaneously developing culture of the modern city. Freud spent nearly his whole working life, relieved by long country holidays, in Vienna, and when psychoanalysis began to appear elsewhere it was in some of the other great cities of the world – Berlin, New York, London and so on. This is a most unsurprising observation: obviously psychoanalysis could emerge only where there were established high degrees of professional specialization and vanguardism, and where there was a potential market for psychoanalytic therapy. These conditions were unlikely to be met outside of the great cities. However we might ask whether specific features of life in these cities are reflected in, and may in some way have helped to shape, the particular directions which psychoanalysis took.

A positive answer to this question does not have to be another version of the cliched notion that psychoanalysis is a product of fin-de-siècle Vienna. Peter Gay has pointed out[16] the absurdity of the argument that Freud's theories were all based on neurotic, middle-class Viennese women, which they were not. He suggests that the idea that Freud's thinking was simply determined by something homogeneous called 'Viennese culture' is a myth constructed by cultural historians (and particularly, I think we can say, by anti-Freudian psychologists playing at being cultural historians). He notes that some versions of this myth are mutually contradictory: both the hypocritical sexual repressiveness and the sexual permissiveness[17] of Vienna have been blamed for Freud's preoccupations. Gay perhaps overstates the case, proposing that 'Freud lived far less in Vienna than in his own mind'. Sociologically we cannot take that to be the whole truth, and the inconsistency of the 'Viennese culture' theories may point to the complexity of the relationships between Vienna and Freud's work, not to the absence of any relationship.[18]

However it is not Vienna as a unique city which is of relevance here, but rather the fact that the environment of psychoanalysis is the urban one, and specifically the most developed and intensive form of urban environment, the administrative and commercial metropolis of advanced capitalism. Lewis Mumford, the theorist of the city, contends that after 1890 there was a shift in the centre of gravity of the advanced nations. The industrial cities, the Coketowns, declined in political, cultural and to some extent economic significance, he argues, as they became increasingly overshadowed by the metropolitan centres, the cities of administration, finance and consumption, which were the growth points of what sociologists were soon to call 'mass society'.[19] These modern cities were never, as Max Weber pointed out,[20] organic communities organized around a military or religious authority, nor around a common industrial enterprise; rather they were shifting aggregations called into being by national and international forces outside themselves.

By 1900 there were eleven cities in the world with populations of over one million, including Vienna, Berlin, New York and London. In what Mumford described as their 'shapeless giantism' and their 'overpowering congestion',[21] these megalopolitan growths on the frontiers of cultural development brought new qualities of experience to everyday life, or at least dramatically intensified certain aspects of the experience of inhabitants of earlier cities.

The historian Norman Stone[22] summarizes under the heading of the 'Cultural Revolution of 1900' a number of changes in art, literature and social life towards modes of immediacy, sensuality and immanence, away from assumptions of durable and transcendent values. This changing vision of the cultural elite expressed a shift in the qualities of popular experience. Amongst the new or intensified qualities was that of the discontinuity and fragmentation of experience. There were many literary testimonies to this, some of them celebrating the exciting variety and 'feverish joys' which were now at hand, but most recoiling in anxiety or confusion from the bombardment of the senses.[23] In the city one is continually confronted by, and is part of, a motley human traffic in which the only unity usually experienced is that of a physical mass; people succeed one another in each other's experience in a disconnected stream, their purposes unknown. Faces, bodies and vehicles are adjacent in time and space, but apparently not linked by anything else. Images, goods and information are presented simultaneously or in rapid sequence, each perhaps with a powerful appeal but with no intrinsic relation to the next.

It is very difficult not to be cliched when trying to specify this disintegrative quality of city life, because complaints about the pace, impersonality and chaos of the city have become routinized in popular discourse. It helps therefore to go back to the earlier statements of distress about the quality of the metropolitan experience, to the attempts of commentators at the turn of the century to articulate what were perceived as the new pressures and costs brought by these unprecedented human settlements.

We can do this by taking not a literary example, but one from early sociology. In an interesting coincidence, Freud's *The Interpretation of Dreams*, though it actually appeared in 1899, bore the publication date of 1900, as did a book entitled *The Philosophy of Money* by the sociologist Georg Simmel. Simmel lived and worked in Berlin, and in this book he set out some observations about the phenomenology of city life. He extended these three years later in his classic essay of urban sociology, 'The metropolis and mental life'. Simmel states very clearly some points which have since been endlessly repeated, usually less clearly, in the everyday critique of the city: the intensity of stimulation and the 'crowding of impressions', the anonymity and the matter-of-fact soullessness. The number and variety of human contacts, he suggested, are such that no individual can respond to them all and remain inwardly coherent. The options for the city-dweller are therefore to become unresponsive, or to disintegrate psychically. In more recent psychoanalytic thinking, a worse scenario than Simmel imagined is described, in which both these alternatives are combined: in the schizoid condition a degree of inner disintegration is characteristically masked by a degree of outward indifference. Simmel's diagnostic framework did not comprehend such ironies of the unconscious, but his analysis of urban subjectivity is nonetheless a rich one.

He described the conditions of life to which, I am suggesting, the technique of free association, and indeed psychoanalysis as a whole, can be seen as a response. At the same time that Simmel and others were charting the fragmenting impact of metropolitan life, Freud was tracing configurations of meaning beneath the senseless fragments of dreams, which tend to collect, as Freud put it, the 'indifferent and insignificant' elements of waking experience.[24] Looking beneath the imagery of the dream, which multiplies the bizarre juxtapositions and disconnections of waking life in the city, he found patterns of personal meaning, threads of association which could be woven together into a restored fabric of experience.

Freud saw dreams as stemming partly from the need to work out ideas, and work through feelings, that had been provoked by some aspect of the previous day's experience, and which there had been no opportunity to deal with during the day. Perhaps this has always been one function of dreaming, but how much more urgent and burdensome a task it must have become in a world where even a few minutes of waking experience in a city centre can generate a mass of unfinished business – desires and fears evoked by passing faces in the street, memories and wishes associated with an advertisement glimpsed on the Underground escalator, and so on.

Why was and is the modern environment so fragmenting in its effect upon subjectivity? Beneath the urban flux Simmel saw the money economy and the dominance of social relations by impersonal calculation. His voice is one amongst a number to be heard in classical sociology according to which the major source of modern dislocation is the capitalist market. By driving out all considerations except ones of profit, market forces tend to dissolve those frameworks of meaning and community which can provide for the deeper coherence of experience. As Erich Fromm was to put it in his description of the dominant psychic orientation of the modern era: 'the premise of the marketing orientation is emptiness, the lack of any specific quality which could not be subject to change.'[25]

The problem with the city is therefore not only nor even mainly one of the sheer quantity of stimulation. Its disorganizing impact is not primarily a matter of its scale, though that is important, but of its soul. It is a problem of the moral quality of interpersonal contacts and of relationships with the physical environment. This kind of picture of modern life is heavily indebted to Webererian accounts of the 'rationalization' and 'disenchantment' of the Western world. The secularization of experience, the weakening of religion as the main source of transcendent frames of meaning, is no doubt the most important cultural underpinning of the developments Simmel described.

To these sociological analyses[26] we can add a psychoanalytic dimension, drawing upon recent debates about the possibility that deep changes in psychic structure have occurred as a consequence of the socio-economic development of capitalism. The dissolution of traditional frameworks of meaning and authority, including and especially those organizing family relationships, has led, it has been argued (most forcefully in the works of Rieff and Lasch) to crises of superego formation and ego-integration. The miscellaneous and atomized nature of the external world is thus impressed upon a psychic apparatus itself beset by internal disintegrative pressures.

Since the initial formulations of this problem, around the turn of the century, things have arguably got a great deal worse. People everywhere in the advanced industrial and post-industrial nations, whether or not they live in the metropolis, live increasingly in the metropolitan mode. Moreover the business of consumption has assumed an increasingly dominant place in the everyday life of the city and its extending hinterland. Social membership and personal identity are increasingly defined in terms of consumership. Marketing, retailing, leisure and service industries absorb larger proportions of the workforce. Advertising comes to dominate the iconics of everyday life. Public space becomes more saturated with the imagery and the practices of consumption, and 'commodification' – treating people and things only in terms of their market value – becomes a powerful trend in all social spheres. All these effects are felt most acutely in the city, where the frontiers of consumption are pushed out the furthest.

The variegated tradition of critique of the 'consumer society' is then relevant here, in so far as it is concerned with the corrosive effects upon psychic integrity of a culture in which the pleasures of consumption have displaced more substantive and ethical codes. Consumption knows no values outside of itself. A malign spiral effect can be discerned,[27] in that the world of consumer goods does offer some kind of integration to the disoriented, disenchanted modern self: an integration into and through the rituals of consumption, and ways to hold the self together in membership of the community of consumers, in a largely spurious sense of agency through the exercise of 'consumer choice', and in regressive psychic satisfactions in fusion with or possession of needed objects.

However, the citizen-turned-consumer is then even further removed, as a result of immersion in the fragmentary imagery of advertising and consumer culture, from any possibility of more authentic integration. At its worst, consumption is a social correlate of the omnipotence described in Chapter 2: things exist only in order to be incorporated, devoured or controlled. There is little basis in successive acts of consumption for an individual's experience to cohere around stable configurations of feeling and value, and for the painful, affective interchanges with other people upon which the development and sustenance of selfhood depends.

The consuming self, bombarded and manipulated by advertising and imagery, is a product of its familial origins, and the family itself has also, on one influential view, been invaded by the market and its values. A key theme in Lasch's work,[28] for example, is the contemporary decline of authority, at the heart of which is the dissolution of parental authority. Confident parental authority, based on a containing discipline as well as on spontaneous love, is a precondition for the child's subordinating its narcissism to its sense of reality, and so acquiring the basis for integrated selfhood. Where the parents lack the commitment or the capacity to sustain their moral authority, and to represent both love and discipline, the child will find difficulty in reconciling itself to the needs of others.

It is the impact of consumer culture upon the family, in this account, which is in large part responsible for the subversion of the moral-affective ties upon which parental authority is based, and their replacement by the shifting imperatives of the market – fashion, youth cultures, mobility and so on. (In Lasch's view, shared to some extent by the earlier writers of the Frankfurt School – see below and note 30 – and, in a different way, by Foucault, another large part of the responsibility rests with bureaucratic regulation of families and with the welfare professionals who claim privileged expert knowledge on how to bring up children, thus de-skilling parents.)

Through these psychoanalytic reflections on the experiential effects of the growing city and of the culture of consumption, we are able to complement the social-historical analysis of free association with a psychoanalytic perspective on socio-historical change, and so move towards a thoroughly two-way strategy for interdisciplinary work.

The related critique of 'mass society' is another tradition of social analysis which is of relevance here, in that it has often included reference to the experiential qualities of life in the city, which is the principal stage on which the 'masses' and 'mass culture' make their appearance. In the classic writings of the Frankfurt School[29] a major theme is the 'decline of the individual', by which was meant the erosion in mass society of an autonomous, rational, integrated individual who occupied a coherent moral space and was therefore capable of moral choice and spontaneous authenticity. The individual is increasingly a passive, de-centred consumer manipulated by the 'culture industry', and is easily seduced, through the process of 'repressive desublimation' (as Marcuse termed the cultural liberalization of late capitalism) into the consumption of commodified pleasures.[30]

However, we are by now in some very deep waters of social theory, and face some serious terminological difficulties and problems in periodization. Take for instance the historical account offered by Fredric Jameson.[31] Under the heading of *post*-modernism, he describes – and locates within the last thirty years – a number of the cultural tendencies which I have been referring to: the fragmentation of the subject, the superficiality of affect, the break-up of stylistic norms. I have been describing such developments as 'modern' (in a sociological if not in a literary or history of art sense), and locating their emergence around the turn of the century. Amongst the questions which then suggest themselves are these. Are there different phases to these psychosocial developments? Are they best described as characteristics of 'modernity', or of 'post-modernity'? And how in *today's* experience do the tendencies towards fragmentation appear? What is the utility in this context of the terms 'consumer culture' and 'mass society'? Both terms are often used in ways that lack precision, and that may associate them with highbrow distaste for anything popular.

Without going further into these issues, I will try to clarify the assumptions which are involved in the broad historical perspective on psychoanalysis being offered here, and which I think remain tenable whatever answers are given to the foregoing questions. I am assuming that although our contemporary world has been in the process of formation for many centuries, a particularly rapid and profound phase of its establishment can be seen to have occurred in a period of thirty years or so across the turn of this century. Some of the cultural phenomena and qualities of social experience which came to prominence in that period, and which were particularly characteristic of the emergent metropolitan environments, are still central to everyday life. (This, though, is not to overlook the profound changes in the 'cultural logic of capital', as Jameson calls it, that have taken place since, especially in the post-World War II 'settlement' and again in the 1980s.)

A particular range of psychosocial phenomena are in focus here, all characterized by the fragmentation of experience and the decomposition of meaning. This focus invokes a central theme in a wide and long tradition of modern lament, in which present-day society (whether defined as capitalist, as market society, consumer society or mass society) has destroyed the old values and regularities. This tradition shades on one side into reactionary or empty clichés about good old days, but also it incorporates some of the most profound sources of social and moral critique, from Marx through Weber to a number of contemporary positions. It is a tradition of some melancholy, but not necessarily of elitist hauteur nor of nostalgic reaction.

Accordingly the reader can appropriately place this argument within that tradition, providing that it is borne in mind that we are not talking about a total description of modern society, but rather about one trend or one set of elements within it, and one important way of evaluating those elements. Nor is it even an adequate account of the principal features of the metropolitan experience, which like the society of which it is a part is a much more mixed phenomenon than the foregoing discussion might suggest. Simmel, though unsparing in his critique of it, was in many ways an enthusiast for the city, for the real gains it could provide in individual freedom. Alongside the reaction against the modern metropolis, there has been a contrary tradition of appreciation, following Baudelaire, which has influenced social thought about the city (e.g. in the work of Richard Sennett, for whom the disorder of the turn-of-the-century city offered rich new possibilities for psychological growth in the diversity of contacts with others that it made possible.[32])

Clearly any one-dimensional jeremiad about the ills of consumption and the megalopolis will match poorly the lived experience of modernity, with the real as well as the illusory possibilities it has brought for individual freedom, expression and satisfaction. Marshall Berman's well known book is an eloquent exploration of the complexity of modern experience, while in Peter Saunders' contribution to a 'new sociology of consumption' there is an example of the argument that consumption can provide a legitimate sphere of choice, control and self-expression, and a genuinely therapeutic way of contending with contemporary disorientation.[33]

Here I am concentrating on just one aspect of metropolitan

culture, and the main argument will probably by now be clear. It is that the practice of psychoanalysis, following the fundamental rule of free association, is concerned with the integration of experience and the generation of meaning, and as such constitutes a potential opposition to the psychologically disintegrative tendency in contemporary culture. In adopting the technique of free association Freud was encouraging his patients to listen to the voices of their hearts, and so to rise above the shouting of the market.

This is not a novel contention, but what may be added to it here is the suggestion that it can be given a concrete grounding in the historical sociology of everyday life. I am suggesting that as well as seeing the application of free association as the outcome of complex developments in the history of psychology, and as a romantically influenced challenge to modernity, we can also see it as a response to more mundane features of the culture in which it originated, as a response to the day-to-day interactions and experiences of people in the milieux of its development. It offered to restore meaning to subjectivities which were increasingly being constructed and maintained in environments of impaired meaning.

'Meaning' is used here more in the senses of affective and moral meaning rather than those of cognitive or perceptual meaning. The issue is not whether people can make logical statements, perceive physical objects correctly, understand messages, and generally perform cognitive processing of information; on the whole they can. It is more a question of whether they can feel that their whole life experience can be contextualized within some encompassing framework of meaning, whether this be in the terms of an explicit ethical code, at a more implicit level of felt values, or simply in relation to their capacity to give coherent accounts of their lives and conduct.

The tragedy of the individual is more, then, than a transhistorical[34] phenomenon without reference to historical, social realities, fixed only in the biosocial facts of our infantile dependence and in our capacities both for omnipotent illusion and for learning about reality. It also has a historical dimension, which mediates the transhistorical, and at least part of which is rooted in the psychic costs of modernity. These are felt most acutely in the metropolitan environment, where meaning is most under attack and where consumption is at its most intense – and where accordingly phantasies of omnipotence are most persistently excited. This environment is also that in which the reality of the other is most pressed upon us – in all the myriad complaints about the city there is inevitably a complaint about the very fact of other people. *They* are the problem – the ostensibly inhuman 'stresses' and 'pressures' of the city can be nothing other than the bodies and noises and needs of others as they too go about their business. Yet the city is also said to be the place where we are most separated from others and least able to make enduring commitments to them. Given this contradiction, the city is likely to pose particular problems for the integration of the self around a renunciation of omnipotence, a toleration of others and a loving internalization of the other.

Having at last arrived at the nub of its argument, I should now explain the title of this chapter. One of my starting-points for this line of thought was a statement attributed to the literary critic Leo Lowenthal.[35] It is a very rich statement: 'Mass culture is psychoanalysis in reverse.' What Lowenthal probably had in mind here was the inter-war experience of fascism, and to a lesser extent Stalinism, which led the Frankfurt thinkers to the idea that modern mass society inevitably generates authoritarianism: authoritarian systems of government, and authoritarian personalities in its individual members. Psychoanalysis, on the other hand (he presumably implied), is concerned with trying to free the individual from the compulsions and illusions produced by repressive authoritarian socialization, and with developing a rational ego in place of a cruel, irrational authoritarian superego. This is a valid and important statement, both about mass society and psychoanalysis, though it lends itself to simplifications by libertarian rhetoric.

However, the statement can be understood in a different way, as a comment on the vicissitudes of meaning in human experience – an observation that in important ways mass culture acts to destroy meaning, while psychoanalysis is about the recovery and construction of meaning. This is one of the most important *social* meanings of the psychoanalytic pursuit of unconscious meaning. What Freud and psychoanalysts since have sought to do, through the arduous process of free association and interpretation, is to sift through the chaotic debris which necessarily constitutes a large part of modern experience, uncovering its abiding emotional content and trying, where necessary and possible, to reorder it around a core of meaningful selfhood – in other words, to act in a reverse fashion to the cultural tendency towards the *dis*sociation of experiences, thoughts and feelings from each other. Moreover it provides a number of ways to theorize the dissociative trend, such that we can talk both of the social meaning of psychoanalysis and of the psychic meaning of the social trends which elicited the development of psychoanalysis.

Freud's own way of theorizing disintegration emerged in the controversial concept of the death instinct, which he conceptualized as a force at work in living matter seeking 'to disintegrate the cellular organism',[36] to dissolve the complex structures of life and return matter to inorganic stillness. This speculative concept failed to establish itself in much post-Freudian theory, yet we can see it as an indirect expression in Freud's thought of actual social trends (characteristically transmuted by him into philosophical absolutes). The strand of post-Freudian theory which has given greatest credence to the notion of a death instinct, namely Kleinian psychoanalysis, has also been the one to explore states of psychic disintegration most fully, and so to provide the most useful vocabulary for describing both the fragmentational and the reparative tendencies in contemporary experience.

It would be pleasing to report that in addition to his oblique theoretical grasp of modernity, Freud's own experience of the city of Vienna was consistent with the features stressed here, that he too felt overwhelmed and fragmented by the clamour of anonymous persons going disconnectedly about their unknown business outside the windows of his home and consulting room at number 19, Bergasse. Promisingly, Freud is known to have disliked Vienna; in letters to Fliess he spoke of his 'loathing' and 'hate' for it, and described it as 'repulsive' and 'extremely disgusting'.[37] However, he did not enlarge on the grounds for these strong feelings, and the quality of his comments suggests more of an obsessional, libidinal involvement with the city than any fear that it threatened him and others with psychic disintegration. (This is also borne out by Freud's admitting to an ambivalence about Vienna: after arriving in London, he spoke of his love for the prison he had finally escaped.)[38]

Freud's feelings about the *filth* of Vienna point less towards the theme of this chapter than to another aspect of the psychohistory of the modern city: the significance for anally dominated phantasies of the new problems in sewage and rubbish disposal posed by the dense squalor of the inner cities and the greedy sprawl of the suburbs. That is another story, though.[39] Moreover Jones suggests that the main source of Freud's feelings about Vienna may have been its illiberal, anti-Semitic atmosphere, and the opposition to his work and the progress of his career which he encountered there. Nor is there much sign in the self-reports given by the early patients of psychoanalysis that they were particularly preoccupied with the problems of living in Vienna. So we must conclude there is no evidence that Freud explicitly or personally registered the disintegrating qualities of urban life, but it is fortunately not necessary for the argument that he should.

Same Problem, Different Solutions

The argument here is not concerned with the conscious aspects of the work of theorists and practitioners, addressed to problems they were aware of. My case for the social significance of free association is rather based on the notion, commonplace in the history of science, that developments in theory and technique can be related to aspects of the social context unbeknownst to those responsible for them. It may clarify the case, briefly to compare psychoanalysis with other roughly contemporaneous developments in psychological theory seen as different kinds of responses to metropolitan disorientation.

Let us turn to Chicago, another of Mumford's eleven monsters of 1900, in the early years of this century. Here American urban sociology was about to emerge, and another very different and influential response to the mass urban experience was being elaborated within psychological theory, one with enormous subsequent influence in socio-psychological thought. This is the tradition of symbolic interactionism, which grew around the notion of the self developed by Charles Cooley and George Herbert Mead.[40] They theorized the self as consisting *only* of the myriad reflections it saw of itself in interactions with others – the 'looking-glass self' in Cooley's famous, though not entirely appropriate, phrase.

Here, and in the subsequent elaboration of the concept of 'role' in social psychology, the shifting, discontinuous nature of the new subjectivity, continually interrupted or intruded upon by others, came to dominate completely the theoretical attempt to grasp the essence of the self. Freud in comparison strove to find the constant interior of the self, the durable and autonomous patterns that lay beneath the kaleidoscopic contents of the urban consciousness. In other words, Freud's response was more to *contest* the exigencies of the new order, while symbolic interactionism tended more to *reflect* them, uncritically, in its theoretical formulations.

A similar comparison can be made between psychoanalysis and behaviourism, and again between a Viennese and a Chicagoan response. In an interesting paper on the origins of behaviourism, David Bakan[41] has suggested that John Watson, the founder of behaviourism, was profoundly influenced by his experience of Chicago when he arrived there to study at the university, also in 1900. Watson was a raw youth from the rural South, and a refugee from a powerful Baptist upbringing. He was ill-equipped emotionally to deal with the new world of the city, where it seemed as if one's very survival depended upon acquiring a dissociated, mobile and instrumental self. His way of coping with this was not, like Freud, to *challenge* the atomization of experience but to embrace it, theoretically – to posit that human mental life was everywhere nothing other than a morally meaningless aggregation of responses to isolated stimuli. This response to the problem of urban alienation could at least help Watson and those who have adopted his theory, to avoid the pain of feeling that there is something better in life that they have missed out on.

Thus, at least in this context, psychoanalysis can be favourably contrasted with interactionism and behaviourism, which are the main sources of most of today's non-psychoanalytic theories of the person. We should beware, though, of heroizing Freud as a lone fighter for meaning in an age of meaninglessness. There is, for example, another John Watson who is closely linked with another contemporary of Freud's – someone probably more famous than Freud himself and certainly more clearly understood as one who could put together the pieces in the shattered life-worlds of troubled individuals.

This was of course Sherlock Holmes, who has been likened to Freud by various writers.[42] Raymond Williams, whose *The Country and the City* is the source of a number of my generalizations about responses to the urban experience, has suggested that one aspect of the Holmes phenomenon is the capacity of his intelligence to penetrate beneath the bewildering surface detail of life in the city, and to understand a state of affairs by revealing the motivated human action which has brought it about. Freud had to find his way through a different sort of fog, but had – in this respect – a similar project.

Stanley Hyman claims that the dramatic, revelatory construction of Conan Doyle's stories was a clear stylistic influence on

Freud. Carlo Ginzburg has discussed the way in which both Holmes and Freud worked by the close examination of detail, apparently trivial, disconnected or incidental fragments which prove to be parts of an important whole. And Michael Shepherd's essay hints at a similarity of the content of their discoveries, in that the two were both centrally concerned with guilt. We should not get carried away with these homologies, striking and significant though they are; Holmes was concerned with the social prosecution of material guilt, and Freud with the psychic management of irrational guilt. As Steven Marcus suggests, the shift in the location of meaning from Holmes to Freud, from external to internal worlds, 'marks a great historical transformation'.[43] Nonetheless Conan Doyle's readers may well be in pursuit of more than a good story on their vicarious visits to the consulting room in Baker Street.

This leaves us on the brink of some crucial questions about the Holmes/Freud method. Both Conan Doyle and Freud were medical men, transposing techniques developed in medical diagnosis to other spheres. Why should we believe their conclusions? Holmes was fortunate: the culprit, when accused, often admitted the deed. Unconscious wishes are rarely so helpful. The truth value and the healing power of psychoanalysis cannot be so clearly attested. I have suggested that the truth and the therapeutic value of psychoanalysis can be understood partly in terms of its confrontation with tragedy and its related capacity to integrate and make deep sense of experience. To extend this argument it will be necessary to specify the differences between the Freudian response to disintegrative modernity and the many unifying balms offered by detective stories, and – often more damagingly – by religious revivals, mysticisms and charlatan purveyors of meaning. The next three chapters will try to work towards that requirement.

4

THE FATE OF FREUD IN
ACADEMIC PSYCHOLOGY

Freud Is Dead

We are now going to look at how some aspects of Freudian theory have fared in the course of its transmission to certain audiences. One might think that the name 'Freud' denotes a formidable and systematic body of theory, unamenable to its incorporation into any other set of ideas, defiantly insisting on its own preoccupations. There is some truth in this, as is suggested by the volume and vigour of work in the Freudian tradition, broadly conceived, and by the fact that in a number of contexts – particularly, for example, in academic psychology – Freud is often regarded as being largely unassimilable to mainstream ideas, and is granted a presence only as, at best, an interesting relic or suggestive oddity.

Certainly, 'Freud' does not have the same kind of presence in official psychology's consciousness of itself as, say, his approximate contemporary the American William James. James is consensually regarded as a major figure in the establishment of modern psychology, even though today there is no systematic position which is recognizable as 'Jamesian'. His influence is diffuse, and his name claimed for competing traditions such as behaviourism and symbolic interactionism. Freud, in contrast, is not seen as such a flexible and benign figure; in the images of familial roles which help to shape our thinking about the history of science, he is most commonly depicted as a *paterfamilias*, sternly possessive of psychoanalysis as *his* intellectual child and refusing to tolerate others lending a hand in its development. He is not presented as a generous, avuncular figure who gave freely of his concepts for others to use as they would.

Given all this, one might expect to find two things in the accounts of psychoanalysis given in psychology texts. One would expect firstly that there would be a high degree of uniformity between these accounts. If Freud was so recalcitrantly Freudian, then there can be little mistaking what he was on about, and whether or not his present-day expositors agree with him they will at least agree on the fundamentals of what he said. Secondly, the ideas attributed to Freud should be markedly different from those found in other major traditions of psychology. Whether our aim or our conclusion is to reject Freud overall, or to pay him some qualified respect as a pathbreaking pioneer (and these are the two options most often offered to readers of psychology texts), we should be able to distinguish him clearly from the other 'founding fathers'.

When we look at representations of 'Freud' in academic psychology, we find that the first of these predictions is verified, but not the second. This can lead us to question whether the *substance* of Freudian theory is really apprehended in quite the definite way, determined by Freud's own work, that the image of Freud-the-paterfamilias suggests it should be. Does the similarity between representations of Freud occur because textbook authors are all accurately summarizing the actual works of Freud? Or does it come about because they are all seeing Freud through the same powerfully refracting lens?

The second explanation is much closer to the truth. Although in a way these accounts certainly indicate something of the uniqueness of psychoanalysis compared to other psychological paradigms, what can be found on closer inspection is that in them Freud is assimilated to a very familiar and pre-Freudian paradigm. At the heart of the Freudian conception of human nature, most psychology texts inform us, is a simple psychological utilitarianism. According to this traditional doctrine we are all essentially isolated individuals struggling above all to find what happiness we can, and we come closer to happiness the more we can secure for ourselves, as individuals, experiences of pleasure. Freud may be credited with having introduced a revised conception of the nature and sources of this pleasure, by tying it to sexuality and by advancing the notion of infantile sexuality as the developmental origin of pleasure, but these revisions seem to place him only more firmly in the utilitarian camp. In the Freudian conception which is outlined for us, the reductive individualism which is always present in utilitarian accounts of motivation is given a very strong expression: it is a person's individual and asocial *body* which is seen as the ultimate source of all pleasure.

As already noted, there is undoubtedly some warrant in Freud's own writings for this rendering of his theory. However, it is remarkable that in giving such emphasis to the utilitarian tendency in his thought – indeed, in presenting a 'Freud' who it seems knew no other way of conceptualizing human need – what contemporary psychology does is to absorb Freud entirely into one of its own dominant paradigms. In consequence, psychoanalysis appears to be essentially the same kind of psychology as behaviourism, the utilitarian origins of which are beyond dispute. There are still differences, of course, due to Freud's arcane concerns with mythology and anatomy, but underneath these it seems that he is, after all, talking a language that we know. So, many a student of psychology has concluded, why bother with the Gothic scheme of Freudian theory when you can get basically the same message (that each individual strives for maximum gratification, the roots of which are bodily) from a few simple pages of behaviourist metapsychology?

It is as if 'Freud' is not after all a heavy, brooding figure in a dark Victorian portrait. He is rather a mirror, at which the writers of many psychology texts have hurriedly glanced as they press on towards their deadlines. They note the main features of what they see, which is the soulless countenance of utilitarianism, and report to the next generation of students that, although Freud is dead, his theory is still with us because we anyway understood it – at least its useful parts – before he wrote it.

Freud is not the only psychologist who is dead. Yet somehow, as one scans introductory psychology texts, he seems to be more dead than others. This may not be entirely an effect of the texts themselves, but be due in part to the mind-sets with which we (at least the Anglo-American we) read: 'Freud' connotes another time and another place. But the texts are also in part responsible, in that Freud's work is portrayed as ending with Freud. We are not linked to him, it is implied, by a living tradition which carries his work forward to today. The gap between him and ourselves therefore seems to be much greater than that between us and, say,

Pavlov, or G. H. Mead, whose works are described in relation to the present-day research and theorizing which are their direct descendants.

Sometimes, Freud is the only person referred to in the section on psychoanalysis. Often, though, others are given some space, and there is a striking consistency about which figures, from the whole range of important psychoanalytic writers, are selected. The most common format is to follow the section on Freud with somewhat shorter sections on Jung and Adler. Indeed, many diligent students of psychology will believe they know that 'psychoanalysis' comes in three varieties, owing to Freud's intolerance of dissent which drove his more able disciples to establish their own schools in which the dogma of sexuality did not hold sway. (These two other schools are also usually presented as starting and finishing with their founders, which is another noteworthy piece of historical 'freezing', although perhaps a little more excusable since there has been less subsequent development of these schools, particularly the Adlerian, than there has of Freudian theory.)

Another common practice is to follow an exposition of Freud with a discussion of some 'neo-Freudians', particularly Fromm, Horney and Erikson. Here, it is true, an important line of *post*-Freudian development is being indicated, but what is frequently stressed in these accounts are the ways in which such thinkers *departed* from the core psychoanalytic tradition. The main refrain is that they sought to correct what had been one of Freud's major errors, his underestimation of the importance of society and environment.

I shall say more later about the question of Freud and environmentalism, but at this stage we can note two points. The first is that the neo-Freudians' critique of Freud is an important one which has a major place in any overview of psychoanalysis. Yet a powerful case has been made (in the radical Freudian analyses of Juliet Mitchell's *Psychoanalysis and Feminism* and Russell Jacoby's *Social Amnesia*) for seeing their 'sociologizing' of Freud as a dilution or obscuring of his central discoveries about unconscious processes and therefore as outside of psychoanalysis proper. If psychoanalysis is defined in a conceptually rigorous way, this may be so, though the mere drawing of a boundary does not of course necessarily entail the rejection of positions which may lie outside it. Some of the neo-Freudians may themselves have seen their work as substantially revising psychoanalysis, as heterodox, but this does not detract from their potential relevance to a critical account of orthodox psychoanalysis.

The second point is that the significance of the neo-Freudian critique, and the conclusions to be drawn from it about the value of Freud's own ideas, can be assessed only in the light of other major developments in psychoanalytic theory by thinkers who see themselves as working very much *within* the Freudian problematic. In short, there have been many attempts within mainstream psychoanalysis to address the problems focused on by neo-Freudian and other less sympathetic critics of Freud. To suggest, as the textbook accounts of Freud do, that these problems – which are basically concerned with the place of the social in mental life – have been identified only by those at the margins of, or beyond, psychoanalysis, and that the Freudian project itself has been unable to reflect on at least some of its shortcomings, is therefore misleading.

Both the recitation of 'Freud–Jung–Adler', and the selection of some neo-Freudians to represent post-Freudian developments, are the effects of a major flaw in the textbook presentations of psychoanalysis, namely a more or less complete absence of any indication of its historical development. If behaviourist psychology were treated in the same way, the result would perhaps be an attempt to give a systematic summary of Watson's work, followed by brief references to Guthrie and Hull, and no more. The radical reformulations introduced by Skinner and Bandura, and the attempts to sophisticate the theory by generations of psychologists working consciously within the behaviourist tradition, would all be omitted. This would be an equivalent of the failure to take account of the post-Freudian developments in psychoanalysis. Although ego-psychology is occasionally mentioned, the whole crucial expansion and reorientation of psychoanalysis carried out by Kleinian and object-relations theorists is rarely even acknowledged (except in a very few recent texts by more informed authors).

The Mysteries of the Consulting Room

We can conclude that much present-day writing in psychoanalysis, with its language of phantasy, internal objects, counter-transference, containment, projective identification and so forth, would be incomprehensible to the authors of today's psychology texts.

They nonetheless feel able to expound on the limits of psycho-analysis to a large and probably impressionable audience.

The reasons for this extraordinary treatment of psychoanalysis – its reduction to an impoverished reading of a selection of themes in Freud's own work – will be discussed later. It amounts to a consistent failure to meet some of the most basic demands of scientific work: the need to consult all relevant authorities, to review all sources systematically, to take account of recent (and not-too-recent) developments – in short, to know what one is talking about. It is quite clear that decades of writing in the psychoanalytic journals, and nearly all key theoretical texts since Freud, are unknown to the textbook writers. Sometimes it is even questionable whether they have read much by Freud himself, since direct references to his work are not always to be found in their bibliographies. Occasionally good selections of introductory readings are listed (say, *The Interpretation of Dreams*, the *Introductory Lectures* and the *New Introductory Lectures*), but frequently the referencing is distinctly thin. (Freud's posthumously published *Outline of Psychoanalysis* is a favourite, being the only reference given in a number of texts. Significantly, this is described by Freud himself as a dogmatic work – it is a highly condensed summary which states many things far more crudely than they are formulated elsewhere in Freud's writing.)

Not surprisingly, given this lack of adherence to the usual standards of scholarly work, and of responsible teaching, important errors can sometimes be found. This is especially so when the textbooks undertake to pass comment on psychoanalysis as a therapeutic practice, a topic into which neither their reading nor their personal, cultural and professional experience is likely to have given them much insight. For example, Eysenck is of the opinion that in psychoanalysis, 'Treatment consists in *uncovering* the original infantile experience which laid the basis for the later neurosis.'[1]

While that may have passed muster as a comment on the psychoanalytic method in 1897, it would certainly not now be accurate as a statement of its primary purpose. Since the effective abandonment of the seduction theory of the aetiology of neurosis, and the gradual establishment instead of the notions of wish and phantasy at the centre of psychoanalytic theory, a process under way by the turn of the century, psychoanalysis has not basically been a piece of detective work in search of a single pathogenic trauma – another difference, incidentally between Freud and Holmes. Eysenck, one of the most contemptuous critics of psychoanalysis, offers this characterization of psychoanalytic therapy as the only description of the treatment itself in ten pages of criticism of it.

For another text, psychoanalysis as therapy is 'a means of obtaining controlled regression back to the psychosexual stage at which the patient is supposed to have been fixated . . . the analyst attempts to right the previous wrongs so that the desired emotional maturity may be reached by the patient'.[2] Here the notion of analytic therapy as a forensic return to the scene of a crime is compounded with an implication that the analyst is an omnipotent healer, bringing justice and maturity to the helpless patient. Any sensible student encountering a practice described in these terms would be wise to reject it as banal and grandiose – which may well be the judgment which authors of such descriptions have already formed of psychoanalysis.

Again, then, a misleading picture of psychoanalysis, derived from partial descriptions of the technique at very early stages of its historical development, is presented with the likely effect (and, we might suspect in some cases, the intention) of discrediting it. Indeed, the picture is *false*: no competent analyst is likely to describe analytic practice as a righting of wrongs, whatever that might mean, and a familiarity with any contemporary analytic literature, or with practising analysts, would make this clear.

This typical misconstruction is again probably the result of a reliance on secondary sources which themselves are fixated, as we might say, on a simplified conception of psychoanalytic technique at an early stage of its development. At least it does not include any frankly imaginative or invented details of what the treatment involves, unlike this slightly earlier report of what goes on in the psychoanalytic consulting room: 'The therapy begins with a physical examination to identify organic causes of the disturbance. Interviewing, testing and personality assessment may then be performed to try to construct a "picture" of the person's personality.'[3] This is a laughable description to anyone today who is at all familiar with psychoanalysis. Where the authors got the idea that an analyst (who is quite likely not to be a medical doctor) physically examines the patient, and may 'perform' a test of some description, we can but guess at. (The only reference quoted with any discussion of psychoanalysis in it is Eysenck's *Fact and Fiction in Psychology*, which just rehearses generalized criticisms with no description of the process.)

An Illustrative Error

When we come to psychoanalytic theory, the picture does not appear to be any better. For Freud, we are told in the same book, 'sex' included 'all the basic drives, needs and motives'.[4] Freud's extensive theorizing about aggression is completely ignored. Certainly Freud saw the expressions of aggression as profoundly interrelated with sexuality, but this relatively sophisticated point about instinctual dynamics is rarely approached in introductory texts.

The two misrepresentations of psychoanalysis just described made their appearance in a widely read paperback (linked to a major series of television programmes), though admittedly one published over twenty years ago. Have things improved since? Basically they have not. One of the best-selling textbooks in Britain and the US is Atkinson *et al.*'s *Introduction to Psychology*. The most recent, ninth, edition of this substantial text still carries the statement from earlier editions that 'Projection is really a form of rationalization'.[5] This particular misconception is worth a brief discussion, since it indicates a general tendency which can be observed, amidst more miscellaneous errors, in the textbook treatments of Freud, and which will be the main theme of the rest of this chapter.

Projection, both in Freud's own work and increasingly since, is a process of a most primitive and fundamental kind, perhaps best understood by analogy with a physical process of evacuation or expulsion. A part of oneself is disowned and projected on to or into another person or other external 'object' (see Chapter 2). Something mentally intolerable is got rid of – only to return, usually, to oppress or persecute the self from the outside (or what appears to be the outside). Along with its opposite, introjection, this process is at work from the beginnings of psychic development. Indeed, it is through the complex interchange between expulsion and incorporation, projection and introjection, that the very boundaries of the self are established. Present-day psychoanalytic theory is far from settled on matters such as the precise origins, scope and interrelationships of the various processes involved here. There is, however, no dispute that projection must be understood as one of a set of fundamental psychic processes, without which the very constitution and being of the self could not be conceptualized.

Yet in Atkinson *et al.*'s text, projection is merely a particular type of rationalization. In psychoanalysis, and similarly in one of its uses in everyday discourse, this latter term refers to the self-deceptive production of rational or otherwise acceptable reasons for one's actions, when their real sources lie in some unconscious, irrational wish. This is by definition a relatively complex process, requiring developmentally high levels of intellectual functioning. It is not one of the psychologically basic defences, like projection, by means of which disturbing psychic contents are repressed.[6] It is rather a way of camouflaging a defence which has already been erected: the wish is already unconscious.

What we then have in this textbook error is the transmutation of a preverbal, elementary and ubiquitous process into a sub-type of an occasional and very intellectual operation. The force and primitivity of projective expulsion is lost in the bland concept of post-hoc rationalization. It is suggested that we project parts of ourselves not because we find them intolerable, and not because projection is indeed one of the main channels of exchange between inner and outer worlds, but simply because by projection we might sometimes be able to account for why we feel or act towards someone in a particular way. This is a complete misunderstanding of the concept of projection, which is intended to illuminate the real reasons, not the rationalizations, for someone's actions and experiences. Paranoid persons have delusions of persecution *because* they have projected into the outer world their own persecutory rage; they do not project because they have delusions.

An error of this magnitude in a description of, say, Piagetian theory would not pass into the ninth edition of a prestigious text. Its effect here is twofold. Firstly, psychoanalysis is trivialized, in that one of its most powerful concepts is assimilated into a familiar observation. And secondly, a concept which is primarily about the affective *relation* between a subject and an object, or between two subjects, is presented as if it were about the solipsistic calculations of an ego concerned only with its own individual coherence. 'Rationalization' is not a relational concept, and in seeing it as more basic than projection Atkinson *et al.* betray one of the main underlying tendencies in their, and others', treatment of psycho-analysis. This is to ignore the possibilities it contains for a relational and communitarian understanding of the individual, and instead to present it exclusively as a rather crude form of utilitarianism.

This tendency is best discussed with reference to the portrayal of the ego.

Ego, Superego and Others

There is a high degree of uniformity in the textbook portrayals of the ego. Basically we find that a conception of the ego drawn from Freud's earlier writings is more or less accurately presented, with no reference whatever to another and in some ways radically different conception which can be identified in his later work and which is the key to much contemporary psychoanalytic thinking. Following Laplanche and Pontalis in their detailed discussion of the complexities of Freud's thinking about the ego,[7] this later conception can be summarized as one which sees the ego as the product of identifications with others (see Chapter 2). It therefore sees the ego as emerging from, and remaining embedded in, inter-personal relations; it is a relational, *social* entity. In the earlier conception, by contrast, the ego is an outgrowth of the id. It is the surface or intelligent cortex which the id develops in order to negotiate its demands with the external world (and with the superego as well). It is in this view a fundamentally biological entity, an organ of adaptation.

Not infrequently this conception of the ego is misunderstood as implying its equivalence to consciousness, where – it is assumed – our most intelligent and adaptive processes are seated. Even an unusually careful and complex account[8] identifies the ego as 'the superficial, conscious self'. Those learning from such a text would be unlikely to know that the ego is also seen as having profound unconscious dimensions.

In a number of accounts, including Atkinson *et al.*'s, a Darwinian model of the ego is translated into the modern language of business: the ego is the 'executive' part of the personality. It is 'a kind of chairman of the board that must find some way of arranging compromises between the demands of the id and the superego'.[9] Similarly, it is 'a kind of referee'[10] in the battle between the other two agencies of the mind. These metaphors are derived more from the social experience of the authors concerned than from Freudian texts, even if they do convey some elements of Freud's thought. The ego weighs the id's demands against the needs of 'society', represented by both the superego and the external world, and tries to arrange a course of action which will bring the maximum possible happiness, i.e. the greatest differential between id-satisfaction and punishment (whether internal, in the form of guilt induced by the superego, or external, in the form of reprisals taken by the external world).

This is a straightforwardly utilitarian conception of psychological functioning, with the ego as the calculator and arbiter of utilities. Freud's message is that 'Man is a pleasure-loving animal', states an A-level text.[11] 'The model of motivation developed by Freud is a hedonistic tension-reduction model, which implies that each individual's primary goal is to obtain pleasure', affirms a leading British textbook,[12] which goes on to rehearse the usual castigation of this model as 'primarily mechanistic'. It is the ego's job to find the opportunities for pleasure, and this defines it as essentially the servant of that from which it came, the id. The ego 'has the task ... of finding ways in the real world to satisfy the id's demands'.[13] Or, as another text[14] put it, in terms that a cognitive psychologist would feel at home with, 'the important point here is that there is one aspect of mind that frames an idea containing certain urges [the id], and another aspect of mind [the ego] that searches for ways to express those urges'.

Freud himself was rather less consistent in his views about who served whom in the psychic household. On the same page of 'The dissection of the psychical personality'[15] he suggests both that 'The ego's relation to the id might be compared with that of a rider to his horse', and that the id (along with the superego and the external world) is one of the 'three tyrannical masters' of the ego. Acknowledging the inconsistency, he adjusts his first metaphor so that the horse is guiding the rider, though as he says this is a 'not precisely ideal situation' – neither for the ego, we might say, nor for the coherence of his formulations: the metaphors will not mix. These largely incompatible conceptions of the ego–id relation provide a choice point in the development of psychoanalytic theory, from which quite divergent tendencies, leading to different evaluations of the ego, may be seen to originate.

However, none of these problems, about whether the ego is or can be in charge of its own house, make an appearance in the texts under consideration. The position usually taken is that the ego is simply an enlightened form of the id. Some support for this position can be obtained from Freud's 1911 work 'Formulations on the two principles of mental functioning',[16] where the 'reality principle', which the ego is usually taken to represent, is characterized as a more sophisticated form of the pleasure principle. 'Actually the substitution of the reality principle for the pleasure principle implies no deposing of the pleasure principle, but only a safe-guarding of it'.[17] The pleasure principle is preserved, in this for-mulation of Freud's, by rendering it more realistic and subtle. While external reality may oppose pleasure, it does so condi-tionally, and to follow the 'reality principle' is not to forgo pleasure but rather to work out, rationally, how pleasure may best be extracted from a reality in which the *un*conditional demands of the 'pleasure principle' would founder.

Following this, one text[18] concludes that the id and the ego are brought together under the control of the 'pleasure principle', and it adds that Freud's is a 'negative' hedonism, since he sees pleasure as *relief* from the suffering of inner tensions and excessive excitation. While we must acknowledge the authorization given to this picture by Freud's writings, it is worth noting that the psychology texts do not consider the extent to which the introduction of the reality principle involves a qualitative change in the operation of the pleasure principle. Predominant though pleasure may still be, it is in such a transformed way – incorporating the idea that pleasure can be found in the most self-denying or sublimatory of pursuits – that the pleasure principle could be seen as having been expanded to the point of subverting itself.[19]

On the whole, then, in these texts the ego is unproblematically taken to be the street-wise agent of the id. It is, to be sure, constrained to act at times in ways that sharply disappoint its employer. But for the most part and in the long run it is seen to be engaged in the pursuit of a happiness defined by the criterion of tension-reduction – that is, in terms of completely individualized pleasure, grounded in the body and of biological rather than social meaning. On this reading the ego is ultimately rooted in biology, whether the emphasis is on the biology of the individual body and its capacity for pleasure (the fulfilment of which is the ego's final goal), or on the biological notion of adaptation as the key concept in understanding the body-environment relation (and as the strat-egy employed by the ego in pursuit of its hedonic goals). There is no room here for any conception of the ego as emergent from intersubjective processes.

It may be objected at this point that this is too harsh a verdict on the textbooks' rendering of the ego, which may be less biologistic than I have suggested. After all, they frequently stress that the distinctive characteristic of the ego's agency is its rationality, and is this not obviously a sign that the ego must in some way be a product of human culture? (Indeed, some critics of Freud, and some post-Freudians, have attacked the concept of the ego – or the ego itself – for its embodiment of a historically specific set of cultural values, namely those stemming from Enlightenment rationality.)[20] This objection, however, begs an important question about the origins and location of the kind of instrumental rationality attributed to the ego: in these texts this rationality is seen as essentially *outside* of human society, as an absolute principle of life. Then Freud's 'symbolic but asocial view' can be unfavourably contrasted with symbolic interactionism.[21] Characteristic of the ego's rationality, it is suggested,[22] is learning not to touch the flame – a kind of rationality shared with non-human organisms.

This concept of the ego as an organ of adaptation is less the product of contemporary psychoanalytic theory, though it can certainly find some justification in Freud and the analytic tradition as a whole, than of predominant modes of thinking in non-psychoanalytic psychology. Octave Mannoni has noted how in the United States psychoanalysis was absorbed into 'a pseudo-Darwinian model of social adjustment'.[23] He refers to a striking example of how this affected psychologists' understanding of what Freud actually said. In 1949 Ernest Hilgard (who was the senior author of early editions of the Atkinson *et al.* textbook) commented that the 'mechanisms of adjustment' were the first aspects of Freudian theory to be taken on by psychology. Mannoni observes with astonishment that there has never been in Freudian theory any concept of 'adjustment', nor even any use of the term.[24] The 'Freud' that some American psychologists welcomed appeared to be a creature of their own imaginations, a projection particularly of their pre-Freudian imagery of the ego.

Thus, as one writer sums it up, 'the ego, like the id, is amoral'.[25] It knows of no transcendent social values and has no commitments to any human collectivity. Although occasionally one comes across references to a superficial sociality of the ego, when it is described as the part of the personality directly interacting with others,[26] there is no trace of a theory of the ego as *constituted* by its relatedness to others. The textbooks reserve that quality for the superego. Here at last we may find a social element in the expositions of Freud, and a powerful one, perhaps.

The superego is the 'internalized representative of society'.[27] In this notion, it seems, is to be found the strongly environmentalist tendency in Freud which the more sympathetic accounts of psychoanalysis often imply is its great merit. Society's teachings are installed in our minds in our superegos, which are therefore the sole repository in our minds of 'social values'. Freud is deemed to have stressed two features of this internalization of society: that it is mediated by our parents, and that it is primarily (sometimes, it is suggested, exclusively) a negative presence, a matter entirely of prohibitions, restrictions and punishments. The superego is 'the parent within',[28] though not infrequently in these expositions the familial focus of psychoanalysis is lost in the presentation of the superego as the accumulation within of *all* social authorities experienced in childhood. Whether at home or at school, though, the function of 'society' and its representatives is clear; it is to prevent the attainment of infantile pleasures, indeed of any pleasures. 'Society' and 'authority' are simply massive interdictions, and their internalization consists primarily of negative limits.

Here we find the basis of the contention that Freud's theory is a gloomy, pessimistic and negative one. 'Freud's view of human nature was essentially negative', state Atkinson *et al.*,[29] and this judgment is endlessly repeated throughout the texts under review. We are driven by the same instincts as animals, Atkinson *et al.* continue, and as such we then can do nothing but struggle with the society which must oppose their satisfaction. It should be noted that consistently though this critique appears, it is not always consistent with other parts of the accounts given. For example, the same authors go on to say that despite the many possibilities for conflict between the three parts of the psychic apparatus, 'More often in the normal person the three work together to produce integrated behaviour'.[30] In this they are anticipating the humanistic psychologists' rewriting of the Freudian tragedy, but they allow themselves to slip into this assertion of psychic unity before they have left the chapter on Freud. Other texts are also remarkably unclear about the extent to which the ego is locked in conflict with the superego. For example one states that, 'The ego must control and refine the promptings of the superego', but also inexplicably defines the superego itself as 'a refinement of the ego-function' (and on the next page it is Freud who is accused of being 'logically incoherent').[31]

Setting aside these particular weaknesses, there are two major shortcomings in the usual characterization of the superego. Firstly no reference is made to a crucial element in Freud's views on the origins of the superego. In the *New Introductory Lectures* he writes:

> Thus a child's superego is in fact constructed on the model not of its parents but of its parents' superego; the contents which fill it are the same and it becomes the vehicle of tradition and of all the time-resisting judgments of value which have propagated themselves in this manner from generation to generation.[32]

This statement establishes the radically unconscious nature of the superego and its transmission, and its non-identity with actual external prohibitions. Times change: culture and mores change. New prohibitions may develop, and old ones may lose their social authority, as we have seen during the Sixties and other periods of cultural flux in this century. But something in the psyche resists these changes; resources of primitive moral feeling remain beneath liberalizing changes in moral behaviour, and threaten to destabilize the changes. Our recent political and cultural history bears some witness to this phenomenon, in the resurgence of self-proclaimed 'traditional' values in the wake of the 'permissive society'.

This conception of the superego as based on the unconscious reproduction of psychic contents, which are not derived from the parents' explicit teachings, is greatly strengthened by the Kleinian formulation of the role of the individual's own aggression in superego development. The harshness and cruelty of the superego, Klein contended, stem from the individual's own endowment of aggression, some of which is masochistically invested in the superego. Freud's conception of 'moral masochism', of our unconscious need for punishment, had prepared the way for this understanding of superego functioning as rooted at least in part *within* the individual, rather than resulting from the straightforward import into the individual of social mores. On the latter view, although intra-individual conflict then occurs, it is really a straightforward conflict between individual desires and social prohibitions, to which some resolution is at least theoretically possible.

The textbook accounts referred to, as part of their general neglect of post-Freudian work, completely fail to mention any endopsychic (i.e. radically *internal*) element in the formation of the superego. Putting that together with their partial grasp of Freud's own thinking, the result is a conception of the superego which is simplistically environmentalist and utilitarian, and which could have been produced (as indeed to some degree it has been) by a behavioural psychologist. It conveys that the superego develops as a matter of simple expediency: it enables the child to anticipate the adverse external consequences of some actions it might take in the pursuit of happiness, by threatening correspondingly adverse internal consequences in the form of guilt. It is thus responsible for the debit entries in the psychic book which the ego is trying to balance, or rather to manage in such a way that there is an excess of credits (satisfactions, entered in the name of the id) over debits (superego/real-world punishments and reprisals).

In this kind of environmentalism, *all* the ills and unhappiness that befall us can be laid neatly at the door of the outside world, since the superego – in its punishing aspects so clearly the source of so much unhappiness – is nothing more than the direct representative of the external world in the psyche. This can be contrasted with another kind of environmentalism which can be attributed to Freud, in which the concept of identification is central. Earlier in this chapter a model of the ego was referred to in which the ego is seen as the product of identifications with others. The same can be said of the superego – indeed, even the psychology texts sometimes say it, usually in describing the boy's 'identification' with his father as the basis of the masculine superego. Identification as they describe it is, however, an instrumental manoeuvre, carried out to avert the father's reprisal and to secure, in the long-term, the desired satisfaction of possessing the woman of the house. It is not seen as the very ground of being, as the basic means by which differentiation and psychic development is achieved, and as the basic expression of our need for others, of our fundamentally relational nature.

This second kind of environmentalism sees identification as an active, assimilatory process, not as the passive registration in the mind of an external figure. Moreover, the person or 'object' installed within as a result of identification is to some degree the creation of the baby or child making the identification, since what is taken in is not an unmodified piece of the external world but an object of experience which will itself have been infused, through projection, with some of the identifier's own psyche. A projective-introjective interplay, constitutive of the self, is thus the context within which the importance of 'environment' must be understood.

While this framework is one which allows clear critiques of certain environmental arrangements to be made, it does not permit the simplistic location of all efficacy – and thereby often all blame and badness – on 'society' or 'environment'. It is an environmentalism within which personal agency and individual responsibility can – albeit at times with some difficulty – be recognized, and it contrasts with behaviourist environmentalism in which, ultimately, the problem is *completely* 'out there'. Just what the relative weights of the introjective and projective components are remains controversial, but this does not vitiate the general formulation of development in these terms.

Banalizing the Unconscious

The accounts that we have been considering of ego and superego therefore complement each other. Both embody a failure to take on board the full psychoanalytic theory of identification, and both are premised on the notion of a preconstituted 'id', a set of impulses (with built-in goals) which 'society' is inevitably opposed to. They add up to a rendition of psychoanalysis which strongly encourages the reader to regard it as at best a rather quaint piece of dated conceptual machinery. It may generously be stated that 'Freud still deserves to be read',[33] but this concession may turn out to be in recognition of Freud's literary stylishness rather than for the content of his work, which is perhaps acceptable as a descriptive language but is 'much more dubious' as explanatory theory.[34] After all, his work was 'speculative rather than substantiated',[35] and 'should not be taken too seriously [since there is] very little evidence that Freud was anywhere near correct in his theories'.[36]

Such condescension and dismissal is, however, often tempered with an acknowledgment (sometimes merely gestural, sometimes perplexed) of Freud's 'greatness' – for example the last-quoted text continues to say that 'Freud's perspectives were profound'. Just why this is so is usually unclear. What is implied, though, is that they do not constitute proper psychology, since the 'ingenious' or 'imaginative' 'inventions' of Freud are not a part of 'the body of established psychological knowledge',[37] into which they must be integrated. Thus Freud is a figure routinely paid homage to but not someone whom anyone would *now* regard as providing a useful framework for *today*'s thinking.

In a few cases one can feel that the authors of these texts are struggling with the limitations and distortions of their discipline, and are trying to offer a more rounded, accurate and sympathetic account of psychoanalysis than they are likely to have received themselves. For the most part, however, there is little to say in mitigation for the repeated abrogation of intellectual standards found in the treatment of Freud. There is a selectivity and one-sidedness not only in the reading to psychoanalysis, but also in the cues taken from within academic psychology itself, where although the main feeling has been strongly anti-psychoanalytic there have also been a number of more sophisticated expositors and defenders of Freud.

Particularly amongst British psychologists trained in earlier, more humanist and cosmopolitan intellectual atmospheres prior to World War II, and amongst those of European origins, there have been some firm pro-Freudian voices. The leading cognitive and developmental psychologist Jerome Bruner has been one of the most eminent of these, as has the social psychologist Marie Jahoda.[38] For some years now her writings on the relationships between psychology and psychoanalysis have been available to psychologists wishing to get a better grasp of psychoanalysis and its relevance to their concerns. Her *Freud and the Dilemmas of Psychology* points out that academic psychology is plagued with the controversies and problems about scientificity and so forth which some psychologists imply are the particular affliction of psychoanalysis. She argues that psychoanalysis, incorporating elements of natural science, social science and 'humanistic' science, is the most complete psychology yet developed, and the one most expressive of tensions and problems within psychology as a whole.

Analyses of this sort have never received space in mainstream psychology texts. The latter's systematic denigration of psychoanalysis, though it may have gained in intensity during the post-World War II period which saw narrowly scientistic ideologies become overwhelmingly dominant in academic psychology, is almost as old as psychoanalysis itself. A 1943 survey of all academic psychology textbooks published since 1900 (a total then of 248 books), and of samples of abnormal psychology and psychiatry texts, found that, 'Rejection [of psychoanalysis] refers less frequently to concrete statements of Freud's theory but rather to a stereotypical concept of psychoanalysis in general'. The dogmatic quality of psychology's response to Freud was evident then – 'little use was made of the legitimate methods of science' to assemble empirical disproof of Freud, or to advance any alternative theories. Twenty years later another survey reported a widespread ignorance of the specifics of psychoanalytic theory and methods, due in part to the unsatisfactory nature of the main secondary sources on which most people relied.[39]

The 1943 survey reported that early moralistic repudiations of Freud had disappeared, and had been replaced by an increase in methodologically based rejections, as a different kind of ideological fire was turned against the unwelcome message of psychoanalysis. Early on it had been the substantive theories of the unconscious and of infantile sexuality which were the most unwelcome aspects of psychoanalysis, the lumps that stuck in the craw of a culture that prided itself on its rationality and on the innocence of its children (and, indeed, of many of its adults). And even today, when objections to psychoanalysis are more often cast in epistemological terms, the distaste felt by some of Freud's contemporaries can still be seen in the choice of words in some psychology texts, in references, for example, to the unconscious as a 'murky and often evil territory of the mind'[40] – Holmes territory indeed! The scenario of sinfulness with which psychoanalysis was associated is still playing on our cultural screens.

But in the argument being developed here, another area of difficulty and rejection in the cultural response to psychoanalysis is being focused on. In an intellectual culture where metapsychology is dominated by utilitarian thinking, the non- and anti-utilitarian aspects of psychoanalysis (as expressed for example in the theory of identification) have been invisible to many commentators on, and consumers of, psychological theory. In a manner analogous to the behaviour of some patients in psychoanalysis, the unconscious is trivialized, and reduced to an object of disdainful contemplation by the sovereign ego. To put the matter this way is to invite the charge that one is trying, in a circular fashion, to psychoanalyse away objections to psychoanalytic theory. That is a moot point, but there is another way of putting it which is not open to the charge of circularity. This is that the banalization of the unconscious involves a systematic refusal to recognize the constitutive role of the other in the formation of the self. In these utilitarian readings, the ego is no more than the psychic form assumed by an abstract, unproblematic rationality; there is no conception of its being built up, slowly and imperfectly, as the precipitates of interactions with others accumulate in the inner world. Only the superego is seen as the product of internalization, and that in a direct, simple way involving only bad, punishing objects; the introjection of a loved and loving object is not part of this picture, neither as part of the structure of the superego nor, certainly, as the basis of ego development.

The presentation of psychoanalysis as a mechanistically utilitarian theory of the mind has facilitated its rejection by a readership which, while in large part remaining dominated by utilitarian world views, is uncomfortably aware of some of their limitations, and yearns for a psychology which will tell a more heartening or a more sophisticated story about human nature.

In one constituency, the radical left, psychoanalysis has in fact been identified as offering such a story, although one with many chapters of unhappiness before the happy ending. That reception of Freud will be considered in Chapter 6. Before that, in the next chapter, we will examine how humanistic psychology, accepting the banalization of psychoanalysis found in academic psychology, strove to find a more uplifting and hedonistic language of individual utilities. In both these areas, as in the textbooks reviewed above, the understanding of psychoanalysis is seen to be conditioned by a similar set of utilitarian assumptions, but combined in different ways with other philosophical influences.

5

HUMANISTIC PSYCHOLOGY
DISPELS THE FREUDIAN GLOOM

Selling Self-Acceptance

The history of humanistic psychology is an exemplary tale of salesmanship. The basic story is this. You enter a market which is already becoming congested with different products competing to meet the same needs. You rapidly develop a new product range, which in many important ways is based on the existing products but which you claim offers more, and more quickly, to those who consume it, and which lends itself to new forms of packaging and advertising. You develop an advertising campaign around a few key words and images, which not only describe your products in appealing terms but also provide consumers with a vocabulary for describing the older products. This vocabulary is basically a simple one, populist, portentous and highly rhetorical. Those who come to use it will inevitably compare other products unfavourably with yours. At your most successful, you have appeared to create not just new products but a new universe of choice. And most importantly, you achieve all this without many people (including perhaps yourself) realizing that this is in fact what is happening. Your entrepreneurial flair disguises itself as a blessed combination of scientific genius and social progress.

The humanistic salespeople have been assisted in this enterprise by an overall (and in some areas very rapid) growth in the market: the demand for psychological therapies and for psychological ways of thinking about all sorts of everyday problems has increased greatly since they came into the business – though they may

reasonably claim to have aided its growth in that their salestalk
has served to create new consumers of psychological products, by
spreading a language of psychological need amongst people who
previously had no ears at all for their inner lives.

In my own case a complicated transition from the highly scientistic approach to psychology, which I had taken on from my undergraduate course, into a less alienated one, which eventually led
me into psychoanalysis, was assisted by a reading of Carl Rogers's
On Becoming a Person, one of the key texts of humanistic psychology.
I was not especially impressed with its conceptual language, but
something about the feel of it was very attractive. It speaks with
a voice that is both permissive and, apparently, secure and stabi-
lizing. It offers a way of introducing the feeling subject (which,
of course, for the average reader means *oneself*) into the domain of
sober scientific inquiry, and so radically extending the reach of
science into emotional life. However, a few experiences of the
contrived spontaneity and ersatz self-disclosure of the 'encounter
groups' which were then (in the early 1970s) sprouting up, and a
second, more politicized reading of Rogers, were sufficient to turn
me away from the humanistic path to self-discovery (and into, as
it happens, the cul-de-sac of another shrill scientism – see Chapter
6). But for many others with firmer commitments than mine,
intellectually or professionally, to official psychology, humanistic
psychology has provided an enduring relief from the impersonal
aridity of their early training.

Outside of official psychology, there is a continuing increase in
the felt importance and the visibility of the psychological, and this
is something for which Freud is often held to be chiefly responsible.
Yet while Freud may be of singular importance in the initial
formation of at least one tradition of psychological thought, he is
no more responsible for the burgeoning in modern culture of
heterogeneous discourses of the psychological than Columbus is
responsible for the development of American society. Critics of
psychoanalysis, seeking to exaggerate the difficulties or the importance of their critical efforts, sometimes grossly overstate the extent
to which psychoanalysis has established itself in contemporary
culture, in their talk of the 'empire' of psychoanalysis and the
'astonishing revolution' it has achieved (see Chapter 1 and note
6). It is often assumed that psychoanalysis is at the heart of a
transformation of our self-consciousness into a psychologically
analytical one.

This may well be true historically, in that psychoanalysis was a crucial catalyst of the psycho-cultural changes which were a part of the installation of modernity and of the modern, reflexive subject. It is not true, however, as an analysis of the present state of affairs. Into the space of self-conscious interiority which psychoanalysis did so much to open up poured a host of non-psychoanalytic theories and therapies, panaceas and philosophies, many of them consisting mainly of *pre*-psychoanalytic notions. Some (not least, as we shall see, amongst the humanistic psychologies) have certainly employed rewritten versions of Freudian tenets, but often do so in ways that subvert their psychoanalytic meaning. Since World War II, as the numbers of psychological theories and techniques have rapidly increased, orthodox psychoanalysis has come to represent a progressively smaller relative share of the expanding therapy sector. Notwithstanding the current growth of interest in psychoanalysis, particularly as a theory, its direct contribution to the psychological preoccupations of contemporary culture is very limited. In particular the influence of the humanistic psychologies now overshadows that of psychoanalysis, and of all other psychological paradigms, in many areas of social life.

Ways of making sense of experience and of responding to others that are derived from humanistic psychology, especially its Rogerian version, are now commonplace. This is most evident in professional welfare sectors such as counselling, social work, and especially education, where the whole development of child- and student-centred strategies now owes more to Rogers than to Piaget. The spread of humanistic psychology techniques has also occurred in other applied contexts across the political and occupational spectrum, from management training in multinationals to anti-racist training sponsored by socialist local government, from 'despair workshops' in the disarmament movement to sensitivity training for police.[1] It is a clear sign that we are dealing with a cultural development of great significance when some both of the demonstrators outside a nuclear base, and of the police who lift them away, have been trained for their roles in groups using similar humanistic methods.

In under twenty years a wide range of practices, loosely connected by a language of self-actualization and self-acceptance, have taken root in many contexts. There has as yet been no systematic historical study of this development (though there has been some good satirical commentary[2]), and it would be imprudent to make claims that a 'revolution' has occurred. Moreover, humanistic psychology is now a term with a very wide meaning, so much so that generalizations about its social significance should on the whole be avoided. It covers work of remarkable banality, but also has its more sophisticated supporters; it is conscripted to serve in both voluntarist and environmentalist, individualist and collectivist causes. Sincere therapeutic efforts sometimes persist amidst its more characteristic charlatanry and glibness, and while it has built-in tendencies towards the inauthentic and the trite, it can also provide for some honest questioning of experience.

I do not propose here to make any kind of overall assessment of the different elements comprising humanistic psychology. For those unfamiliar with its terms, I will first of all give a brief summary of what are usually taken to be its main contributions to psychological theory, looking at the writings of Carl Rogers and Abraham Maslow, and of Frederick Perls and other exponents of 'gestalt' therapy. Its representation of psychoanalysis, and of its own relationship to it, will then be considered, and this will lead to a discussion of certain undercurrents in the broad stream of 'humanistic' work. In all, this will tell us something of the ways in which, in the post-Freudian world, the search for happiness is still being conducted.

The Cult of the Organism

At least in its earlier days, humanistic psychology was often spoken of as the 'third force' in psychology, as a new and better alternative to the tired orthodoxies of psychoanalysis and behaviourism. It promised to transcend old disputes, and to overcome the sterility of the established paradigms by its concern with *self*-discovery as well as with scientific discovery. Although more recently it has acquired a substantial influence and respectability in mainstream professional and academic psychology, it began less as a development within psychology than as part of the wider cultural changes of the post-war period, particularly those embodied in the 'human potential' or 'growth' movement of the 1960s and 1970s.

This account of the triumphal progress of humanistic psychology, from counter-cultural frontier to the citadels of legitimated knowledge, can easily be overdrawn in the interests of mythologizing its achievement. It should also be noted that the self-styled 'third force' was basically consonant with much that was already consensual. For instance, Maslow and Rogers, its two main theoreticians, were throughout their careers leading figures in the American psychological establishment, each serving as President of the American Psychological Association. Nonetheless the active interlocking of humanistic psychology with developments outside of all specialist communities, professional and academic, was and is an important feature.

Psychology's response, which on the whole has been to try to assimilate the humanistic challenge, contrasts with its marginalization or rejection of psychoanalysis. Scientist dogmas have similar criticisms of both humanistic psychology and psychoanalysis, but mainstream psychology, while still committed to its identity as 'science', has found room for the humanists. Unlike psychoanalysis, humanistic psychology is above all an attempt to articulate the demand for happiness. The popularity of this articulation in the wider culture, and its generally welcoming reception by mainstream psychology, both testify to the urgency with which the demand is being felt and expressed.

Where then is happiness to be found? The answer apparently given by the humanistic psychologists is not, at root, an original one: it is, they say, to be found in one's body – but the body reconceptualized in such a way as to connote personhood. This is most clearly and influentially expressed in Rogers's concept of the 'organism'. He wished us to understand by this term the totality of experience, the sum of everything which is going on in the individual at a given moment. Within the organism there is an area of experience Rogers termed the 'self', that part of the organism composed of perceptions of 'I' or 'me', and of my relationship to the rest of the world. One is in the desirable condition of 'congruence' when there is harmony between the experiences of the self and those of the rest of the organism, i.e. when there is nothing going on in the organism which the self cannot accept. Incongruence arises when some experience within the organism is rejected by the self, which is thereby constricted and defensive.

Incongruence is the product of our dependency on other people, our need for their 'positive regard'. Where positive regard is given unconditionally, there is no problem, but where (as is more often the case) it is conditional, we find ourselves driven by our need for it into acceptance of the conditions imposed by others. This means that we tend to exclude from the purview of the self those aspects of our organismic experience which have not gained the approval of others. Thus the child may come to reject or deny its own sexuality or naughtiness, indeed any of its actions, feelings or aspirations, if it seems that these will bring the loss of positive regard. Incongruence between organism and self therefore opens up under the pressure of social censure (though it can be reduced in the context of a relationship in which *unconditional* positive regard is offered, one of the aims of Rogerian 'client-centred' therapy).

Incongruence is therefore a state of conflict, based on two basic human needs. On the one side there is our need for positive regard – or rather there is a set of conditions laid down by others for satisfying our need for positive regard. On the other there is our drive towards 'self-actualization', to become congruent and 'fully functioning persons' able to experience and develop all aspects of ourselves. Put differently, there is a conflict between the judgments of others and the individual's 'organismic valuing process', the spontaneous capacity of the organism to know what is right and best.

In the writings of Maslow, the self-actualizing tendency is not, as for Rogers, something constantly at work against the ignorance and repressiveness of social judgments, but is rather something which can come into play only when other, more rudimentary needs of the organism have been met. He is famous for his theoretical construction of a 'hierarchy of needs', up which we move in steps through a series of physical and emotional needs (for physiological sustenance, safety, belongingness and love, and esteem) to the 'growth' needs or motives, the needs for self-actualization. Here, at the top, we find the Nietzschean drive to become whatever one is capable of becoming, and here again we find that the *body* is the motor of self-fulfilment: the tendency to self-actualize is an 'instinctoid' one. It is continuous therefore with the lower-level needs which must be satisfied before actualization is even a possibility. 'Growth values' and 'survival values' are fundamentally of the same, *biological* kind; the insufficient realization of either is a 'deficiency disease'.[3] We must 'trust in the organism', in the aura of the body; 'a state of subjective well-being is a pretty good guide to what is "best for the person".'[4]

Growth values (also known by Maslow as 'metaneeds', needs beyond what we normally think of as our needs), are at some points in his writing fused with what he calls 'B-values'. These are the values associated with 'Being', with a sublime cosmic consciousness.[5] Growth and actualization are therefore identical with the attainment of these B-states of mystical transport. At other points, though,[6] it is only a *sub*-group of self-actualizers who operate with 'B-Cognition', namely those most given to 'peak experiences', moments of ecstatic transcendence, of complete spontaneity and receptivity. The impact of oriental mysticisms is particularly clear in these parts of Maslow's writings, but in the urge to synthesize so characteristic of the humanistic thinkers he seeks to fuse his borrowed Taoism with his understanding of scientific materialism. The ground for this fusion is the body, the organism: 'the so-called spiritual or value-life ... is on the same continuum (is the same *kind* or *quality* of thing) with the life of the flesh, or of the body'.[7]

In gestalt therapy, too, the conceptualization of psychic functioning rests upon a notion of the organism. We spontaneously give our 'organismic attention' to anything which is important to us, to whatever 'organism-environment transactions' of significance are taking place at a given moment between the individual and the world. Psychological malfunctioning consists in our failure to become aware of what our organisms are attending to, in the failure of mental awareness to match organismic attention. The aim of therapy is to reintegrate *attention* and *awareness* – to make us aware, for example, of our non-verbal behaviours and what they mean.[8] This distinction between attention and awareness is very similar to Rogers's distinction between organism and self, though in gestalt work there is more specification in actual bodily terms of what the 'organism' is up to. Much emphasis is placed in gestalt therapy upon the development of body awareness and the decoding of body language.

In the fundamentals of humanistic psychology, then, the body is the repository of authenticity, and the core of healthy selfhood. A deference to nature, found in some psycho-physiological theorizing about the 'wisdom of the body',[9] is elevated here into the basic article of faith. In this faith, the body is not mere flesh, but is a knowing organism, 'autonomous, self-governing, and self-choosing'.[10] Our unhappiness is our punishment for failing to trust our bodies, for cutting ourselves off from the organismic ground of our being. As such, however, it can be cured: we must simply submit ourselves to the guidance of our organismic processes, and open up our selves to their spontaneous beneficence.

The organism is basically good; 'The facts are friendly', assures Rogers.[11] His organism is a mild and sober one; nothing unpleasant or unmanageable will emerge from it.

This philosophic veneration of the organism rapidly gained an enthusiastic following which, in the more diversified therapeutic and theoretical culture of the 1980s, it has largely retained. The speed and scale of its success suggest that it expressed simultaneously a number of different social forces. Most obviously, it rationalized and amplified the demands for certain kinds of sexual licence that came to prominence in the 1960s. Another feature of the youth-based cultural phenomena of that period was the revolt against the conventional regulation of social encounters, against formal codes of civility. This revolt was powerfully expressed in the 'encounter group' movement, with which Rogers was particularly associated. In these groups the attempt was made to establish new ways of regulating interpersonal interactions, based on principles of organismic spontaneity, truthfulness and trust (and, sometimes, degrees of sexual disinhibition). More generally, the preoccupations of humanistic psychology closely matched the romantic trends of the 1960s – the concerns with self-expression and the holistic outlook.

The social and intellectual agendas of the 1960s are not, though, the only ones that need to be considered here. The humanistic valorization of the organism was also in part a consummation of older, religiously inspired tendencies in American thought and culture, which had already profoundly shaped the development of American psychology. An optimistic belief in nature had been, in various forms, an important influence on psychological theorizing, and the dogma of the good organism was an extension of this belief into a new wave of personality theories and therapeutic techniques. Piety and science could be combined in doctrines of the wholeness and integrity of organisms and the goodness of evolution.

However, as Robert Fuller (1986) has described, this new wave of religious sentiment did not originate in the humanistic psychology of the 1960s but very much earlier. He demonstrates that in the early American responses to Freud of William James and others we can see essentially the same rewriting of the concept of the unconscious as in the later humanistic texts. The growth movement simply rediscovered a nineteenth-century vision of harmony, thus sacralizing the unconscious in a way parallel to the simplistic 'Darwinizing' of Freud described in the previous chapter. As Rogers put it, 'My main thesis is this. There appears to be a formative tendency at work in the universe which can be observed at every level ... what Whyte (1974) calls the "morphic tendency", the ever operating trend toward increased order and interrelated complexity evident at the inorganic, the organic and the human level.'[12] Speculative cosmology of this sort is on the whole more characteristic of Maslow's grand theorizing than of Rogers's more homely style, but here we glimpse the wider context of the 'organismic valuing process'. It is an expression of a cosmic Eros, which is also at work in the speck of dust and on the international stage, bearing us all on to greater order and integration. We can gain access to this power through fidelity to our organismic being.

So, life is good (in fact, simple material existence is good). This celebratory stance of humanistic psychology distinguishes it, perhaps more sharply than any specific theoretical differences, from psychoanalysis and other philosophies of endurance. Yet in some ways there seems to be an overlap between the humanistic and psychoanalytical approaches. Psychoanalysis is, too, at some level a theory of the body, of body-experience as constitutive of the psyche. The Reichian development of this theme in psycho-analysis, into the theory of character as residing in muscle tone ('character armour') and into therapeutic techniques involving massage, was taken up into the 'growth movement' and seen by many as kindred to humanistic psychology.

Reichian ideas have been one of the most important sources, in contemporary culture, of the notion that the route to happiness is through the body. Yet these ideas are completely at odds with almost anything that can now be described as psychoanalytic, and certainly with the position outlined in Chapter 2. For psycho-analysis, the body is indeed fundamental to psychic life, but this is a *developmental* truth rather than a prescription for adult conduct. Bodily experience is crucial to our emotional development, but this does not imply that the moral horizons of the adult must be drawn in some concrete way upon the body – the achievement of maturity is to have extended and transformed our loving and reparative feelings towards bodies out into the non-corporeal uni-verse of the social and moral. Bodily experience is anyway always socially mediated; and, moreover, it is never far from frustration, conflict and loss. It is the work of the caretaker upon and with the infant that determines what kind of psychic presence the infant's body will have for it. How then does humanistic psychology sustain its claims for the possibility of happiness, and for the organismic basis of self-actualization and contentment, in the face of the longer-standing psychoanalytic rebuttal of such claims?

Flushing out the Evil Unconscious

The relationship between humanistic psychology and psycho-analysis is a complex and at times contradictory one. Common ground between the two is not hard to find, and not only at the Reichian margins of psychoanalysis. The major example is in the use made by humanistic theorists of Freud's concept of repression. It is difficult to understand Rogers's notion of 'incongruence' as anything other than a partial restatement of this concept, with the repressed unconscious transmuted into a benign phenomenological field called the 'organism'. In this restatement, instead of the unconscious as a domain of mental life, operating according to distinct principles of its own and full of irrational and sometimes destructive feelings, we have the gentle wisdom of the organism. The notion of an inner split, resulting in our not knowing who we are nor what we feel, is retained, but the negativity and dynamism of the unconscious is cast off.

Rogers was exposed to an 'eclectic Freudianism' when he worked at the Institute for Child Guidance in New York City in the 1920s, but was never much impressed, his biographer tells us, with the complex theoretical system of Freud.[13] He objected to the view he attributed to Freud that human nature was intrinsically evil. Like many others, Rogers took some of Freud's diagnoses for prescriptions. For example, he discusses Freud's analysis of the bases of the authoritarian's need for authority in the persistence of an unsatisfied longing for the father. For Rogers this is, quite illogically, evidence that Freud's own stance was 'very autho-ritarian'. Freud was typical, so Rogers implies, of an old, fearful school that could feel safe only if human nature were bottled up. It was left to brave pioneers such as himself to risk putting their trust in people, and to begin to demonstrate the gains that can be made in all areas of life if people are allowed to be themselves.[14] His reading of Freud was 'relatively shallow',[15] which may account for why he did not come to test the accuracy of some of his paraphrasings of Freud. It does not, though, fully explain how he was able to overlook the psychoanalytic underpinning of his most basic and appealing concept, the debt owed by 'incongruence' to the theory of repression.

Maslow was more generous, and somewhat more informed, in his citations of Freud and acknowledgment of the elements of Freud's thought upon which he drew. His understanding of Freud is, however, as questionable as that of Rogers: for instance psychoanalysis teaches us, so Maslow believed, 'that repression is not a good way of solving problems'.[16] To self-actualize is to break through all repressions and defences. Maslow also shared Rogers's rejection of the negative unconscious: Freud's 'one big mistake, which we are correcting now, is that he thought of the unconscious merely as undesirable evil',[17] with the corollary of a 'necessary, intrinsic, built-in opposition between the needs of the individual and the needs of society and civilization'.[18]

In this view, and in his general representation of Freud, Maslow is much less attentive to the work of Freud himself than to that of the 'neo-Freudians', particularly Karen Horney and Erich Fromm. It was they who most fully developed the critique of Freud's allegedly undue emphasis on the anti-social nature and the recalcitrance of unconscious impulses. In his brilliant, enraged assault on 'conformist psychology', Russell Jacoby[19] attacks the neo-/post-Freudian/humanistic tendency for its attempt to humanize the dehumanized, for its asserting the possibility of fulfilment and happiness in a world of alienation. When social relations require inauthenticity and suspicion, claims to realize authenticity and trust can only be bogus and misleading. One need share neither Jacoby's Marxism nor his 'instinctivist' Freudianism to agree with his basic assessment of some of the theoretical propositions and therapeutic claims of humanistic psychology as, at best, naive.

Perls had much less opportunity than either Rogers or Maslow to neglect or misunderstand Freudian theory, since he was trained in psychoanalysis in inter-war Europe, and continued in analytic practice after emigrating in 1934 to South Africa (where he was involved in the founding of the Institute for Psychoanalysis). There is in the conceptual language of gestalt therapy a quite detailed indebtedness to various psychoanalytic insights. As with Rogers, we find in gestalt a rewritten version of the concept of repression, in the notion of our failure to become aware of the full range of our organismic doings and beings. But we also find, beyond Rogers, a specification of various ways in which we keep our self-functioning out of our awareness. The psychoanalytic theory of defences is clearly influential here, especially in the concept of projection, though the primary debt is to Reich. 'Retroflection' is a way of blocking an impulse by setting up an opposing sensorimotor tension. Chronic retroflection produces Reichian 'character armour'.[20] 'Desensitization' is the perceptual analogue of retroflection, referring to denial and selectivity within sensory processes. What such concepts add up to is a *somatization* of the notion of defence, and thereby of repression.

The psychoanalytic term 'introjection' is also part of the gestalt lexicon, though used in a way that is at odds with current psychoanalytic theory. The gestalt use is based on Ferenczi's definition of introjection as being a process mainly involving *bad* objects (see Chapter 2), with an additional emphasis on the subject's failure properly to digest the introject. It refers to ways of behaving 'adopted wholesale ... from significant others *without assimilation or integration with the self*'.[21] The introject is thus an alien presence within the soul, a triumph of other over self. The unintegrated introject, seen as pathological in psychoanalytic theory, is here taken as the primary and dominant form of internalization.

The contrast here with the psychoanalytic concept of introjection as encompassing both good and bad objects is a sharp one, but despite such divergences we might expect to find in gestalt writings a general acknowledgment of the debt to psychoanalysis. And quite often we do, but it is usually *Reich* who is being acknowledged. Of Freud, Perls has this to say: 'It took us a long time to debunk the whole Freudian crap.'[22] His need to evacuate the Freudian 'crap' is an urgent one: this pronouncement is the second sentence of one of his best-known books. A contemptuous and throwaway style is characteristic of Perls, and also we should note that he is talking here about his own history. Of the humanistic writers it is the one who had the history of most involvement with psychoanalysis and who tried to internalize it in the most extensive way who later develops the most violent rejection of it, for its failure to provide him with the kind of salvation which he needed and which he subsequently found in a school of his own making.

Nonetheless we might still ponder on Perls's choice of words, and on whether his experience of psychoanalysis as something bad inside him, which has to be got rid of, tells us something of more general interest about the relationship of humanistic psychology both to psychoanalysis, and to things (whether ideas or images or other people) felt to be inside the self. The humanists have taken in something of Freud and psychoanalysis, and they find it deeply distasteful. In part this is because they are not satisfied with the kind of mechanistic utilitarianism which, following academic psychology, they attribute to Freud. And, in another respect they again receive without modification academic psychology's picture of psychoanalysis: its equation of psychoanalysis with Freud alone. They appear ignorant of most of the post-Freudian developments, which could provide them with some very different images of the unconscious, but which they have chosen not to take in.

The Badness Inside

One fairly consistent theme, explicit and implicit, across much of the humanistic canon, is the attack on repression. From the complex psychoanalytic account of this process, only one dimension is taken. Repression for humanistic psychology is nothing but self-deception, distortion, alienation, self-oppression; it is the opposite of self-knowledge, freedom, integration and fulfilment. Those allegedly less repressed than others, such as children and artists, are held in particular esteem.

This simplified rendering of the notion of repression is powerfully convincing for any reader who has not already been schooled in the more subtle psychoanalytic understanding of inner conflict, according to which the repression of impulse is, at least to a degree, part of the acceptance of reality. It is the outcome of a real struggle with one's impulses and needs, rather than being an omnipotent denial of them. This reading of it is easily lost, not least because of the connotations of the word 'repression' in everyday language. There, 'repression' is something carried out by military dictators and the like; it refers to brutal attacks upon innocent persons and just causes. When this same word appears in a psychological text, most readers are not going to think that repression, despite its drawbacks, is overall in some ways a necessary and good thing. Perhaps psychoanalysis will have to find a word to replace 'repression' if there is to be a wider understanding of the theory of the unconscious.[23]

As we have noted, the force which the humanists wish to free by breaking the chains of repression is that of organismic goodness. However, it is only in gestalt therapy that this objective is actually carried through in a more or less literal way, in the detailed conceptual and technical attention paid there to the body. Even then, there prevails a Reichian understanding, of the body not as a thing in itself but as the inscription of *psychic* and *social* forces (though there may be a tendency for this to slip, in practice, into a prioritization of bodily experience). Moreover, despite its somatization of basic psychoanalytic concepts, gestalt theory criticizes psychoanalysis for underplaying the creative, synthesizing capacity of the ego to integrate bodily impulses into the totality of the person. So, even in gestalt work, the organism finds it hard to fill the central role allotted to it.

Outside of gestalt work, the invocation of the organism seems to be a completely empty rhetoric. The main thrust of both Rogers's and Maslow's theorizing is not literally towards the organism but rather towards the interpersonal domain, and what might loosely be termed the 'existential' – towards a concern with certain questions of choice and agency in everyday life. The main impact of their work, especially in recent years that of Rogers, has been in support of stronger 'social' and 'political' orientations in psychology and psychotherapy, and humanistic psychologists are in self-conscious opposition to reductive biologizing. The occasional references that Rogers made to actual organisms are more to plant life than to human bodies – he saw psychotherapy as analogous to horticulture. A potato sending out sprouts in the dark is for him a good metaphor for the strength of the actualizing tendency – hardly a powerful theoretical appeal to the human body. Biological knowledge he saw as being of no special value to the psychotherapist.[24]

Some aspects of humanistic thought, including key notions of transcendence, have on occasions been combined with the results of psychophysiological research into the relationships between brain functioning on the one hand, and experience or behaviour on the other. Maslow himself referred[25] to research on 'pleasure-centres' and biofeedback as evidence for his contention that we have an intrinsic capacity for happiness. Yet for all his enthusiasm for a 'humanistic *biology*', Maslow is most at home in the environmentalist preoccupations of pragmatic American social science.

What then is the persistent rhetoric of the organism all about, if not about actual organisms? Why turn to an apparently biological category, if one's programme is not to biologize psychology, but rather to render it less amenable to reductive materialistic science?

The humanists' organism is, on closer inspection, a negative entity: it is the negation of something else, and it is with the unconscious aim of negating that something else that the humanists are in fact primarily concerned, not with offering some substantive conception of the organismic.

That something else is society, the external world of others. As Ray Holland[26] has noted, in Rogers's work there is a split between the organism and society which is in effect a split between 'good' and 'bad' respectively. The flip side of Rogers's praise of the organism is his denigration of the social, or more specifically of what the social is alleged to have done to the individual. This theme is by no means peculiar to Rogers, but runs throughout the humanistic world-view. It is similar to the split described by Raymond Williams[27] in existentialist thought between 'social man' and 'authentic man', and indeed in so far as European existentialism can be regarded as a source of American humanistic psychology[28] then its equation of the social with the inauthentic is one source of the humanistic rejection of the social.

At times this rejection may be of some relatively specific social relations or institutions; more often it is of some vaguely described quality of the social environment and the psychological normalcy which it allegedly demands.[29] And sometimes it is simply implied or assumed that society in a most general sense is an alien and damaging force from which we must extricate ourselves, and outside of which we must define ourselves. There is an obvious and important critique of this aspect of humanistic psychology, of what might be called its humanistic essentialism. It is intellectually sterile, and politically dangerous, to postulate that our finest qualities and most precious experiences are products of our individual effort, *as opposed to* being expressions of the social traditions and matrices within which we live.

This individualist, voluntarist strain of humanistic psychology, and the ideological critique it invites, will be discussed further in Chapter 7. But it must also be observed that many of those influenced by, or even committed to, humanistic paradigms would wish to distance themselves from such individualism. In practice the political affiliations of humanistic psychology, especially in the therapeutic field, are predominantly leftist or left-liberal. The social meaning of its conceptual individualism is therefore not, at present, to underwrite strategies of political disengagement or of aggressive neo-liberalism.

Further consideration of the characterization of the 'social' in humanistic psychology actually suggests a different and rather more subtle effect. The characteristic hostility to the social is not a hostility to the actual, external social world. The humanistic world-view is a benign one, apparently, and within it the social world is seen as being subject to the same happy laws of integration and actualization as are the natural and personal worlds. The social dimension which is the object of humanistic reproach is rather that of the internalized social. It is the presence that society has established in the mind of the individual which is the object of the critique. It is assumed that anything that has been taken in from others is by definition inimical to authenticity and spontaneity, unless (as the gestalt critique of 'introjection' requires) it is subordinated to the 'self'. Gestalt theory does admittedly have a place for a constructive process of taking in: introjection is contrasted with 'assimilation', which is analogous to good digestion. But there is little further study of what assimilation might mean in interpersonal terms; when the actual, formative relationships an individual has experienced are addressed, it is usually through the notion of introjection, of alien impositions upon the self.

In any case, we might ask, what is the substance of this self? For the psychoanalytically based position outlined in Chapter 2 (and also, though in different ways, for other fundamentally *relational* perspectives such as symbolic interactionism) it is itself the legacy of the other. The substance of the self gathers around the imprint of the other upon the protoplasmic psyche of the infant. The protoplasm is not of the same quality in all infants, there apparently being variation in constitutional levels of such general traits as activity and reactivity. However the protoplasm does not in itself have the degree of determinativeness that humanistic psychology ascribes to the 'organism'.[30] It simply has the potential for receiving the determinative imprint of the other.

In favourable conditions, this will be the imprint of love. The high frequency of *un*favourable conditions allows the humanistic theorist to equate the internalized social other with badness, and to forget the role of good internalizations in providing the basis for emotional development, for 'growth'. The mythic talk of the 'organism' fills the gap; it claims to account for where the goodness comes from, on the assumption that it does not and cannot come from outside, from others. There is little specification of what the substance of the 'organism' is; it stands merely as a grand and empty principle by which the internalized *other* can continue to be seen as bad.

Thus Rogers contrasts 'organismic' values with 'introjected' ones. We should abide by the former, those from within. Without, are the alien values of others – but not the 'generalized other' of Mead's cerebral society: the humanistic sensibility attends to the specificity of feeling, and so it cannot fail to notice that *some* others are more important than other others, and that parental others are the most important. 'Most of us', wrote Maslow,[31] '... listen not to ourselves but to Mommy's introjected voice or Daddy's voice or to the voice of the Establishment, of the Elders, of authority, or of tradition.' His focus on the *familial* matrix is weak, and slides into an easy adolescent lumping together of all forms of authority as alien and bad. But the message nonetheless comes over that parental introjects are, in general, things we should expunge. There are no distinctions here between a persecuting superego and a protective superego, and no hint of the possibility that the voices of persecutory repression could be at least in part the creation of the individual – that is, that the bad parental introjects may be *re*-introjects, of voices which are themselves the results of projection on to the parents of sadistic feelings.

What role is left for the parent whose voice must not be heard? And what possibilities are there for the teacher or for the therapist, if they too must not be allowed to interfere with the spontaneous inner voice? The concept of facilitation provides a humanistic answer here: the aims of child-rearing and teaching, as of therapy, must be to encourage that inner voice to speak up, to provide the facilitating conditions within which the 'morphic tendency' is most able to unfold. Authority must be, in a deep sense of the word, permissive, giving permission to grow. For Maslow, even this may be too active a posture for the elders to adopt; he preferred a Taoist let-it-be principle, or at most an attempt to find out what is *inside* the child. The most extreme 'hands-off' position is stated in Perls's oft-quoted and infamous 'gestalt prayer': 'You are you and I am I/And if by chance we happen to find each other, it's beautiful/If not, it can't be helped.'[32]

In the more considered versions of this argument, though, there is much that is appealing and important. The principles of trying to work out what one feels about something, of distinguishing one's deeper responses from less abiding ones, and of clarifying the extent to which one may be irrationally pacifying internalized others, are ones shared with the psychoanalytic and some other traditions. They may at times be formulated by humanistic psychologists in particularly sharp and effective ways. At its best, humanistic psychology can embody an exemplary tolerance and generosity of spirit. But this is mixed up with, and ultimately dominated by, other currents of feeling of a more pathological kind.

There is for instance an almost paranoid quality to the insistence on expelling all traces of introjected others. The only alternative imagined to permissive facilitation is dominative control; the imprint of the other is necessarily a threat, a scar, or a prohibition. The demands of the other inevitably conflict with the inclinations of the organism. The individual as posited by humanistic psychology experiences introjected others as alien, invasive and constricting. What this can amount to, somewhat paradoxically, is a eulogization of the spontaneous inner organismic *potential*, while everything that is *actually* currently inside, the total of internalizations that constitute the self, is denigrated. The humanistic position reveres inner goodness, but can see no basis for it in the actual process of psychological development. Hence the recourse to the notion of the 'organism' as the repository of goodness.

On this analysis, the most important social meaning of the cult of the organism is not as a biologistic or individualistic ideology, but as a veil of illusion behind which a deep disillusionment might be hidden. A profound lack of faith in the capacity of human beings to give anything of permanent value to each other, and mutually to constitute themselves, is obscured behind a cheerful, vacuous dogma of the good organism. The repetitive humanistic charge against psychoanalysis, that it is pessimistic, that it dwells unwholesomely and needlessly on human weakness and pathology, can now be seen as a projective defence. The deepest pessimism can be found between the lines of the uplifting humanistic texts. While Freud is castigated for postulating an irreconcilable conflict between society and the individual, the alternative vision we are offered is of a society which at present is wholly negative in its relationship to individuals, and which in an ideal world would have *no* intrinsic relationship to them.

In place of the 'evil' of the unconscious we have the evils of introjection. The humanistic temperament, ostensibly so outgoing and tolerant, is intolerant of the other within. There is a link here with another intellectual current in the 'Sixties counterculture' of which the first phase in the popularization of humanistic psychology was a part. The 'psychedelic' project, based on the use of 'mind-expanding' hallucinogenic drugs, was another kind of assault on the established structures of the psyche – not in this case on internalized persons or parts of persons but on the bio-cultural inheritance of perceptual categories which are either a precondition of, or are amongst the earliest achievements of, psychological development. The purpose of an acid trip was to dissolve the impoverished, instrumental way in which one habitually saw the world, and so to open oneself to new modes of sensuous and spiritual engagement with it.[33]

Again, it is important not to be one-dimensional in evaluating this assault, containing as it did something of a creative and inquiring impulse, and some benign affective loosening. However, it shared with the growth movement, with which it was to some extent allied, the belief that truth and salvation could be found in some organismic inwardness of the individual, and that the presence in our emotional make-up of introjected values was a pathology from which we needed to be delivered. There was no psychedelic critique of psychoanalysis,[34] but notably the term 'ego' was often used with inverse connotations to those it has in psychoanalysis. It was used in psychedelic thinking to refer to the *undesirable* qualities of structure in the mind, to the unholy alliance of insrumental selfishness with oppressive tradition. The antidote to the ego was the pharmacological dissolution of ego-boundaries, creating a state of selfless merger with the material world, and of transcendence of the social world. The traces of others, especially of those who taught us to see and hear and touch in particular ways, were to be washed away on this voyage into inner 'space'.

This kind of craving for oceanic oneness is frequently to be found in and around Maslow's work. Peak experience is the 'merging of subject and object'.[35] He preferred regressive modes of identification, involving 'a melting of the psychological skin between two entities',[36] to the idea of identification as essential in the *differentiation* of self and other. Rogers's notion of empathy also involves a measure of de-differentiation, as a requirement of good therapeutic technique. Empathy is not simply knowing how the other person feels, it is knowing it from the 'inside', without many of the frames and responses which make up one's own distinctive psychological being. Notwithstanding the exhortations that the therapist be 'genuine', you as therapist must do all you can to avoid presenting the client with the configurations of your own self as a moral agent: this would be to have expectations of the client, to seek to control. It is assumed that when you really peer inside someone, behind all the introjections, you will find only good, and so you will not be required to merge empathically with something horrible. It is thus technically necessary to immerse oneself in the idealized image of the client-as-organism. Any other form of contact or engagement is seen as oppressive.

Psychoanalysis suggests that these themes of transcendent merger are only superficially different from exclusive preoccupations with the autonomy, originality and sanctity of the self. In both cases the tensions and conflicts of our real interdependent yet separate condition are set aside. Further, psychoanalysis predicts that where these visions of sublime unity are found, however innocent or attractive they may in themselves be, then we should also expect to find impulses of a sinister kind, omnipotent and domineering. The common factor in beatific visions of merger, and in totalitarian visions of an ideal society, is the refusal to recognize the irreducibility of the *other*. The very existence of other people is a constant insult to our infantile omnipotence, and a constant reminder of our vulnerability to psychic pain.

An Uncertain Humanism

Despite gestures of acknowledgment that sorrows cannot be avoided, indeed are a part of life's rich tapestry, Maslow was not interested in the toleration of psychic pain. For him, the prospect of unending unhappiness was tantamount to the end of the world. 'We must have better human beings or else it is quite possible that we may all be wiped out, and even if not wiped out, certainly live in tension and anxiety as a species.'[37] Around this vision of the 'better human being' collect the most alarming elements of his thought. He returned frequently to the idea of the 'superior specimen', the person who is a better perceiver of facts *and values* and who is therefore fit to prescribe for society as a whole. His glorification of his eminent 'self-actualizers' is at best a crass elitism, and at worst a sub-fascism. Forgetting his manifesto for a contemplative, Taoistic approach to science, he was so animated by the problem of producing more 'better people' that he became an extreme advocate of aggressive social engineering, demanding that a research programme as big as the Manhattan Project (which led to the first nuclear bombs) be set up to solve it.[38]

Maslow is often regarded as the chief pioneer of the humanistic tradition,[39] and we may well pause for thought on how and why the term 'humanistic' became regarded as the appropriate one for this tradition when we discover its founder in the grip of such a technocratic fever. We might begin to think that the name was hijacked as part of the marketing strategy for the 'Third Force'. Our doubts about this choice of name should intensify when we read Maslow's bold declaration that, 'Or even we could say: This person is *more* human than that one.'[40] A chilling arrogance begins to emerge from inside the relaxed colloquialism of his writing, with potentially terrible implications for politics. The meanings of 'humanist(ic)' are broad and contentious, but it is widely taken to refer to some kind of assertion of 'humanness' as an absolute, unquantifiable characteristic of all individuals, the basis of all principles of universal equality and 'human rights' (however they may be defined). When, then, we find someone talking of *degrees* of humanness, and developing the corollary that some lives are worth more than others, we feel that we are stepping outside of any discourse deserving to be described as 'humanistic'.

Maslow himself was not as a whole a potential fascist, and in so far as he elaborates the possible political significance of his ideas he moves more in the realms of liberal utopias than of totalitarian scenarios. He invokes Ruth Benedict's concept of 'synergy' to define 'social orders in which the individual by the same act and at the same time serves his own advantage and that of the group'.[41] Healthy, actualized people are 'good choosers', and they will tend to choose those things which are not only good for themselves (so they will not choose to smoke, or lead over-stressed lives), but which are also good for others. There is no necessary conflict between the interests of individual and society, and in a synergistic social order the dichotomy between selfishness and unselfishness will be transcended. What precisely such an order would be like, and how we arrive at it, Maslow does not know. Yet vague though his social programme is, we shall see in Chapter 7 that it testifies to a close fit between the whole structure of his thought and the broad intellectual matrices which have so powerfully influenced the reception of psychoanalytic ideas in the wider culture of market society.

The Authority of Others

Maslow's vision of a synergistic, 'eupsychian' social order, in which individual needs can find spontaneous, natural expression amidst harmonious social relations, depends upon the validity of his 'cleansing and correction' of Freud.[42] Rogers's vision of 'person-centred organizations', of 'collective organisms' in which both productivity and happiness are increased, similarly requires a rejection of some basic elements of Freud's thought. Such ideal worlds could exist only if the unconscious as described by Freud did not exist, only if the complex and conflicted nature of psychic needs could be done away with. Hence Maslow's creation of a 'happy unconscious', as Holland termed it,[43] and Rogers's search, in the footsteps of Adler and Rank, for the 'positive will', the 'will to health', in the 'trustworthy organism'.[44] Hence the belief, as expressed by the British humanistic psychologist John Rowan, that, 'Deep down underneath it all, where it really counts, there is the self. And the self is all right. There is nothing there to be afraid of.'[45]

There is only goodness within, it is repeatedly asserted. That we may have to struggle, at the deepest levels of our being, with emptiness and rage is simply ruled out as a possibility. Whether one agrees with this assumption, or sees in it a kind of narcissistic complacency, it has to be recognized as an assumption, and its corollaries can be explored. Chief amongst these, I have been arguing, are the proposition that any badness that is within must come from outside, and the extension of this proposition into the claim that anything that has come from outside must be bad. The latter proposition is clearly not a corollary in the sense of a logical deduction from the first assumption, and indeed stated in this stark way it may be widely seen to be absurd. Yet as an informing spirit, if not as an explicit premise, it is of great importance in the humanistic philosophy of the individual. Even those things which may be ostensibly good, like morality, are seen as bad if they have been 'imposed' from outside, rather than springing from inside, for example from Rogers's organismic valuing process described above, or from 'intrinsic conscience' (Maslow).[46]

The use of psychoanalytic thinking in the elaboration of this outlook is contradictory. On the one hand, the irrationality and negativity of the unconscious, if not the unconscious itself, has to be eliminated from consideration. Psychoanalysis becomes the representative, in the world of theoretical ideas, of an interior badness which has to be expelled, shat out and flushed away. On the other hand, as noted earlier, the essentially psychoanalytic concept of repression provided a necessary basis for much humanistic thinking about psychic functioning, though not without some violence to its meaning. And moreover, much of what psychoanalysis has to say about the social constitution of health as well as sickness is completely ignored in the humanists' attack on the outside world.

Not surprisingly, the humanistic picture of psychoanalysis is actually an unintentional parody,[47] constructed at some distance from the real thing. It is typical of the humanists' approach to scholarship that in Maslow's *The Farther Reaches of Human Nature* there are more index references to Freud than any other person, except Maslow, yet there are no works by Freud in the bibliography. As in academic psychology, it seems that Freud is more often spoken of than read, and that the 'Freud' whom the humanists believe themselves to be cleaning up or cleaning out is in no small part a figment of their imagination.

Rogers made no attempt to conceal his lack of scholarship. On the contrary, it became like almost everything else in his life a source of satisfaction to him. 'He was always grateful that his thinking did not come from the teachings of one special mentor ... [but] primarily from his own experience.'[48] This suggests something about the specific qualities of the humanistic hostility to the internalized other. The difference between self and other is most sharply felt in relation to others who are in authority.

This is partly because one's prototypical others, the parent in whom one first encounters the limits of one's self, are in authority over one. It is also because authority marks a *difference*, often an ineradicable one, between two persons. It can bring home the fact of one's aloneness, and one's vulnerable dependence on others. For these reasons, a successful identification with and internalization of authority figures is an important achievement, a coming to terms with one's limits and dependencies. And for these same reasons, the humanists' discomfort with their internalizations is particularly acute with their internalized authorities, such that they would prefer, like Rogers, to do without them. To live by their 'own experience', rather than by the teachings of others, enables them to continue to live an illusion of inner sufficiency. Authority signifies limitation and interdependence; it is the most potent and standardized embodiment of society, of the other.

Barry Stevens, a co-author of Rogers's, wrote: 'In the beginning was I, and I was good. Then came in other I. Outside authority.'[49] From this viewpoint, much of the rest of one's life has to be spent, if one is to be happy, in dissolving or avoiding this 'other I', in both its inside and original outside forms. A pathway to the dissolution of authority was found in the therapeutic techniques advocated by the leading humanistic psychologists. Maslow, taking an idea from Adler, proposed that the therapist should be like an 'older brother' to the patient, rather than being a remote, 'qualitatively different' figure.[50] This de-oedipalized relationship is then the model for education and social reform generally.

Rogers sought to avoid even the limited judgmental responsibilities of the older brother, in his prescriptions for non-directive empathy and for 'unconditional positive regard'. Time and again he deplores the need to have power over others, and criticizes the making of 'decisions which ... regulate or control the thoughts, feelings or behaviour of others or oneself.'[51] An authoritative judgment passed by one person on another can only be baleful in its effects, since it will make the person judged dependent upon the expertise of the one making the judgment. In a common misunderstanding of the psychoanalytic clinical concept, Rogers[52] takes this form of dependency to be the essence of 'transference' – so preoccupied is he with authority as an enemy invader of the person, he does not register that transference may take any form out of the full range of regressive relationships, of which only a minority will be manifest in overt dependence.

Rogers's difficulty is that he cannot conceive of a benign and facilitating authority, so much does he experience the other's moral agency as a malign attempt to 'control'. It is okay if you tell me what you feel, but if you tell me what you *think* than you are trying to get inside me and shape me to your desires. There is here both a philosophical naivety (feelings and judgments cannot be so neatly separated) and an enormous clinical naivety (about the vast possibilities for manipulation – by therapist or patient – through the ostensible disclosure of feelings). And as in all the key texts of humanistic psychology there is the insistent demand that we keep, so to speak, out of each other's organisms.

In all, humanistic psychology like academic psychology makes unwitting use of Freud as a mirror. It holds up what it takes to be a picture of psychoanalysis, and it sees to some extent the same simple utilitarianism recorded by academic psychology. The reflection is more complex than this, however, and more powerful. It also sees an evil expression on Freud's face, the overpowering stare of a hated authority. 'Freud ' and psychoanalysis are the symbols, in the domain of psychological theory, of the radical alterity of authority. In their images of him the humanists therefore contemplate themselves, their internalized others whose presence they find so intolerably oppressive. Appalled, they turn away from the mirror, to look instead at idealized portraits which they take for mirrors.

Thus humanistic psychology, whatever else it may do, rewrites the psychoanalytic doctrine of repression, and puts it in the service of an attack upon the internalized other, experienced as controlling, dominating, poisonous. Happiness must consist in the expulsion of the other, particularly of the internalized *authority* of others. In his later work of the 1970s and 1980s, Rogers caught up on the political element of the Sixties and began to direct his work towards social and political issues such as racism and inequality. The authorities which came under scrutiny in this work were predominantly *external* ones, such as bureaucracies. Rogers saw them as inimical to the fulfilment not only of the individuals subjected to them but also of the group. Again, the alternative to authority was to trust the organism, but now it was the organism of the group.[53] This move of Rogers's brought humanistic psychology, already grounded in the *cultural* trends of the 1960s, into explicit convergence with Sixties *political* radicalism, with the tradition most characteristically concerned with attacking external authority. To the uses of psychoanalysis in this tradition the next chapter will turn.

6

FREUD ON HIS HEAD:
PSYCHOANALYSIS AND THE LEFT[1]

A Long Relationship

In this chapter we will consider some aspects of the part played
by psychoanalysis in left politics in Britain since 1968,[2] through a
broad and critical characterization of the major uses to which
psychoanalytic theory has been put in political discourse during
this period. There will be very little material in this that will be
new to readers already familiar with this field, but my arguments
are illustrative of a critique which has yet to be fully faced by
many of those concerned with the political applications of psychoanalysis. Further, a review of this area should serve to emphasize
that issues of political vision as well as of psychological understanding are involved in the cultural transmission of psychoanalytic ideas.[3]

This account is based in part on retrospective research into the
publications and activities of the last twenty years, and in part on
my own experience of involvement (since 1974) in work concerned
with the problems and challenges posed by psychoanalytic thought
for socialist politics, and vice versa.[4] This experience has inevitably
been partial, and so some areas of work are given less detailed
attention than others in what follows. This will detract from
my argument only if I have misrepresented any of the positions
discussed. I hope to use personal report illustratively and as an
expository convenience rather than as a substantive basis for argument. It would, though, be an odd thing if some personal reflection
did not have an important place somewhere in any intellectual

engagement with psychoanalysis, and this chapter contains more than others in the book because of the greater involvement I have had in this area.

The use of psychoanalytic thinking in political philosophy and in analyses of specific political situations dates back to the earliest phase of the psychoanalytic movement. *The Psychopathology of Everyday Life*, published in 1901, was concerned mainly with mundane phenomena in the life of the individual, yet was also a first systematic demonstration by Freud of how psychoanalysis could be used to examine non-clinical domains. The second step in its development as an instrument for the analysis of political life was its application to *collective* phenomena in Freud's first sociological essay, '"Civilized" sexual morality and modern nervous illness' (1908). Here Freud argued that the limitation of legitimate sex to monogamy, the product of civilization's tendency to increasing sexual restrictiveness, was probably not worth its costs in increased neurotic misery.

In Britain the leading Freudian Ernest Jones was quick to see the potential of psychoanalysis as a framework for political comment. In 1915, the year that Freud published 'Thoughts for the times on war and death', Jones also published two papers on war, thus initiating in British psychoanalysis a tradition of writing about socio-political matters. Jones himself, Edward Glover and Roger Money-Kyrle were subsequently leading contributors to this tradition, for which war remained a major concern and in which a spectrum of reforming ambitions were represented.

It is in its links with more revolutionary ambitions, however, that psychoanalysis is best known as a contribution to political thought, particularly in the forms of Wilhelm Reich's Freudo-Marxism and the Freudian cultural critique of Herbert Marcuse and other members of the Frankfurt School of 'critical theory'. In fact, though, the writings of the Frankfurt School do not point one-directionally towards *revolutionary* politics as the requisite framework for psychoanalytic insights. And the work, also, of more recent American writers such as Philip Rieff and Christopher Lasch, linked in some ways to critical theory, has established powerful claims for more liberal and democratic-socialist directions for psychoanalytic cultural theory. In the history of psychoanalysis itself such directions can be traced; for example in the minor tradition in British psychoanalysis already referred to, and in the Austro-German beginnings of psychoanalysis. Russell Jacoby's explorations of these in *The Repression of Psychoanalysis* have brought to light the less well known contributions to political Freudianism of Otto Fenichel and others from the end of World War I to the 1950s, and indicate the variety of socialist and communist, revolutionary and reformist politics with which the development of psychoanalysis was closely interwoven until World War II.

This evidence of the diversity of political perspectives with which psychoanalysis has been associated should make clear the inadequacy of any dichotomization between 'revolutionary' and 'reactionary' applications of psychoanalysis in political thought. A substantial amount of left intellectual effort has been expended within the terms of this dichotomy, usually in order to recruit Freud, despite himself, from where he is usually assumed to stand, on the side of reaction, to the side of revolution. This effort has been comparable to the Marxist inversion of Hegel in order to render his insight into historical change of service to revolutionary politics. While Hegel had to be transposed from idealism to materialism, Freud has had to be removed from the pulpit of ahistorical bourgeois fatalism and repositioned at the barricades so that his message reads not downwards as a ruling class prescription disguised as natural law, but upwards as a demand for libidinal freedom or the recognition of desire. The notion that psychoanalysis is essentially 'ambivalent' moves decisively beyond the seizure of its essence for one side or the other, though even then the complexity of its political meanings is still not fully heeded.[5]

Why Psychoanalysis?

In the early 1960s some paths which could have led towards psychoanalysis were struck by some on the emergent New Left, notably Ronald Laing and David Cooper in early articles in *New Left Review*. However, it is since 1968 that increasing numbers of people who would identify themselves as of the radical left have turned towards psychoanalysis, or have sought to bring together in some way what might otherwise have been their disconnected or divergent interests in socialism and psychoanalysis.

Two simple, apparently competing, explanations for this development suggest themselves. One is that there was something, in the cluster of political, cultural and philosophical forces which have been identified as comprising the 'moment of 68', which prescribed or pointed towards a political appropriation of psychoanalysis. The other is that the turn to psychoanalysis was a *post-68* phenomenon, part of a reaction to an experience of the failure of the millenarian ideals of 'May 68'. An analogy here would be with the reasons why Herbert Marcuse and others became interested in psychoanalysis in the 1930s, in response particularly to the experience of what seemed to be the corruption of the revolution in Russia, and of mass support for fascism in Germany. If successful revolutions were so difficult to achieve, then perhaps there were deep intrapsychic impediments to them which needed to be understood and which psychoanalysis could illuminate.

In other words the turn to psychoanalysis can be seen as either positively or negatively produced by 68, as a direct development of it or as part of the attempt by a new New Left, sadder and wiser, to make a fresh start in the aftermath of 68. I will argue that in general the first of these explanations provides the more basic truth, though it is importantly qualified by the truth, at a certain level, of the second.

I will first of all consider two very different kinds of possible reasons for intellectuals (of any political stripe) to turn towards psychoanalysis, namely the experience of therapy and the search for a philosophically satisfactory psychology.

The Experience of Therapy

In many cases the decision to enter psychoanalytic therapy, as opposed to seeking some other form of therapy or eschewing all expert help, is determined by a pre-established familiarity with and sympathy for psychoanalytic discourse. However, there may well be some people for whom the experience of therapy came first, and was followed by an interest in psychoanalysis as a theory and as an input to politics. My own impression is that such people are few, which is not surprising given the relatively small and circumscribed scale of psychoanalytic practice in Britain, and the tendency for patients to be already familiar with some ideas about psychoanalysis.

Whether for any particular individual the experience of therapy is the cart or the horse, it is clear that therapy and politics can become intertwined in the lives of some individuals, such that the work of therapy (whether as therapist or patient) becomes experienced as part of a *political* life-project (though probably in some tension with other, more conventionally political, parts of

that project). The growth of 'feminist therapy' is the most important example of this phenomenon, but this takes us largely beyond
the sphere of psychoanalytic work, within which it is not usual to
recognize such a sociologically defined specialism. Within psychoanalytic work, the only distinctions which can be recognized are
those which depend on what the analyst or therapist brings (in
theoretical orientation, personal technique) or on the clinical
context (e.g. whether long- or short-term work is planned, what
the institutional setting is). Otherwise, each patient is unique, and
the socio-political categories within which the patient (and the
therapist) lives, and the belief-systems with which the patient
may try to interrogate the therapist or the therapy, are basically
material for the analytic work of interpretation, not a way of
classifying or qualifying that work.

Thus, at least in the case of orthodox psychoanalytic practices,
there is a considerable distance between the experience of analytic
therapy, and the political project of engaging with psychoanalytic
insights and their implications for understanding society. In those
few cases of people for whom there has been some direct and
major initiation of an intellectual/political interest by therapeutic
experience, it is likely to be in a non-specific way, in that, for
example, a helpful therapy may establish psychoanalysis in the
mind of the patient as a good thing, a tradition to be regarded
with respect.

In his sustained analysis of the relationship between his clinical
work as a psychoanalyst and his political commitment as a Marxist
(and psychoanalytical) intellectual, the American writer Joel
Kovel presents an unresolved contradiction, in which the problem
is not one of mere distance but one of disjunction. For example:
'Psychoanalysis is a practice which belongs to bourgeois experience
in late-capitalist urban society ... Perhaps someone also will be
able to figure out how to do an authentically proletarian psychoanalysis. I can't.'[6] One need not share Kovel's historical judgment
on psychoanalysis to concur in his practical judgment that psychoanalytic therapy and political work are at the least separate
spheres, and may in some way be incommensurable or immiscible.

We can take Kovel's failure to synthesize his clinical work with
his politics to be definitive, and not only for the Marxist position
which he represents. For me the experience of a (Kleinian) analysis
was itself a very important factor in bringing about a shift of
outlook, from viewing the world in the totalized terms of a

Marxism tending towards the monolithic, to a more pluralistic conception of the autonomy, within historical contexts, of specific social practices. Here in the session, and in the analytic process as a whole, was an instance in which the primacy of the conflict between class interests clearly did not obtain. A practical struggle about being honest with oneself has little to do, for practical purposes, with class struggle (though it may well be possible to describe some of its phases in terms of their mediations through class, gender and other social-structural relations). In the intensity of its refusal to become preoccupied with the 'real event', psycho-analysis may more easily be the vehicle for such a change of outlook than would other less reclusive practices, but its autonomy is not of a fundamentally unique kind, being based as it is on a technical procedure, more or less rigorously adhered to.

I am not claiming the complete autonomy of technique from social context; the point is rather that psychoanalytic therapy has a technical interior which, though historically produced and not fully insulated, has a large degree of discursive autonomy from its currently prevailing political exterior. As was noted for psycho-logical theories in Chapter 1, there is no simple relationship between psychological techniques and political ideologies. Like theories, techniques are subject to some very immediate social and ideological pressures, but also like theories they exist in a particular social space which is partly insulated from the world outside.

In the case of psychoanalytic technique, it occupies a social space structured by considerations of competence and ethics which are unusual in that they require a high and explicit degree of screening out of the world. This point helps to explain the generally low participation of psychoanalytic therapists in the public domain, notwithstanding their spontaneous political sympathies (Richards, 1986). It should also clarify that the personal change of outlook to which I referred above was not the result of my becoming imbued with 'reactionary' ideas in the form of a radical–Kleinian doctrine of the pure endogeneity of unconscious phantasy. The technical specificity and relative autonomy of psychoanalysis as an interpretive exploration of personal meaning and self-deception is independent of specific theoretical positions, and holds just as much for an environmentalist neo-Freudian or object-relations position as it does for any more instinctivist theory.

At the same time I do not want to imply that psychoanalytic experience has no relation to politics; there are various reasons for insisting that it does, or should. A particular school of clinical work may dispose its participants more towards some political concerns, and less to others. Also, my self-example above illustrates how the acquisition of a general political conception – of the practical autonomy of social spheres – was facilitated by analytic experience. Moreover it is sometimes justly complained that one of the most serious weaknesses in much of the discussion about psychoanalysis in political theory is that it is cut off from clinical work, and from the major developments in psychoanalytic theory which are – in the empirical, though not unproblematically so, nature of psychoanalysis – closely tied to the clinical literature. While radical theorists, like academic and humanistic psychologists, have been rearranging some early Freudian concepts, freezing them at one stage or another in the process of their formation and change, many actual psychoanalysts have been transforming the theory in practical contexts. It is only in some areas of the interchange between feminism and psychoanalysis that clinical experience (which is not necessarily understood by those involved in it as 'feminist therapy') has been at the heart of the theoretical effort.[7]

Overall, then, some personal experience of psychoanalysis, and strong links between the communities of clinicians and of intellectuals, are prerequisites, or at least very beneficial conditions, for interesting and useful work on psychoanalysis and politics. Yet the clinical and political domains are fundamentally distinct, and simple, direct movement from one to the other is not on the whole possible. The growth of interest in psychoanalysis amongst political intellectuals cannot be attributed to their having had good experiences of therapy. While some connections between therapy and politics are desirable, a deep interlocking between the two domains is neither desirable nor possible.

A Philosophical Quest

Philosophical debate about psychoanalysis has tended to be mainly in the philosophy of science, which is perhaps symptomatic of the general cultural response of marginalizing the substantive and moral questions raised by psychoanalysis. Nonetheless, the debate about scientificity has provided for some people an approach to psychoanalysis. In my case, an attachment to a particularly scientistic form of Marxism–Leninism, which persisted until the mid-1970s, meant that I was looking for scientific truth, and hoped to find that psychoanalysis was epistemologically more sophisticated and sound than other schools of psychology, trapped as they were in empiricism and positivism. (It was of course very helpful in this that the judgment of bourgeois philosophy on psychoanalysis was in general so damning.)

Accordingly I attached great importance to the advocacies of psychoanalysis found in the left scientism of Louis Althusser and in the feminist scientism of Juliet Mitchell (1974). A little later I found that realist philosophy expanded and improved the philosophical armamentarium with which to install and defend psychoanalysis in the citadel of science.[8] It offered the grounds for a sophisticated rebuttal of the charge that the concept of the allegedly unobservable unconscious was outside the scope of empirical science. Realist theory argued that science was characteristically concerned with real things which underlay the pattern of events and which it imagined to cause them, rather than just with the observable events themselves (as is the case for much empiricist psychology). Thus the unconscious could be establishd as a proper object of scientific inquiry.

However, this kind of philosophical preference can serve only as a rationalization obscuring other reasons for turning to psychoanalysis, or as the basis for an empty and formalistic approach to it. I had already become interested (through experiences in training as a clinical psychologist) in varieties of psychoanalysis (the Kleinian and object-relational schools) which are very little troubled by the question of scientificity. They occasionally advance a claim to a particular scientific method (e.g. in Harry Guntrip's formulation of what a 'psychodynamic science' should look like),[9] but on the whole they are notable more as expressions of a certain kind of psychological humanism. They tend to stress elements of human need and feeling which for most practical purposes can be regarded as universals; they see the individual subject as a basic entity, as potentially coherent and as a moral agent; and they at least implicitly support the notion that the most fundamental kind of discourse is moral.

Of course none of these features is necessarily incompatible with some kind of concern with scientificity. However, there is an important difference of emphasis, and the compassionate understanding and emotional truth of this humanism came to seem of greater value for me than the search for scientific truth, notwithstanding the tendency of some object-relations writers particularly to slip into somewhat sentimental and rhetorical styles of humanism, in which the individual or self is naturalized and elevated into an absolute principle, rather in the manner of self-styled 'humanistic psychology'.

Moreover, despite the present growing interest in realism, the issue of scientificity has now lost some of the topicality it had on the left in the 1970s, in so far as that was generated by the Althusserian influence. Work on a number of fronts continues, however, and the characterization of psychoanalytic method and epistemology remains an important task. The consideration of psychoanalysis in terms of realist theory has been carried forward by a number of authors.[10] An explicitly humanistic perspective, proposing biography as the core discipline of psychoanalytic human science, has been put forward by Robert Young.[11] And while the Althusserian flame may have flickered, the torch of Lacanianism which it helped to light continued to burn quite fiercely, such that from some viewpoints one of the main commendations of psychoanalysis was its allegedly *anti*-humanist theory of the subject, or its claimed potential for circumventing the humanism/anti-humanism debate.[12]

One other bridge from philosophy into psychoanalysis must also be mentioned, since it is part of a body of work which has been steadily gaining influence since 1968. This is the work of Jurgen Habermas, who in fact provides the most explicit and elaborated model for a philosophical appropriation of psychoanalysis. Habermas proposes that psychoanalysis is the only example of an emancipatory, self-reflective science, or rather that this is so once it is shorn of Freud's theory of biological instincts, a physicalistic misunderstanding by Freud of his own discoveries. However, Russell Keat, in a critical discussion of Habermas's use of psychoanalysis, argues that he departs from Freud in ways other than those which he announces. Joel Whitebook makes a similar criticism of the neglect of the body by Habermas, whose 'etherealized' picture (Keat) of the psyche, in which the unconscious functions not as the ground of all experience but only as the source of distortions of communication, is certainly far removed from the pictures of mental life found in British psychoanalysis (and, in a different way, from the Lacanian picture). This may partly account for the lack of impact in Britain of his reading of Freud.

Despite the interest in his work as a whole, it has not been a springboard for a wider engagement with psychoanalysis.[13]

The Multivalence of Psychoanalysis

Thus, neither personal experience of therapy, nor philosophical commitments, are in themselves likely to provide much of a basis for a political appropriation of psychoanalysis, and if for particular individuals they are important factors then they may each be linked with one of a number of very different kinds of psycho-analytic politics. The brief historical background sketch given earlier established that psychoanalysis is available to diverse and often quite divergent political appropriations. True, there is a notional common element in all these appropriations, which is some kind of stress on unconscious interiority. However, as noted earlier (p. 77), Mitchell argues persuasively that in the cases of Reich and Laing no real conceptual commonality with Freud existed, since the genuinely interior, unconscious and psycho-logical dimensions were lacking in the work of the more 'political' thinkers. Likewise Jacoby offers a somewhat similar critique of the Adlerians, neo-Freudians and ego-psychologists as well as the Laingians. Even if this commonality is not regarded as superficial, it is very secondary in political terms. What can be the political significance and value of a concept of 'the unconscious' if it can be inserted with equal conviction into both historical materialism and classical liberalism?[14]

This is actually the wrong question, although it is based on a fact which must be observed, namely that psychoanalysis does not bear with it a stable set of political values which act as a constant factor in different combinations with other intellectual elements. It does not follow from this, though, that it has no political effectivity; although it has no general political impact, it is at least potentially important in the specific contributions it makes to particular political outlooks, in the ways it may extend, inflect or enrich them.

These contributions are not a matter of logical affinities between abstract forms of discourse (e.g. the question of the philosophical compatibility, or otherwise, of psychoanalysis and Marxism) but of whether there are the people around, able and willing to do the intellectual work required to establish cooperative relationships between psychoanalytic thinking and any particular kind(s) of

political perspective (e.g. the question of whether sufficient philosophers are interested in establishing the compatibility of psychoanalysis and Marxism). In other words, the political value of
psychoanalysis is a historical, conjunctural matter, its content and
impact open to negotiation between contending social forces. Of
course particular forms of psychoanalysis may lend themselves
more easily to certain kinds of appropriation, and some political
traditions may be hostile to all forms of psychological thought, but
these limits are very broad ones, and even quite well defined
schools of psychoanalysis have been claimed by very different
political interests.[15]

The right question to ask is therefore an empirical one: what has
been the political significance of psychoanalysis in those theoretical
appropriations of it which have been made? There are three very
broad problematics or political agendas from which people have
sallied forth to lay hands on psychoanalytic theory. They are distinct and will to some extent be discussed separately, though the
main argument advanced here is that at an important level they
draw upon a common source, psychodynamically and ideolog-
ically. Empirically, they have no doubt been frequently associated
with each other in individuals' political outlooks. For each I will
suggest an alternative reading of psychoanalysis, more in keeping
with that indicated in Chapter 2.

Feminism

The feminist interest in psychoanalysis has been one of the main
reasons for its coming to be placed on the agendas of the left. This
interest, to the extent that it has been a positive one, was at first
mainly in psychoanalysis as an instrument for the critique of
patriarchy and for the promotion of anti-familism. Work here was
mainly around the classical Freudian texts, and was usually either
part of the Lacanian 'return to Freud' (see below) or was seen to
involve an inversion of Freud similar to that described above,
though here the emphasis was on inverting Freud-the-patriarch
rather than Freud-the-bourgeois (if such a distinction was recognized). Partly through the influence of Kleinian and object-
relational ideas, the feminist critique of gender difference shifted
its focus to mothering and to the gendered division of labour in
child-care, developing a highly influential rationale for the abol-

ition of that division as the key to the general subversion of gender identity and the overthrow of patriarchal power.[16]

For almost everyone, the first other is a woman. In Dinnerstein's view, influenced by Klein, the infant's first experiences of the other necessarily bring terrifying intimations of its separate individuality and mortality. As a defence against this, the realm of sensuous experience embodied by the (m)other is rejected in favour of rational worldly activity. Hence the splits between heart and head, feeling and reason, private and public. Woman is continually invested and reinvested with the first half of each of these splits, and man with the second, so that both gender identities are dangerously impoverished and fearful. Chodorow's thesis is similar, but stresses the mother's different cathexes of boys and girls. Daughters are more narcissistically identified with, while sons are related to as different others. Thus boys are driven into a harsh separateness in which they cannot adequately feel with or for others; girls are unable to differentiate themselves sufficiently and to transcend their pre-Oedipal mother-love.

It was in these forms that the feminist appropriation of psycho-analysis was, for a period around the end of the 1970s, a major influence upon many of us interested in the political meanings of psychoanalysis. However these ideas, despite their still current dominance on the left and their popularity beyond, have been subjected to powerful criticism. For example, the political theorist, Jean Elshtain found these uses of psychoanalysis to be schematic and prescriptive, while a paper by the psychoanalyst Jane Temperley showed that a more thoroughgoing engagement with Kleinian theory can see specific patterns of early psychic development, not intrinsic to the general structure of heterosexually differentiated parenting, as major sources of the damage represented by adult 'femininity', or rather by particular organizations of femininity.[17] (And it might be said that the clinical literature has always been replete with evidence that this is also the case for 'masculinity'.) Thus some alternative positions are being articulated, linked to wider and more sympathetic re-evaluations of gender difference, and more concerned with clinically observed qualities of parenting than with abstract notions of patriarchal power. In many readings of it, psychoanalysis teaches that gender is the most fundamental dimension of identity, and that a model of cooperative complementarity, based on good relations between the sexes, can be posited as an ideal for human relations generally.

'The Personal Is Political'

The second political agenda which included an opportunity to explore psychoanalysis was that headed by the slogan 'The personal is political'. The hope that the theory of the unconscious could provide a deeper and more truthful version of this statement was at the heart of much of the feminist involvement in psychoanalysis, but was also a crucial element in the motives of those coming from other, though overlapping, political directions. Earlier versions of the personal/political equation had tended to collapse the personal into the political, but as time went by it became clear that this would not do. Working in the mental health field, for example, it was difficult not to be impressed by the inaccessibility of personal madness to political analysis, let alone to political intervention, as long as one worked only with a rationalistic psychology of 'environment', 'stress' and other similar concepts.

Psychoanalysis was thought to promise to deliver the mediations; the concepts of internalization, introjection and identification, for example, seemed to offer a vocabulary for talking about the political and historical constitution of our inner worlds. The concept of the unconscious was the key to a new way of understanding the totality of our social life, in that it could illuminate how the social outside gets into the psychic inside, and vice versa, and provide the most sophisticated account of how the personal and the political are interwoven. The essential unity, beneath our segmented experience, of all oppressive structures, and of personal and political domains, is implied by this view, which thereby is a point of convergence of an otherwise disparate set of libertarian, (post-)structuralist and critical theory perspectives.

However, this project was from the start in a deep tension with itself. The attraction of psychoanalysis was that it provided the most radically personal and internal account of subjectivity, in comparison with which most other theories of personality seemed banal. But for that same reason it was likely to buck the theoretical burden it was being required to carry, whether that was the Marx–Freud synthesis or some other programme of specifying an inner-outer dialectic. In its core conceptual range, psychoanalysis has a radical uninterest in the external. (It may nonetheless accommodate an interest, in particular cases, in the significance of external events, and individual practitioners may or may not be justly criticized for failing to take sufficient account of the external world in particular cases.) This leads to several points of tension in the project of totalization.

One, already discussed above, concerns the relationship of therapeutic experience to the intellectual agenda. Another is related to the theory of narcissism, which has rightly occupied a central place in a number of debates during the last decade about the input of psychoanalysis to social theory.[18] The equation of the personal and the political may in some contexts be seen as a narcissistic inflation of the self, a view consistent with the non-psychoanalytic criticism of the 'personalization' of politics for which '68' is sometimes held responsible.[19] Not only may *individual* misfortune or responsibility be projected out into the public domain, but personal investments in group and sectional interests and demands may lead to their being presented as a general interest.

The third and major difficulty which psychoanalysis presents for the personal = political formulation stems not from a particular diagnostic category but from the routine and general nature of psychoanalytic discourse. Let us take the example of domestic violence, and the view that wife-beating is no more nor less than a public, political issue, that of patriarchal violence. This rules out of consideration any specific familial or personal factors, and exploration of how the wider societal dimensions are potentiated into violence in some families and not in others. It empties the particular family of its own emotional content, immobilizes those professionals wishing to make helpful interventions, and liquidates the personal responsibilities of all those involved for the violence and its consequences. A psychoanalytic approach is necessarily concerned with putting all these questions back on the agenda, by examining the psychodynamics of the family as a private, partially bounded domain, and seeing the personal and interpersonal specificity of the situation as crucial to understanding it.

In the case of domestic violence, one psychoanalytic hypothesis likely to be of central importance, both in practical understanding and in theorizing the personal/political relationship, is that individuals are usually partly responsible for the relationships which they find themselves in. To raise the question of personal responsibility here is of course a controversial move, but a necessary one. The tendency of left-radical thinking in the 1970s to find victims everywhere, and to project the blame for many ills on to some ill-defined society or environment, left the ideological counter-insurgents of the New Right with the opportunity to win a series of easy victories on a number of social and moral issues, by restoring the widely held concern with personal responsibility to a central role in public debate.

Another example involves the implication of psychoanalytic theory that there is a need for some firm distinction between the private and the public, in order to establish the conditions for trust and intimacy. In psychoanalytic theory, deep emotional attachments are generally seen as forming slowly, on the basis of repeated experiences of reciprocity, security and satisfaction. These experiences are available only within a bounded (not necess-arily physically so) interpersonal space in which the distinctive qualities of the other, in relation to oneself, can be registered.

It has been a main feature of some of the techniques of human-istic psychology that the personal/political boundary is breached at just this point. The best example is probably the encounter group, introduced to Britain around 1970, in which intimacy and confession are demanded in a semi-public setting of people who may be in contact with each other only for a matter of hours. In other words, intimacy and trust are demanded when the conditions for their development – essentially those of longer-term relation-ships – are absent, and consequently the intimate relating which ensues is necessarily in part fake. This at least is a psychoanalytic view and correspondingly it is towards humanistic psychology rather than psychoanalysis that some radicals who have remained committed to a personal/political fusion have turned.[20]

Thus, far from showing us how the personal and political are fused, psychoanalysis offers ways of theorizing the inauthenticities which result when the public–private distinction is eroded such that neither domain can sustain the forms of relationship appro-priate to it – authentic intimacy in the private domain and auth-entic civility in the public. In this role, psychoanalysis is at odds with simple equations of the personal and political, and instead is in keeping with more pluralistic understandings of where power is located, and whom it oppresses. This is not to jettison the insights gained in the more totalizing moment, nor to abandon the research programmes which we are now only beginning to project in, for example, the historicity of subjectivity.[21] It is, though, to introduce a quite different orientation, for which psychoanalysis is of interest to social theory partly because it can inform the argument that the personal sphere not only is but also *should* be a distinctive segment of social life, and that in general the principle of boundaries and segmentation is a crucial element in good social organization.

The Revolutionary Programme

The most general feature of the left-political context within which interest in psychoanalysis took initial shape in 1970s Britain was the frustration of the aspirations of '68'. For many of us psychoanalysis held the promise of revitalizing those aspirations. A major problem with the revolutionary programmes, it seemed, was that they had overlooked the *internal* resistances to social change and to socialism, resistances which psychoanalysis could illuminate. Of course this hope had been entertained before, by Reich, Fromm, Marcuse *et al.*; an important difference was that we could bring the conceptual gains of more recent developments in psychoanalysis to bear on the problem, and not be shackled by the limitations of classical Freudianism. Psychoanalysis was the theory which could help to explain why socialism had not yet arrived, and to do so in a way that sustained the belief that when it does arrive it will enable us to *transcend* the world as we know it. Capitalism is still strong because of its anchorage in inner repression, but if that repression could be undone then an unprecedented condition of psychic fulfilment and harmony would ensue, as part of the social transformation.

This political appropriation of psychoanalysis cannot accurately be called utopian, since those who advanced it were generally Marxists for whom the idea of utopia was, at least in theory, impermissible. But to borrow – with due irony – a term from Maslow, it might well be called 'eupsychian', since the transcendent condition to which it aspires, though not necessarily one of social perfection, is one of intrapsychic ease, release and satisfaction.[22]

Two major routes to this condition have been mapped out. One is via the overthrow of the capitalist *state* and the undoing of the repression which is the psychic basis and effect of its authority – the Reichian route of which Kovel is today's most eloquent and subtle advocate. The other is that which leads away from the capitalist *market*, and leaves behind the psychic splitting which is the consequence of engaging in instrumental exchange relationships with other persons. Erich Fromm in various writings was an early guide to this route, which takes one through the extensive post-Weberian critique of rationality, and is one of the main highways of critical theory. This latter route is sometimes seen as leading towards the re-establishment of social authority in a remoralized world, and may not include a critique of repression, in which case[23] it would diverge from the more libertarian path of the first. Often, though, the two routes are felt by their would-be travellers to be running in parallel towards the same destination, where the deep psychic organization of the majority will be different to what it is now.

This is certainly a simplification, though it falls far short of parody. I am referring most obviously to Reichian and some Marcusan doctrines, though I have not indicated the important differences between the two. Whereas Reich's attack on the ego, on 'character' and repression was unremitting, Marcuse sought to salvage a necessary minimum of 'basic' repression, and his hostility to the ego was historically relative – he objected to particular kinds of egos, not to the very idea of one. But there is little argument that Marcuse as much as Reich was interested in a wholesale transcendence of our current structures of repression.

Traditionally posed against this revolutionary appropriation of Freud is the view that psychoanalysis offers both an analysis of why 'revolution', as theoretically imagined, is impossible, and a diagnostic critique of revolutionary politics and of the personal motives at work in them. In many of its specifics (though not as a general rule) the latter has been welcomed by the psychoanalytic left (indeed, has sometimes been seen as the major contribution psychoanalysis has to make), but the former, understandably, has not. Yet this kind of selectivity is hard to maintain, say the critics of revolutionary aspirations, since the two anti-revolutionary arguments are linked. The theory of the post-revolutionary ideal society is simply an intellectual expression and corollary of the same delusions and defences found in the paranoid machinations of sectarian politics, which rest upon the preservation of the ideal programme.

We need not rehearse the main forms in which this attack on the revolutionary impulse has been put. It will, though, be useful to mention a recent exchange in which the two traditional antagonists have once again been tested against each other. In the mid-

1970s, when the left's romance with psychoanalysis was at a peak in France, two analysts working in Paris wrote a book in which they posited a fundamental opposition between Freudian theory and the ideas of Reich, whose work they rejected not only as anti-psychoanalytic but as exemplifying clearly the omnipotence of the revolutionary imagination. *Freud or Reich?* by Janine Chasseguet-Smirgel and Bela Grunberger, has recently been published in Britain, and a commentary upon it written by Joel Kovel. Despite the clinical sophistication and intellectual breadth of the combatants, this exchange demonstrates the limits of the debate as it has been characteristically constructed. Chasseguet-Smirgel and Grunberger combine a clear-headed argument for the intrinsic anti-utopianism of psychoanalysis, and an analysis of Reich's regressive wish to dissolve the Freudian insistence on conflict, with an outlandish assertion of the endogenously individual roots of social life. Kovel, on the other hand, disposes most effectively with the claim for the primacy of internal factors, but does not respond to the substance of the critique of Reich.

Even Philip Rieff, the most profound expositor of Freud's anti-utopianism, does not provide a fully adequate alternative to the terms of this debate, since in his account the *whole* terrain of politics is at risk of reduction to illusion and the search for consolation. Nevertheless he compellingly shows psychoanalysis to be primarily a doctrine of tragedy and forbearance – to be none the less political for that, but to be opposed (at least in the context of the liberal democracies) to programmes of revolutionary political change. It is difficult even to allow these programmes the status of innocence, since we must now admit, to put one aspect of the matter rather crudely, that the impulse to destroy a society is usually a basically destructive impulse, whatever altruistic and reparative motives it may trick into acting alongside it. Even where a milder language of social transformation is used, one which in its imagination of the transformative scenario does not give licence to envious or retributive feelings, then a psychoanalytic scrutiny would still be uncharitable, focusing on the grandiosity of the political vision and its denial of destruction and loss.[24]

This is by no means an apolitical counsel of despair. There are a number of other suggestions in the literature of recent years about the directions which a *positive* psychoanalytic input to political thought might take. For example, Jeffrey Abramson makes an interesting attempt to proceed from Rieff's exposition towards the recovery from Freudian theory of a more 'communitarian' vision of psychic development in which the satisfactions of public life play an essential and honourable part. He stresses those elements of Freudian thought, such as identification, which posit the relational construction of pleasure, and also he contends that psychoanalysis does not theorize the richer civic aspects of character. If some virtues can be realized only through and in the public sphere, then politics must take up where therapy leaves off. There may yet be a bridge between the radical disillusionment of psychoanalytic self-knowledge, and a radical engagement in political life.[25]

The Pursuit of Transcendence

Can any common themes be drawn out of these accounts of the transmission of psychoanalytic ideas into the sphere of left politics, and if so can they be linked to the previous analyses of the fate of psychoanalysis in official and humanistic psychology? All three political agendas – the feminist, 'personalist' and revolutionary – have in common a wish to transcend some existing set of structures or boundaries. The distinctions between men and women, private and public, libido and ego are all under attack – to a great variety of ends, but all sharing in some vision of transcending both oppression and misery.

In the left's use of psychoanalysis, from Adler and Reich on, social justice and individual happiness are characteristically fused together. It is assumed that a single, psychoanalytically informed political project will necessarily change both inner and outer worlds to the same degree. The construction of a basically non-oppressive social order, it is assumed, will result in (or could only be achieved along with) radically different states of mind from those obtaining at present. This eupsychian prescription is most obviously spelt out in revolutionary Freudo-Marxism, as noted earlier, but is also present in the other agendas – in visions of a healing psychological androgyny, and in psychoanalytic contributions to the study of the capitalist totality and its 'social reproduction'. The vision of *psychic* emancipation, as an integral part of social liberation, is as much a part of the scholarly and intricate work of Habermas as it is of sub-Reichian banality.

Eupsychian images of fulfilment, wholeness and happiness therefore underly and unify many of the concerns of the psychoanalytic left, including and especially the attacks on patriarchy and on repression. The lifting of repression promises to remove not only unnecessary frustration but also the painful experience of being divided against oneself. The ever-provisionally *integrated* self offered by psychoanalytic therapy is spurned or devalued as mere palliative; the desire for a *unified* self predominates, and may interact with the desire for an idealized social unity.[26] Any programme for the dissolution of structures of authority and difference in the external world may carry, for its proponents and opponents alike, the unconscious meaning of the dissolution of *inner* structures and divisions, whether or not such psychic de-differentiation is explicitly advocated – though in much of the work I have been discussing the transcendence of inner conflicts is often consciously the aim.

As in humanistic psychology, a romantic yearning for transcendence supplies the main energy at work in the theorizing. And again, albeit with due caution and care not to disguise political dismissal as diagnostic insight, we can employ the same psychoanalytic critique of the romantic values of unity and liberation. Chasseguet-Smirgel and Grunberger suggest that underlying Reich's politics, and any other promises of heaven on earth, is the narcissistic wish for fusion with the ego-ideal. They advance a strong form of the hypothesis that utopian politics are at root an expression of emotional need, by claiming that the aim of such politics is the restoration of the experience of narcissistic perfection.

One does not have to accept their political judgments, nor even their specific psychoanalytical formulation, to take this hypothesis seriously and consider that the eupsychian tone of much radical psychoanalysis may be the product of deeply regressive wishes, and of omnipotent beliefs that the pains of separation and vulnerability can be avoided. Take for example the closing statement of *Repression*, a book in which Gad Horowitz argues carefully for a moderation of Marcuse's theory such that the ego and genital primacy are re-established as indices of health, with re-eroticization and pre-genitality envisioned as deployed *within* the ego's organization of libido. Despite these substantial revisions, the wish for transcendence is preserved, to emerge fully in his closing description of 'communist man' as one for whom 'the pain of separation is no longer experienced as the essence of selfhood'.[27]

This can be seen only as wishful thinking when set against the increasingly well documented post-Freudian conception of selfhood as intrinsically rooted in the pain of separation, though also – crucially – thereby rooted in the satisfactions and compensations that can come from struggling with separateness and from building bridges to others. Again, the alternative to transcendental eupsychianism is not necessarily reactionary despair, since the makings of quite optimistic fortitude are to be found in the psychoanalytic tradition precisely as it focuses on the constitution of subjectivity in the experiences of loss and guilt, and on the intrapsychic embrace of the other as the founding moment of the differentiated self. The transcendent aspirations of much politicized psychoanalytic theory are, like the humanistic psychologists' reworking of Freud's model of the mind, the expression of a wish to be free of others: of the limits and demands that others represent, of the differences and separations they require us to tolerate in the external world, and of the structures and conflicts which form in the internal world around our representations of them.

Again, authority is the most powerful symbol of the other, and is therefore the focus of much of the rejecting effort. Hence the regrettable truth in the arguments of those[28] who wish to write off completely the politics of the 1960s by arguing that the radical impulse is an intrapsychic one, a need to attack authority. Yet in so far as this is true for particular people, it may still be only half the truth – the internal object under attack may not be authority as such, but the other. As one (fictional) woman member of the '68' generation put it, looking back twenty years later in conversation with a male friend and fellow iconoclast: 'Your revolt against authority was also somehow a revolt against me.'[29]

The Lacanian Influence

In this chapter's discussion the main bodies of work implicitly centralized have been the classical left Freudianisms of Reich and critical theory, and psychoanalytic feminism, with a counterplot emanating from the psychoanalytic theory of omnipotence. What then about that range of political appropriations of psychoanalysis, based on the work of Lacan, that emphatically distance themselves from all the classical revolutionaries? Despite a growing mood of re-evaluation in the Lacanian constituency, his influence is still strong and widespread. Both the journals founded in Britain in the 1970s with the aim of incorporating psychoanalysis into a politically defined project (*m/f* and *Screen*) were strongly Lacanian, as are some non-clinical psychoanalytic societies founded in the 1980s.[30]

At first sight it seems that the critique of the transcendent impulse is not relevant here. A major complaint about Lacan has been that far from holding out a promise of a eupsychian paradise in some future society, he did not even concede the possibility of moderate psychic improvement through psychoanalysis in the present one. The inevitably fractured, alienated condition of the human subject is routinely enunciated in Lacanian texts, and a similarity with existentialist negativity can be discerned.[31]

However a number of convergences with other strands of the Freudian left can be noted, some of them at points found on the agendas discussed earlier. Firstly, Lacanian theory has been very suitable for incorporation into the attack on the patriarchal family, which Lasch (1981) sees as having been the central purpose of the Freudian left. Secondly, the radical decentring of the subject and the evacuation of the subject into language is, at a very intellectualized level, a manoeuvre equivalent to the collapsing of the personal/political distinction. As personal subjects we do not exist; our scripts are written for us by the language we speak. Thirdly, the psychoanalytic critique of the market, though most often associated with critical theory, has received analogous formulations within Lacanian paradigms, via the equation of the Symbolic with the realm of exchange.[32] Fourthly, and most importantly, the Freudo-Marxist tirade against repression and against the ego is profoundly matched by Lacan, whose bitterness against ego-psychology exceeded that of Marcuse, and who built upon it a theory of the ego as intrinsically narcissistic and paranoid.[33] Also, the Marcusan critique of heterosexual 'genital tyranny' and celebration of polymorphous sexuality[34] is comparable, as rhetorical cultural analysis, to the Lacanian description of our uncertain sexual identities.

Points of similarity are sometimes noted, too, between Lacan and British psychoanalysis, which has also developed a picture of the ego as necessarily split. Here, however, the differences are more important: the multiple egos of object-relations theory are not the equivalent of the shifting identity of the Lacanian subject, but are the dynamically interrelated agencies of the mind. Whereas Lacan concluded that if there is inevitably multiplicity and conflict within the psyche, then there can be no stable identity nor integration, most other schools of psychoanalysis (not only ego-psychology) have continued to believe (as, it might be claimed, did Freud) that coherence and stability can be achieved, though they must continually be re-established as the dominant moment in the inner struggle with fragmentation.[35] Since the Lacanians dismiss this hope as adaptationist and humanist fiction, it leaves them with only a romance of 'desire'.[36] At worst, it leads to a celebration of psychosis and delirium.[37] It also leaves them with a shadowy transcendent image of psychological de-alienation. The locus of transcendence, for semioticized psychoanalysis, is not so much, for practical purposes, in the political institutions of society as in the literary and cinematic text and its deconstruction, but it is none the less transcendent for that, as can be seen in its precursors in the surrealist movement.[38]

Thus although Lacan's thought may address the utopian mentality of transcendence, it does not do so to offer us psychodynamic clarification of a particular pathological state of mind. Rather he claimed to be reflecting upon our collective and absolute lot – transcendence is largely ruled out on metapsychological grounds as an actual possibility, yet it is all that the Lacanian political imagination has to work with.

For a number of reasons, then, the Lacanian development is appropriately included in a discussion of psychoanalytic leftism and the pursuit of transcendence. Jacqueline Rose observed that, 'The political use of Lacan's theory therefore stemmed from its assault on what English Marxists would call bourgeois individualism.'[39] The assault is, however, not only a philosophical one on the 'myth' of the unitary, coherent subject; it is also an emotional and political one on the ego and its cultural representatives. On to the rational ego of the 'bourgeois individual' is projected much that is limiting, bounding, untruthful, frustrating and oppressive, and here we have the most striking parallel with German and American traditions. This is clearly illustrated by reference again to the work of Joel Kovel, whose most powerful influences are Reich, Marcuse and his clinical experience. Kovel has on that basis brought American Freudo-Marxism and the psychoanalytic castigation of the bourgeois individual to its most sophisticated form, and yet he has also absorbed into his language some key Lacanian terms and thus created a neo-Reichian discourse of Desire.

Social Justice and Individual Happiness

Political radicalism is linked to the eupsychian impulse by the assumption that social oppression and personal unhappiness more or less reflect each other, with the social as the ultimately leading moment. Challenging oppressive social relations has been seen as necessarily involving the goal of *psychic* transformation.

Any social changes which were effective in reducing the misery of those millions of people in the Third World living in or on the edge of destitution, or in making life and health more secure anywhere, would bring in their train inestimable relief of mental suffering, and reduce the mental disorder which is the precipitate of suffering. To that extent the causes of justice and happiness are one. But a measure of security from the pains of hunger or torture is not by any means the same as the psychic transcendence of the pains of loss and guilt. The conscription of psychoanalysis by the left has been in the main according to this transcendent, distinctly metropolitan, project.[40]

This eupsychian project is not the same as, and cannot be hitched to, the socialist project in the liberal democracies. The latter must include plans for changing the social arrangements for *responding* to distress, but it is an error to confuse these with the totality of the distress and its sources. This is not to say that much mental disorder in our present society is not socially produced and historically specific in content, but it is to stress that some considerable part of the social means of its production may, as discussed in Chapter 2, be transhistorical, or pansocial – at least in the universe of modernity. The management of unhappiness is clearly and directly a matter of mutable social institutions (and is of great political significance in that unhappiness may assume many different political expressions, depending on how a culture is able to manage it), but the reconstruction of basic forms of the psyche is something else. This sounds like Freud, though it is more the Freud of *Civilisation and Its Discontents* than that of '"Civilised" sexual morality and modern nervous illness'. It is the Freud who pointed towards a possibility for uncoupling political visions of justice from the intolerance of psychic conflict and pain. Post-Freudian psychoanalysis has pressed along this line of analysis, and yields the disquieting conclusion that the ostensible pursuit of the welfare of others through programmes of political transformation may be linked to an inner refusal and rejection of the other.

POLITICS AND ENDURANCE

7

PSYCHOANALYSIS AND MARKET IDEOLOGIES

Market Individualism

On the arguments and evidence of the last three chapters, it is possible to identify some elements which appear to be common to otherwise very different responses to psychoanalysis. These elements are at an unconscious level; they involve pre-verbal states of mind, and so can enter into conceptual thought only in subtle ways. They are concerned with the capacity and readiness to give the existence of others, and their constitutive and limiting role in the formation of our own selves, as fundamental a place in theory as they have in the realities of emotional development. What might seem to be an obvious and incontrovertible principle – that each is in the other – is persistently disregarded or overruled by theories of mind which prefer to see the ego or self as original, to view internalizations of the other as generally malign, and to preach the possibility of transcending the limits and conflicts of differentiated selfhood.

The anti-social and omnipotent qualities of these theories are not usually explicit, and their identification is in large part an interpretive procedure to which numerous objections can be made. Yet without necessarily being convinced of the accuracy of the interpretations, we can regard them as documented well enough – and as significant enough in their implications if there is truth in them – to merit further consideration. They are not matters of theoretical dispute in a value-neutral zone of scientific inquiry; they are moral issues, with a broad reference to everyday life and to questions of policy and politics. It would be evidence of a bizarre and fragmented world if such illusions prevailed in the realms of psychological theory yet had no existence or effects elsewhere. While the world may be bizarre and fragmented, the contrary has been assumed throughout this study. The unconscious meanings of the responses to Freud are of importance not only in themselves but as samples of what may be prevalent trends in the wider intellectual culture, and also of what may be important features of conduct in the social world.

There are two sorts of question that can be asked about the relationship of various readings of Freud to actions and practices. Firstly it can be asked how these ideas may guide and inform courses of action – what their practical implications might be. Some observations on the political implications of these issues in psychological theory have been made, and will be developed in the concluding chapter. Secondly it can be asked whence the ideas came – what their sources and supports in actual social relations are, how their emergence and prevalence can be sociologically understood. In Chapter 3 I suggested one way in which the project of psychoanalysis itself might be understood as an engagement with particular historical conditions. In this chapter we will consider firstly how the responses to Freud which have been described can be placed in a broad social context.

A helpful starting point is the following list of assumptions which comprise part of a particular model of human nature and society:

(i) What makes a man human is freedom from dependence on the wills of others.

(ii) Freedom from dependence on others means freedom from any relations with others except those relations which the individual enters voluntarily with a view to his own interest.

(iii) The individual is essentially the proprietor of his own person and capacities, for which he owes nothing to society.

This could quite accurately be from a description of the utilitarian vision of personhood around which academic psychology fixes Freudian theory; it could even more appropriately be a summary of some of the key features of the transcendent model which humanistic psychology opposes to the 'gloomy determinism' of Freud. It is in fact the first three of a list of seven assumptions which C. B. Macpherson, in his classic work on political theory,[1] attributes to 'possessive individualism'. This is the philosophy, utilitarian at heart, which Macpherson claims to have been dominant in liberal political thought from the seventeenth-century to the present, from Hobbes via Locke to present theories of liberal democracy.

Macpherson sees this theory as having its origins in, and as being maintained by, the social relations of market society. He goes beyond this to suggest that a further assumption, that 'Human society consists of a series of market relations', could be regarded as the primary one from which the above three can be deduced, on the grounds that contractual market relations require the kind of freedom and proprietorship specified by the earlier assumptions. In the terms used so far in this study, we can say that Macpherson points to a socio-historical basis in market society for the illusions of the radical separateness and autonomy of self which can be seen, albeit in different colours, in the declamatory responses of official and humanistic psychology to the psychoanalytic assertion of our basic intersubjectivity. Even the theories of radical psychology, usually committed on one level to an absolute opposition to market values, betray in the texture and scope of their aspirations an origin in the market's promise of a satisfied selfhood, sufficient unto itself.

Macpherson's analysis converges with our earlier discussion of the market and consumer society. Market society is both the context which called forth psychoanalysis as a restitutive challenge to market relations, and also the context in which these regressive responses to psychoanalysis have occurred. The critiques of the consumer society, especially when informed by psychoanalysis, have suggested that one of its features is the powerful encouragement to believe that through the freedom of the market and through inspired acts of consumption one may become anything, that the self is infinitely plastic and capable. If, as Colin Campbell has recently argued,[2] the major source of the principles of consumerism is the 'romantic ethic', then we have a firm set of links between those forms of psychology influenced either by romanticism or utilitarianism, or both, and the demands of a market-led, consumption-dominated society.

In brief, the argument is this. The advanced capitalist market acts at two levels to potentiate illusions of omnipotence: directly through the pressures towards the narcissistic use of consumer goods, and more insidiously (as discussed in Chapter 3) in the basic psychic development of the individual, through the tendency of market relations to subordinate affective ties and to corrode all forms of traditional and moral authority. One product of these processes, mediated through the philosophies of romanticism and utilitarianism, is the continual reappearance of the illusions in new waves of psychological theory, as if a new truth were being discovered each time. When a form of psychological thinking emerges which contains elements of a challenge to these illusions, it will be assimilated or revised in such ways as to conform with them.

The Missing Essence

At this point it may seem as if we have a neat and encompassing scheme to hand for conceptualizing the two-way relationships between forms of psychological knowledge and technique on the one hand and social processes on the other. Market society has generated various forms of psychology which unwittingly and uncritically reflect both its utilitarian workings and its omnipotent phantasies about itself. It has also given rise to psychoanalysis as a contrary and reparative project, an attempt to renew our personal matrices of meaning amidst the amoral disorder of the market. At the same time psychoanalysis offers us ways of theorizing both the general psychic damage done by market relations and the specific illusions expressed in other psychological theories.

This is an appealing interdisciplinary cluster of hypotheses, for which some evidence has been presented here and which would merit further study. They tap into some deeply felt and widely found features of contemporary society. However they also have some shortcomings, which it is now necessary to consider. The main problem is the degree of generality and abstractness with which they have been expressed, both here and in the literature which has been drawn upon. A more empirically grounded approach, paying attention to the specific historical locations and variations of the processes under discussion is also necessary. (In Chapter 3 we noted some of the problems about historical location which arose immediately in relation to the definition of the 'modern'.) The more general level of analysis may be of great value as a guide to research, and in the clarification of overall priorities and perspectives. It is, though, important to emphasize the inadequacies of such analysis.

Here the notion of 'market society' has been at the centre of the discussion around the trends observed in the transmission of psychoanalytic ideas. However no single exhaustive definition of market society or of a market has been offered, and none will be. The reason for this is that in reality markets exist in many diverse forms, and it is not possible to get very far in establishing a general definition of a market. The term may be used to refer to any situation in which the supply of a commodity is not monopolized by one agent or one set of interests, or to any situation in which the distribution of a commodity is determined by a price mechanism. Or it may describe any situation in which the production or distribution of a commodity is not subject to (or is minimally subject to) governmental regulation. Moreover, there are markets in consumer goods, in labour and in capital, with profound differences in their overall social effects. (Today's 'market socialists' are often in favour of the first kind but not the latter two.)

None of these uses specifies what the relations of ownership might be: various forms of private, collective and state ownership could all be compatible with situations falling under any of the above definitions. The sociologist Barry Hindess[3] has recently pointed out that much political debate about the market has been based on a tendency to 'essentialize' the notion of the market, that is to assume that there is a general category of 'the market' which can be defined in terms of some essential features. In reality, he argues, so-called market situations vary enormously, and should be discussed only in terms of their *specific* features. The particular institutional arrangements comprising a 'market' need to be clarified before any conclusions can be drawn about its social and political implications. The essence of the problem of trying to define 'the market' is that there is no essence common to all markets.

Where then does this leave the projects of trying to understand the receptions of psychoanalytic ideas in terms of the pressures of a market society, and of trying to use psychoanalytic insights to learn something of the psychic meanings of the market? It leaves them viable, but in need of further specification – for example narrower and more empirical statements of just which features of market relations and their cultural effects are being considered as giving rise to particular theories or techniques, or to particular states of mind. The diversity of 'markets' must be recognized and any description of experience and behaviour in market relations must be made in specific terms. We cannot postulate a single, constant self present in all forms of market exchange.

This has been a serious flaw in many of the attempts made, for example within the 'Freudo-Marxist' tradition, to develop a psychoanalytic theory of the market or indeed of capitalism as a whole, as the most developed form of market society. For example Erich Fromm[4] took the descriptions of the anal character proposed by Freud and Abraham,[5] and a characterization of the 'bourgeois-capitalist spirit' based largely on the work of the German sociologist Sombart, and claimed that the two corresponded. This kind of anal theory of capitalism has found some more recent advocates. Michael Schneider's polemical work presented the anal character as the dominant type in capitalism because it is the most closely allied to the preoccupations with abstraction and calculation which are dominant in the exchange relations of market societies. In both anality and exchange there is a compulsion to treat things quantitatively; also anal reaction-formations (habits of extreme order and duty developed to counter anal-erotic tendencies) are useful in producing dutiful and docile workers for the labour market.

Schneider's thesis is incidentally a powerful example of the eupsychian impulse discussed earlier. Schneider expands his critique of capitalist anality into an assault on the 'bourgeois' ego, which he sees as fundamentally an anal structure. The ego is an agency of abstract, calculating rationality, the psychic representative of the exchange relation, while true humanity lies in libidinal needs (the equivalent of 'use values' in Marxist economic theory). Social transformation will therefore entail a psychic revolution in which repression, which secures the domination of exchange value over libidinal need, will be overcome, along with the ego which is built upon it. Inner division and longing will thereby be transcended, once there no longer is any fundamental badness outside (capitalism) to take in.

Such diagnoses of capitalism in terms of anal character organization are not the exclusive preserve of the radical left. Christopher Badcock, for example, wishes to reclaim Freud for liberalism, and has a positive view of capitalism. Yet for him, too,[7] it is reaction-formations against, and substitute gratifications for, repressed anal eroticism which are the source of capitalist dynamism.

This one-dimensional kind of formulation, though inadequate as general theory, may be used in the analyses of specific market situations, where relevant. Working for a wage, paying someone a wage, buying and selling shares, applying for a job, choosing a present for one's child or a friend, deciding on a holiday, buying a car or a record, and going to the cinema are all market behaviours, but they entail widely different kinds of emotional involvement. Interpretations in terms of anality may, for instance, be of relevance to understanding some of our attitudes towards saving, whereas the analysis of Oedipal ambitions may have much to say about one person's leisure choices, and another person's career choice. What is always necessary is a grasp of the plurality of relationships between inside and outside, at the same time as one may be trying to derive a more general overview.

The profusion of generalizations about 'the market' in political debate suggests another question, the answer to which will prove to be of relevance to this study. Why do such generalizations come to hand so easily when they are – or should be – so difficult to make? Furthermore, as Raymond Williams has argued,[8] images of the market and of ourselves as individual 'consumers' dominate our conceptions of economic and social relations even where the actual relations are not (or not yet) predominantly privatized market ones (as in health care). Notions of the market are central to our commonsense and academic cultures. A simplified, naturalized vision of the market is the bedrock of many everyday understandings of social life, while the concepts of the market economy and of the abstract agent within it have for two centuries or more underpinned much mainstream thought and debate in the social sciences and in social and moral philosophy. Yet there is a relative paucity of explicit discussion of the content of these concepts.[9]

In view of this, it is plausible to suggest that we must have some reasons for imposing this generalized discourse of the 'market' upon a range of diverse and perhaps non-market realities. This takes us away from the question of what market relations are actually like, whether in economic or psychological terms, into a discussion of what the significance may be of certain *representations* of the market. As we shall see, this will connect in an interesting and meaningful way with our analyses of the various representations of mental life found in the responses to Freud. There are also other reasons for pursuing this suggestion. At this time there are compelling political reasons for bringing all available conceptual equipment to bear on the problem of the status of the market in political debate.

In Britain, as well as elsewhere, the 1980s have seen the political triumph of neo-liberalism and its strident philosophies of the market. For a number of reasons, this has occasioned a renewal of interest amongst socialists in markets as a distributive mechanism. Thus from several directions images of the market have acquired a particular dominance in present-day political culture, mainly through the rhetoric and policies of the Thatcher government but also through the attempts of some people in the opposition parties to challenge the extraordinary hold which 'Thatcherism', as it is sometimes referred to, has established over the terms of political debate in Britain. We have seen the emergence (albeit transitional) of the Social Democratic Party and its philosophy of the 'social market'. Within the Labour Party there has been a reassertion of markets as a necessary and desirable component of socialist policy. Not everyone on the left is happy with this development, of course, and there has in recent years been a renewed debate amongst socialists about the merits of markets.[10] Opponents of markets stress their injustice, inefficiency and ecological blindness; supporters see them as providing the framework without which the positive achievements of capitalism – above all the development of subjective individuality and choice – could not be realized.

While there is real substance to the questions involved in this debate, Hindess's argument suggests that we cannot take them all at face value. It is necessary to ask why so many issues are posed in terms of the largely unexamined category of the market, and in particular to inquire why – at the unconscious levels of theoretical formulation – the market has been so enthusiastically promoted as a social panacea.

Markets of Desire

One usage of the notion of 'market', favoured by many of its protagonists, consists of contrasting it with activity which is subject to governmental regulation. Hindess observes in his critique of essentialism that 'the market' is placed in absolute opposition to a notion of 'planning'. The dominant rhetoric traditionally used by advocates of 'market' solutions to economic and social problems is one of 'freedom'. It is clear what 'freedom' is referred to: the freedom to act in the market as one chooses, both as seller and buyer. Since, however, 'the market' does not exist as a generality, there can be no such general freedom. What then is the meaning of the marketeers' slogan of 'freedom'?

Freedom in this context has a composite rather than a general meaning: it serves as a rallying call for various parties with diverse interests in such things as, at present, deregulation of the media, privatization of health services and public utilities, the growth of house and road construction, the weakening of trade unions, and so on. Different people stand to gain in different ways from these 'freedoms' (and of course others stand to lose in different ways), and many logical contradictions and inconsistencies have been observed in the present government's pursuit of 'market freedom'. It may be that there is nonetheless an economic programme of some consistency behind these diverse initiatives, but this still does not fully explain the unusual ascendancy which the accompanying rhetoric of 'freedom' has achieved in present-day political culture, nor its powerful electoral impact, which suggests it is influential amongst people who have little or nothing to gain, and may have something to lose, from its practical applications, and who are unlikely to be concerned about recent debates in economic theory.

What then might be the emotional basis of appeals to the freedom of, and freedom for, the 'market'? Freedom from what exactly is being demanded and celebrated? And freedom to do what? The market is posed in the most general terms as the alternative to 'command' methods for regulating production and consumption. It is often seen as the repository of spontaneity, creativity, and energy, in contrast to the dead hand of bureaucratic control. The state, in this scenario, represents all things restrictive and prohibitive; it is the voice of arbitrary negation, of hostile, forbidding authority. Understood in this way, the advocacy of the market has the quality of a revolt against the superego and against the parent-figures, which are experienced as wholly bad. As Winnicott[11] pointed out, a government is in a sense a 'temporary parent', albeit elected by ostensibly mature people. As the ultimate authority in many areas of our lives, it receives many kinds of projections derived from our phantasies about authority. Where these phantasies are predominantly of authority as sadistically denying or persecuting, then government is likely to be experienced in related terms.

The state is particularly resented for some of its interventions to control the circulation of money. Some theorists[12] have suggested a link between money and libido: both are abstract, infinitely transmutable forms of general energy, in the external and psychic economies respectively. There is no evidence for these speculative conceptual equations, but if there were such a link, either in our actual experience of money or in our more abstract understanding of the world, then in seeking to control the flow of money around markets the state would be felt to be impeding the flow of libido towards objects. This might help to explain something of the strength of feeling some people have about personal taxation and the government's appropriation of 'their' money.

One phrase revealing of this sort of emotional undertow in the market/state dichotomy is the scornful description of a welfare-oriented, interventionist government as the 'nanny state'. The images deployed here are of a fussy, restrictive female, imposing her own ideas about what is good on her charges and thereby keeping them, emotionally at least, in the nursery. Nanny is a bad object, desexualized and desexualizing. We will set aside consideration of the irony that nannying, in the sense of private home-based child care, has probably increased considerably in the last decade or so, particularly amongst supporters of the attack on the nanny state. We will also ignore for the moment the irony that this attack is led at present by Britain's first woman leader, who has herself been likened by some of her detractors to a malign nanny. We will, however, note one connotation of the attack on the nanny. She is by definition a substitute for the parents, and so the attack on her could be seen as a displacement of hatred from the real parents, who are possibly remote or absent, and continually disappointing. There is no adequate substitute for real, good parents, and any person or institution (whether nanny or 'nanny state') playing a pseudo-parental role is likely to be attacked, especially by those who do not feel that they have had a decent share of real parenting.

This image of the 'nanny state' thus discloses three strands of feeling in at least some varieties of the radical pro-market, anti-interventionist position. Firstly, there is a protest against the allegedly anti-libidinal restrictiveness of the state or government, portrayed as lifeless or inhuman. Secondly, there is a rather violent rejection of dependency: nanny's apron strings are a major threat in life, to be avoided at all costs lest we hang on to them. And thirdly, there is perhaps the hint that a sense of major disappointment with real parents is helping to drive forms of anti-statism up to the surface of political culture. These feelings are important enough to merit some further discussion.

If market freedom is a libidinal demand, then it has not usually been explicitly so. The manifest content of the demand has usually been for individuals to be free to pursue their own choices in life, these being seen as rational, conscious choices. Typically this has been met with the counterargument that it gives licence to selfishness and to lack of consideration for the consequences of one's choices, but in this critique the freedom is again seen as something consciously and logically pursued. My suggestion is that there is an unconscious and non-rational, latent content to the demand, namely that it is at one level a demand to be free of restraint upon impulse. Sometimes this libidinal quality seems to be near the surface. Calls were recently made by some members of the Federation of Conservative Students (FCS) for the legalization of various drugs and sexual practices, that is, we might say, for the abolition of official prohibitions upon certain libidinal satisfactions. The FCS had been closely associated with extreme libertarian fancies, which the Conservative Party leadership largely disowned. Yet while it could hardly be suggested that British Conservatism is now inspired by libertarian hedonism, the FCS demands became utterable because radical market ideologies enjoyed great confidence and pre-eminence.

Similarly, though in less extreme form, the Thatcher 'revolution' in British culture has brought a new glamour and dynamism to the public image of greed. In this connection it is interesting to note the transformation in the image of the City of London, the home of money in its most abstract, most money-like form. There used to be 'City gents', bowler-hatted epitomes of stuffy respectability trapped in dull routines of commuting. Now there are brightly clad City 'Yuppies', racing in fast cars from penthouses to wine bars. Their candid single-mindedness about the pursuit of money is both a shock and an example to others. They are not loved, but they are accepted by most and emulated by many. Greed, even without any other motive to temper it or rationalization to clothe it, has acquired a sort of legitimacy denied to it by post-war welfarism.

Dependence and Hatred

However, the deepest and most prevalent meaning of the marketeers' demand for us to do as we choose is not in terms of simple, hedonistic libidinal release, or the licensing of greed. It is in terms of a different conception of psychic freedom, at once more subtle and even more primitive, more fundamental in its pathology. It is freedom from the impingements, the infringements and the limits which other people, one way or another, necessarily represent to or impose upon the boundaries of the self. Again, this aspect of the demand for freedom has been noted, though in a different register, by well established critiques of the market, which is often seen as atomizing society into individual (or possibly family) units, insulated in their private spaces and lacking real interchange and community.

What I wish to point to here is a psychoanalytic way of conceptualizing this critique. We can understand the demand for freedom in the market as in part a rejection of the anti-libidinal superego, but more fundamentally as a rejection of the reality of the *other*, as a narcissistic refusal to accept the boundaries of the self, to recognize the demands of others for our emotional attention and to be prepared to negotiate one's needs with those of others. While critics of the market lament the isolated individual bereft of community, pro-marketeers celebrate the omnipotently free individual, unfettered by binding forms of relatedness to others.

When considered in these terms, the second strand of feeling noted above – the hatred of dependency – makes considerable sense. The deepest reason for refusing to recognize the other is that to do so entails recognition of one's *need* for the other. The fear of disappointment or abandonment which is evoked by such recognition may be so intense as to result in a denial of the need, and thereby implicitly and ultimately in a denial of the other's reality. Concomitantly, the needs (experienced as overwhelming) and the relationship of dependency are projected elsewhere, particularly on to welfare clients and their relationship with those who would succour them. Of course there is a *real* relationship of dependency between welfare clients and the welfare bureaucracy, and it is in many ways a tragic and crippling one. In the free marketeers' perception of this relationship, however, the real dependency is largely overlain by the projected dependency, by rage at nanny and by contempt for those who still need her – and the contempt itself is a cover for envy of those same people, whose needs are expressed and met.

One corollary of this rage and contempt is the desire to annihilate the offending relationship and its parties, to cleanse the social world of the signs of dependency. 'Smash the NHS' is another recent demand from Conservative youth; the National Health Service is still a powerful and consensual symbol of caring, and this slogan was obviously calculated to shock. However it also expresses very clearly a particular set of feelings about the nurturing object, which is experienced as so poisonous or treacherous that it must be destroyed.

Hayek, Freedom and Guilt

In the work of Friedrich von Hayek, the most influential and sophisticated of modern champions of the market, there is a fundamental distinction between two kinds of order. In both the natural and social worlds, there are spontaneous orders and directed or commanded orders. The market is a spontaneous order – provided actors within it follow certain rules, an orderly condition will result without the intervention of any outside agency. Spontaneous orders are not the result of deliberate, purposive acts of creation, and so cannot in themselves be said to serve any particular ends: they are abstract orders. A directed order, in contrast, is the product of a purposive arrangement of things, and must therefore exist to serve particular purposes. Directed orders cannot achieve the same complexity as spontaneous orders can, because the information needed to make very complex human arrangements is greater than can be held in any one mind or agency. Directed, designed orders may be appropriate for organizing the relatively less complex social tasks, but society as a whole must be a spontaneous order, or degenerate into a primitive condition.

This is a justification of the market in terms of its superior information-processing capacity – the familiar notion of the price as a peerlessly efficient means of communication between all interested parties. Purposive human intervention cannot improve, and can only reduce, this efficiency (though it may be able to facilitate the action of the spontaneously ordering forces). Hayek's philosophy of two orders contains no more substantive arguments for market forces than have often been put in less elegant terms since classical economics: that these forces are best left to themselves, only the wheels need oiling, the market alone can generate the only adequate distributive arrangements, and so on. However, his clarity and explicitness give us a particular access to the unconscious significance of those arguments.

Firstly, the libertarian, amoral impulse to break free of the superego is clearly stated. Hayek wishes to correct 'the error that men must first be good before they can be granted freedom'.[13] The value of our services to others, i.e. the scale of material rewards we obtain, is quite separate from our moral merit as individuals. Material usefulness to one's fellows must not be confused with 'the ends which men ultimately serve'.[14] Ultimate moral ends do not enter into market relations, because the spontaneous market order is morally neutral. Hayek equates planning, direction and command orders as a whole with the imposition of specific moral ends, and at the centre of his whole philosophy is the contention that questions of ultimate ends are not – or should not be – raised in the market-place. He therefore makes no attempt at a moral defence of the market. Indeed he believes pro-marketeers have been in error in believing themselves to be obliged to make such defences. The market, he argues, is a means not an end, and it is the *only* means for securing an order of freedom within which specific moral choices can then be made.

Rather than trying to pretend that market forces do reward people according to their deserts, i.e. their moral worth, Hayek believes that supporters of the free market should recognize that material rewards ought to be separated from moral worth. Where they are not, as he believes they are not in all directed, state-collectivistic societies, then morality collapses into materialism, since people will pursue moral principles not for the esteem of others but for material reward. Thus the spontaneous order of the market is the only secure foundation for morality of any sort, since morality requires freedom of choice. Yet that order can be guaranteed only by exempting the market from moral judgment of any kind. It would be an exercise in social and moral philosophy to assess whether this somewhat paradoxical position is actually coherent; the concern here is more with its psychological significance.

In Hayek's work the dissolution of the moral superego is combined with a rejection of the *protective* parent, who, it is argued, cannot know best. Only individual agents can know their own desires, taking into account their unique needs, circumstances and aspirations. They must be allowed to conduct themselves in market transactions on the basis of the calculations they make about the effects of such transactions upon themselves. They can expect material rewards for doing so, but not moral esteem, which is distributed upon a different basis. No outside agency can know what individuals know about their own desires, so no outside agency can prescribe or guide individual behaviour in the marketplace The necessity of the market is grounded in the privacy of the soul. Psychologically, this expresses a lack of belief in the possibility of an adequately knowing parent, able to intervene in an appropriate way to protect and facilitate as well as restrain. Without such belief, the subject's relationships with any representatives of authority are experienced as invasions. The 'loving and beloved' aspects of the superego[15] are, implies Hayek, fictions of the socialist imagination.

This argument blends an existential truth with a psychological falsehood, and uses the combination to conceal the tensions and complexity of the actual social world. Of course our desires are in a sense essentially private (and market relations are an important means of their satisfaction). But we are able to enter into discussion and into collective actions concerning our desires and the means for their satisfaction. To put this in a psychological way, an individual is able to enter into a relationship with another in which his or her needs, and when necessary the other's, can be negotiated, i.e. can be met but at some cost, or can be partly met. In Hayek's eulogization of spontaneity there is no such conception of the fulfilment of needs involving some cost, in accommodation to others' needs. He argues that our desires need not and cannot be negotiated – the needs and the very existence of the other does not, or should not, transgress our spontaneity.[16] No benign, facilitating parental figure can be imagined within this life-space, and so no basis can be laid for balancing assertion of needs with a reparative concern for the other in the work of negotiating needs.

The subject in the market is thus unencumbered by moral authority of any kind. Furthermore, says Hayek, individuals must not be expected to take remote and unintended consequences of their actions into account – for example, presumably, the destruction of the ozone layer, of forests in other countries, or deaths by cancer of workers in other continents – since this could be done consistently only on the basis of an omniscient grasp of all interrelations between all events the world over. Hayek points out that such knowledge is impossible; more crucially, he does not believe in the possibility of anything less than complete omniscience which would still be an adequate basis for rational design – and this is the logical basis of his rejection of any planning and direction.

Yet behind this imagery of vigorous free agents, untrammelled by moral constraint or by speculation about the distant effects of their actions, Hayek speaks to a profound sense of impotence. The wish and capacity to plan for improvements in the human condition are projected entirely into the state; that is, we might say, some crucial ego functions are externalized, returned to the parents. Those projected functions are then denigrated in the external object: the parent-state is seen as hopelessly unable to deliver on its plans. The achievements of human purpose are seen as paltry fragments compared to the work of evolution, which has brought us market mechanisms (since they generate the most effective and stable social orders), and to the course of which we should submit.

So behind the throwing off of parental supervision in the form of the state, there is a total submission to another, cosmic authority, one beyond the reach of all reason and protest. Thus the free marketeer, while rejecting the constraints of specific, fallible human authorities on the free play of desire, yearns for the ultimate authority which creates and satisfies all desires. The spontaneous order of the market is identified with the very omniscient and omnipotent force which Hayek believes to be humanly impossible, and which he criticizes governmental institutions for trying to be. The sense of impotence encouraged by market philosophies (and found so frequently in contemporary political culture) is therefore the obverse and complement in those philosophies to the phantasy of the idealized, omnipotent parent which the market represents.

Psychoanalytically, this is not a surprising discovery. The presence of this phantasy can almost be deduced from the doctrine, in which the rejection of human, constraining authorities involves more than arguing their incompetence to run the world. Their *malevolence* is also asserted. They are experienced as anti-libidinal, as prohibiting individual satisfaction, and thereby as tyrannical and persecutory. Psychoanalytic theory would predict that where real parents, or quasi-parental authorities, are experienced in these ways (whether or not they are *actually* like that), then phantasies of the idealized parent will be mobilized to preserve some representation of goodness in the internal world.

Hayek is careful to stress that in individual cases there may well be undesirable outcomes: market forces cannot ensure the ideal distribution of goods in all instances. But he enjoins us to keep in mind that in the long run and overall they serve to ensure the best possible outcomes. Thus secure in a belief in the ultimate and absolute beneficence of the market, we can safely merge with its idealized omnipotence and so circumvent the tasks of reconciling our interests and impulses with the needs of others. As Adam Smith had told us, no conflicts with or impingements from others need occur in such a universe of oneness. 'It is the glory of the free enterprise system that it makes it at least possible that each individual, while serving his fellows, can do so for his own ends.'[17]

Hayek is able to confront head-on the moral critique of the market because of his general alertness to moral questions, especially those involving the confusions and obfuscations of his opponents. He makes a particularly telling point in his discussion of the word 'social'. Tracing the importance of this word in the development of an interventionist consensus, he implies that the exhortation to be aware of the 'social' implications of our actions (i.e. those beyond the immediate calculable sphere of individual interest) places upon the individual an impossible responsibility. Again his reference is to the *limits* of our knowledge: we cannot know the remote effects of what we do, and so such a vague and inoperable moral principle serves only to confuse and blunt our sense of responsibility.

Hayek identifies an important problem here, but there is another way of stating it, which is that in an advanced market society individuals are *inevitably* subject to particular burdens of guilt about the consequences of their actions. We may know or sense that some things we buy, use and perhaps depend on are produced and delivered only at great cost to others or to the environment, but lacking the means of individual or collective political control over market forces we feel powerless to prevent or mitigate this. We know that certain abstentions on our part might reduce our complicity, but often feel that these are too costly or difficult in personal terms to be fully implemented (e.g. using only public transport, or only recycled paper). Moreover although it might reduce one's complicity, an individual abstention is rarely seen as able to affect the problem in any significant way, since millions of others may be involved. The problem is not in the moral consciousness which seeks to trouble us with necessarily incomplete knowledge about the consequences of our market behaviours, but in a social order which gives us few opportunities for making effective responses to our guilty consciences. The free market ideology would prefer to abolish the need for response by liquidating the superego.

The Return of Conscience

Psychically speaking, though, this is a high-risk and relatively short-term strategy. The functions of the superego cannot simply be dispensed with in one whole area of life, not least the broadest and most fundamental to our wider social existence. In clinical psychoanalytic work, the poor development of a moral sense is not taken to indicate the absence of a superego, but rather as a sign that a mature, benign, integrated superego has not developed well or has been weakened, and that the prohibitive voices in the psyche are therefore likely to belong regressively to a more primitive, punitive superego. If states of mind and the relationships between them can be observed in a similar fashion in the analysis of ideological positions as in that of individual persons, then we would expect to find indications of this more primitive superego somewhere in the discourse of market libertarianism. In other words, we would expect to find the fear and violence characteristic of authoritarianism beneath the libertarian bravado.

It is not difficult to do so, since in several governments of the present day there is some combination of free-market permissiveness and punitive authoritarianism, in particular areas of policy and in general political style. My examples must be restricted to the British situation. A well known one is a speech given in 1985 by the leading Conservative Norman Tebbit,[18] in which he blamed many of the social ills of the 1980s on the permissive hedonism of the 1960s. His attack was wide, simplistic and bitter, in a way that is characteristic of the more regressed, sadistic modes of superego functioning. Other leading figures have frequently made more moderate pronouncements but with the same rhetorical thrust. Margaret Thatcher herself is well known for her support for the 'family', in many statements which are as vague in content as they are authoritarian in tone.

It is not only in the sphere of 'social' and cultural issues that the severe voice of censure is heard. In economic policy too it is possible to identify ways in which the need for a restraining power is answered not by a mature and protective superego but by a harsh, retaliatory command. This can be seen in Britain in the success of the present government in reducing inflation.[19] 'Inflation', in some at least of its connotations, is a condition of excess. It is, literally, a swelling, a condition resulting from pumping up or engorgement. As a phenomenon of economic life, it involves us all in demanding more and more from each other: more at the till or on the bill, more on the pay slip. It undercuts the rationales of prudent saving, inciting us instead to spend, borrow and consume – more, now. It is, in short, a condition highly expressive of uncontrolled greed and its sorry consequences, and the Thatcher government has regarded controlling it as a number one priority.

In times of persistent high inflation, as in Britain in the 1970s, we are pressed into a preoccupation with its effects. As we demand more, inflation devalues the very thing we have most need for more of: money. It is thus a moral lesson to us on the effects of greed: excessive demands can despoil that which is demanded. Inflation is the come-uppance of the glutton, and because it imposes on us all it makes us all feel like gluttons. It presents us with the prospect of an ever-ascending spiral of greed. It is a sign of overheating, of an economy that is overexcited, of a society in which the immoderate demands of its overly libidinal subjects have got the better of government.

In controlling inflation, which at least for some years it undoubtedly has done, the Thatcher administration can therefore be experienced as one which restored governmental authority over the greedy disorder of the British people. It has offered us protection against our neighbour's greed, and alleviation of the guilt felt at our own. It has bathed the nation in a flow of harshly moralizing language, which has presented inflation as the product of years of greed and indulgence, and offered a cure for it in bracing regimes of public spending. High unemployment, large contractions in public services, and the brutalization of many lives and sensibilities are all part of the package of cure. At election times a sufficient number of the British people have continued to express their gratitude for this punishing treatment of their guilt.

As a part of this process there has occurred a significant transformation in the characterization of the interventionist, welfare state. As noted earlier, it is usual for market ideologies to portray the state as a dreary *anti*-libidinal bureaucracy, against which the free spirits of individuals must struggle for their satisfactions.

However, in the fight against inflation (which has coincided in Britain with this administration's programme for reform of local government), certain formations of state power, especially at local government level, are portrayed as corrupt authority in league with the rampant forces of desire, and as stoking the fires of inflation. Accordingly local government must be prevented from raising the rates to indulge in Dionysian politics of cultural plural-ism, and especially the incitement of homosexuals and lesbians. Similarly, central government must not throw money around and consume our resources in wanton mismanagement and in the misguided pursuit of welfare.

The Chancellor of the Exchequer reports[20] that previous govern-ments were 'addicted' to borrowing. With the use of this image, an *anti*-libidinal superego can be mobilized in an attack on a condition – addiction – which is simultaneously one of dependence and desire. Better a parent whom we can trust to be harsh, than one who might start an orgy, or at least empty the larder. Within this discourse of fear, the image of a bulging, parasitic greed is fused with that of the collectivist state (rather than finding a home in, for example, the new public perception of the deregulated City as mentioned previously), and an anti-libidinal, sadistic impulse is recruited to the same political cause as the libidinal trend described earlier.

The freedom demanded by market ideologies, and to various degrees actualized in market relations, may generate guilt around a number of issues – the damage done, or phantasied as done, to others in the battles of competition; the remote human or eco-logical costs in particular acts of consumption; the wastefulness and greed encouraged by the culture of consumption. Yet in the forms of markes ideology discussed here the possibility of such guilt is not recognized, since the world of market relations is seen as morally neutral. Such frames of reference cannot help in the containment of such guilt, which in the absence of social possi-bilities for its more constructive expression is likely to attach itself to the more punitive moralistic tendencies of the sort deployed in the fight against inflation.

Inflation is a problem, and it is far better to be without it, but whether its control is worth the price paid in the other social effects of the monetarist facilitation of market forces is another question, one which the sadistic superego does not ask. The individual in the market may be free to pursue happiness, but is likely to suffer guilt at so doing and may not be helped much to confront that guilt, to understand its sources, to assess which parts of it are unavoidable or irrational, and in general to contain it. Market societies powerfully amplify and elaborate our inner reserves of guilt while also eroding our resolve and our resources to acknowledge guilt. The result is likely to be a displacement and resurgence of prohibition and punishment, both in theoretical defences of the market and in actual political developments in market societies. Conscience returns, as it nearly always must, but in a debased and dangerous form.

The analysis offered here of some leading neo-liberal texts and themes gives a clear indication of how the conclusions drawn from the study of responses to psychoanalysis may be of wider cultural and political significance. The same sorts of implicit meanings can be found in the discourses of economic and political debate as were observed in the field of psychological theory. Compare for example Hayek's praise for the 'glory of the free enterprise system' with Maslow's belief in the possibility of 'social arrangements in which a person seeking his own selfish good necessarily helps people whether he wishes to or not'.[21]

Maslow is referring here to Benedict's concept of 'synergy' (see p. 114). He might not have agreed with the particular way in which Hayek operationalizes this concept, but there is no contradiction between their two positions. Indeed, we can see Maslow as having provided something of a psychological underpinning for Hayek's social vision. The radical 'hands-off the individual' stance, on the grounds that only individuals themselves can be the arbiters of their needs, is the same in each man's theory. For Maslow, in the field of psychological research the only alternative approach to dominative control was a 'leaving it alone' attitude. For Hayek, the only alternative to 'directed' orders is the absolute sovereignty of the individual in market relations. In Maslow's opinion, 'we enjoy what is good for us, at least with fairly good choosers and under fairly good conditions'.[22] In Hayek's argument, it is a key principle that only individuals can choose for themselves.

So, although actual market relations may be difficult to link in a generalized way to the kinds of pressures and trends which can be observed in psychological theory, some very clear homologies between psychological ideas and market *ideologies* can be recorded.

In each case we are taking only one reading of the bodies of work under consideration. In some of the more subtle and competent works of academic and humanistic psychology, and certainly in many of the positions outlined by radical psychology, different forces can be seen at work to those of the market individualism focused on here.

Yet this focus is not just one amongst many possible and fruitful ones; it has a leading political relevance and a sharp moral edge. It does not imply an absolute, utopian rejection of actual market relations, but is rather concerned with separating rational critiques of non-market arrangements (e.g. pointing out the disadvantages of centralism, and the problems of coordination in planning) from emotionally laden attacks on conscience and the other. In considering both psychological and socio-economic theories, we have been concerned with the ways in which traditions of thought can be described in terms of their unconscious meanings, and how they can act as carriers of those meanings in the wider culture. The meanings at stake here – of individuality and obligation – are particularly important ones, and it is generally to the credit of psychoanalysis that it has been more aware of its active role in the creation and propagation of such meanings than have some other schools of psychology. However, we should not expect less of a tradition which has as its main task the bringing of meanings into awareness.

8

POLITICAL DISILLUSIONMENT

The Return of the Religious

> One is in danger of overestimating the frequency of an irreligious attitude among intellectuals.[1]

The responses to psychoanalysis which have been described add up to the working out of a familiar cultural drama, in which the burdens of living are triumphantly lifted by a spirit of spontaneity and freedom. This story is most clearly and insistently told in advertising, but we have been tracing a similar narrative at work in the conceptual play of responses to psychoanalysis. The defeat of suffering also involves a defeat for philosophies of suffering, which are decried as determinist, negative or reductive. Academic psychology sets the scene, by proffering a 'Freudian' model of human nature that is so devoid of imagination and mystery that it becomes the target for a series of well practised rebuttals on behalf of the richness and complexity of human experience. These responses have been predominantly secular ones, but we have seen how close the humanistic response is to the dominant religious traditions of our age. Furthermore the radical–political response is often based upon a quest for transcendence which, like much romantic thought, is characteristically religious in its redemptive promises.

Within the ostensibly secular debates about the standing of Freud in modern psychology there moves the figure of faith. The drama enacted around Freud is but one partly secularized version of a major argument in modern culture. The general pattern of this argument is that rationality and science have obliterated all the finer and deeper aspects of human experience, and that some resurgence of faith is required to balance or to consolidate our precarious modern identities, by restoring to us both a sense of connectedness and a vision of the transcendent.

Freud is sometimes seen as the arch-fiend of rationality, the one who carried the empty reasoning.of modern psychology into some of the innermost regions of the soul, and mistakenly believed he could see what was there. Sometimes he is seen as a rank practitioner of and apologist for *ir*rationality, the one who concealed a virulent dogma of human bestiality behind the respectable skirts of science and the ego. And sometimes he is seen as the one from whom we can derive a solution, a synthesis of rational inquiry and transcendent spirituality. There are many different Freuds, and quite a number of them have been recruited to play different, often opposing roles in this modern drama of how faith must respond to science.

It is possible to see a large part of the history of psychology in the terms of this drama, as a series of secularized performances of what was originally a religious script, and essentially remains so. In the development of theoretical psychology there have been a number of waves of reform, each one consisting of a recitation of the limits of a narrowly scientific psychology and a resolution to transcend these limits with a more humanized, holistic approach. This stereotyped, repetitious impulse to infuse science with the vitality of the human spirit can be seen at work particularly clearly in the histories of personality theory, of social and developmental psychology, and of clinical and other applied psychologies. This characterization of the history of psychology[2] makes it possible to suggest some links between psychology and the political sphere. Psychology and its tempering of scientific rationality can be seen as an equivalent, in the spheres of ideas and of professional practices, of *political* programmes of economic and social reform which sought to mitigate the corrosive effects of *market* rationality upon human experience and community.

There is in this way an important relationship between modern psychology and modern programmes of welfare reform. At its best, psychology has reflected the kind of realistic and communitarian altruism that characterizes the most successful welfare institutions.

At its worst it has been, in its promise of reconciliation between science and humanism, as platitudinous or as dishonest as the most empty rhetoric of 'caring' and 'community'.

However, the observation that *religious* traditions underly much of the humanistic rejection of psychoanalysis, and that quasi-religious sentiment informs much of the radical embrace of it, suggests that religious feeling and its struggle with the rational spirit provide an older and more general basis for the major concerns of psychology. Philip Rieff has said as much, some time ago, yet the idea that religious feeling and theological concepts may have been woven into the textures of rational thought and empirical inquiry in contemporary psychology may not be an easy one to take on board. It is particularly difficult for those of us who are products of post-war social-democratic-scientific rationalism, for whom religion tends to connote primarily the antique or the bizarre, to contemplate the persisting importance of religious impulses, especially in those areas we might have thought were most inhospitable to them. Yet the fate of Freud in many areas of contemporary culture indicates that we need to do just that.

This is of course no simple task. Above all, there is no single religious impulse. Once again, we have to start from the recognition that there is no one essence of the problem, although we can group and order its features. It would be reductive, to say the least, to proceed as if the massive historical complexities indicated by the term 'religion' were encompassed by the accounts given here of particular kinds of psychological vision. To draw attention to something fundamentally religious in the cultural responses to Freud is to refer to only one of the many meanings and uses of religion. As we have seen it involves focusing on the craving for transcendence, for release from the pains of existence by the transformation of psychic and/or social reality into another order of things where loss and conflict shall lose their sting.

It was Freud's view that consoling functions of this sort were the primary meaning of religion, and psychohistorical research could probably make a very powerful case for this position. Yet there are also the meanings of religion as explicit modes of engagement with politics, from liberation theology through Northern Ireland to Islamic militancy, and as languages of moral value. These meanings may overlap with each other, and one could argue that all of them draw upon a psychological root of religion in the intolerance of pain, but clearly they cannot all be reduced completely to such a root.

The Limits of Endurance

Freud's critique of religion is his most explicit and sustained contribution to ideological disputes. He consistently saw religion as a means for the preservation in adult life of the illusions of childhood, and for protecting us from the bitter truth of our loneliness and helplessness. As Peter Gay has recently reminded us,[3] Freud was a thoroughgoing atheist who stood four-square in the most uncompromising traditions of post-Enlightenment rationality.[4]

When we turn to assessing the political meaning of Freud's thought, and of psychoanalysis generally, we might expect that this philosophical commitment of Freud's will be amongst the largest and most positive features of his significance as a social theorist. One may not agree with some of his specific hypotheses about the psychopathological bases of religious belief and practice. However, if we are interested in the development of a political culture based on the rational consideration of human needs and the critical analysis of belief systems, then the psychoanalytic deployment of rational critique in the study of religion and ideology is at the very least a challenge to be taken up. So on the face of it there is a strong case – which could be put from a range of political positions – for seeing psychoanalysis as having a contribution to make to a politics of reason, in which empirical inquiry and rational argument are the dominant modes of public discourse.

Needless to say, things are not that simple, because 'reason' is not so simple and stable an entity. And Freud's work has come under attack precisely because of his commitment to an Enlightenment, liberal model of reason as an absolute value. The sociological and especially the Marxist critiques of knowledge have castigated the scientific spirit which Freud lived and breathed, pointing out that appeals to the alleged neutrality of 'reason' and 'science' may disguise social values or interests, particularly class interests and the forces of racism and sexism. Freud has of course been accused of propagating the most extreme right-wing and sexist views under the guise of science, and even if we can set aside such ill-informed attacks we cannot be satisfied with as unreflective and unsophisticated an adherence to the scientific Weltanschauung as Freud himself displayed,[5] however much we might admire and sympathize with the depth of his commitment to reason.

There is another problem for those of us who would like to recruit psychoanalytic insights to the cause of a democratic political culture. Freud feared that the mass dissemination of his insights into the illusory nature of religion might result in a massive destabilization, both of individual psyches and of the social order. If people were to learn that there never was to be a Day of Judgment, would they continue to tolerate the severe restrictions on their libidinal pleasures which, Freud believed, were the price they paid for their citizenship? This is not a prominent theme in Freud's writing, but it has been picked out by a number of commentators,[6] and whatever Freud's view on the matter this is a question which points towards the heart of the interdisciplinary potential of psychoanalysis.

With the more relational conception of human nature developed in later psychoanalytic theory, and adopted in this book, we might see Freud's anxiety to have been partly misconceived: we are not Hobbesian animals, cowering before a sovereign authority that is actually a figment of our imagination, and ready to go on the rampage once we realize its imaginary nature. We are more trustworthy than that, as in their way the humanistic psychologists have pointed out, and so there is some substance in the complaint that Freud's outlook was an elitist one. For Freud, only an elite of psychoanalytic intellectuals could be trusted to tolerate the anxieties released by psychoanalytic knowledge, although there is also in his work a strong sense of mission, of the long-term contribution to political society which psychoanalysis could make.[7]

Freud's question about the possible effects of the dissemination of psychoanalytic knowledge can be substituted for by two others, which do not rest on Hobbesian assumptions and the answers to which will define the kind of impact psychoanalysis might have upon social and political thought. The first is whether we can necessarily equate the illusory and the untruthful with the unworthy – that is, whether we must assume that the abandonment of illusion is always the morally necessary choice. Is it such a bad thing that people should ruminate on horoscopes? How compelling is the case for irreligion, when put to some of today's South African churchmen? Should the cancer patient be talked out of a spiritual path towards holistic regeneration? We have noted Freud's comment that illusion can have no value if it makes life more difficult to endure. However the question of what makes life more difficult to endure is not easily answered, partly because of the complexity and ambiguity, also noted earlier, in the notion of endurance. Trying to take a consistent stand against illusions of transcendence and happiness in one's own life is one thing, while insisting that other people do the same may well be another, especially when they are in more painful positions than oneself.

In the psychoanalytic tradition as a whole there tends to be a certain lack of charity towards the terms people come to with themselves and others, the compromises and settlements that we all negotiate, sometimes through long struggle. In therapeutic work, what we need is the clarity and firmness of the best psycho-analytic insights, not charitable tolerance, and the intolerant strain in psychoanalysis is a small price to pay for the light it can cast. However in seeking to incorporate psychoanalytic thinking into a discourse of public affairs, a more flexible or differently toned diagnostic language may be required, one less ready to seize upon self-deception and more ready to moderate its judgment with a sense of pathos.

The second question is, depending on how one asks it, either a corollary of, or a disrespectful alternative to, the first. It is whether the abandonment of illusion is actually a possibility. Why should the future of human society be in this respect any different from the past? Freud, the nineteenth-century son of the Enlightenment, believed that civilization was incremental. But few people can find a basis today for a ready belief in the inevitability of moral advance. If illusions of transcendence are in any case the best or the only liveable alternatives open to people in some situations, their dissolution may well be impossible. Or worse, they may be morally and politically disastrous but be impregnably lodged in the intractable weakness of our psychologies. Either way, the hope – which Freud sometimes allowed himself – that psycho-analytic understanding might become commonplace would be a vain one.

Such a pessimistic view, sometimes associated with melancholic reflections upon 'mass culture' and its deceptions, would tend to return us to a conservative and quietistic approach to politics, of a kind which psychoanalysis has at times been accurately criticized for supporting. But the issue is – or should be – the *truth* of such a view, not whether we find its consequences congenial. To judge a theory on the basis of its congeniality would be to reproduce the most indolent of the rejections of Freud discussed in this book, those which declare him to be wrong because he is 'gloomy'.

Racism is an important example. Psychoanalytic explorations of racism[8] agree that it takes shape at the deepest levels of psychopathology, and that it is sustained by illusions of a most primitive kind. Rationalistic education and social reforms are not, on a psychoanalytic view, an adequate response to racism: there must also be some address to the racist unconscious.[9] This clearly has serious implications for anti-racist politics, which it would be wishful incompetence to ignore. However, these implications are at the level of strategy, not of final social goals. There is nothing in a psychoanalytic approach to refute the idea that non-racist social relations remain a realistic social goal, even though it may be recognized that race will continue to be an important dimension of phantasy life, and that some elements of racist sentiment will persist in a great number of minds.

Racist and sub-racist propaganda may have an important psychological advantage over anti-racism in that it implicitly recognizes the depth and vigour of racial imagery in the unconscious. It deploys that imagery in the pursuit of a transcendent release from the tragedies and limits of life, which are represented in the form and presence of the racial other. In the transformed and purified nation of the racist imagination, life will be *completely different*. Anti-racist work must try to explore racial imagery, and to contain rather than to ignore the more omnipotent and destructive phantasies with which it may be associated.

Many racist ideologies have another psychological asset in that they speak explicitly to the sense of loss. They invoke some past time and disappeared place in which things were different, before the other came, in which the characteristic pains of life today did not have to be faced. Psychoanalytically understood, this lost community is not a community at all but a unity, the state of oneness and of omnipotence which we all feel we have lost in the course of learning to live in the real world with other people. Racism is an intolerance of others which is bottled into and felt as an intolerance of *certain* others. Rational anti-racism which simply argues historically that Eden has never existed is an important line of attack, but not in itself adequate to the problem. The sense of loss around which racism often crystallizes is not a historical but a psychological one.

The same sense of loss may be found in many political ideologies and movements other than those organized around racism. Their appeal may rest upon the extent to which they can inspire belief in the possibility of recovering that which is felt to have been lost – a sense of community, of national integrity or greatness, of class identity, of moral strength, or whatever provides the imagery for the idealized lost object. The cultural successes of Thatcher and Reagan in the 1980s appear to be partly due to the generation of a feeling that something in the nation is being regained. It has been an inbuilt impediment to many of the ideologies of the left that they cannot appeal to these reservoirs of nostalgic feeling since they can look only forward to the golden age. While visions of future deliverance may also receive powerful unconscious confirmation, they are not derived so directly from the core experience of loss and separation as are those of paradise lost.

Some conservative ideologies have also had an advantage in basing much of their rhetoric around some notion of the limits of the human condition. Moves towards equal opportunities for men and women, for example, and towards greater social justice in many spheres may be met by an argument that there are natural limits to the improvements we can make. Completely wrong though such arguments may be, in fact and reasoning, they can nonetheless gain some credibility from their superficial similarity to the kind of considered resignation to human limits that we can find in the Freudian philosophy. However prevalent may be the illusory and evasive aspects of psychological functioning, there often remains a fragment of a deeper awareness such that some sense of the intractability of suffering remains – not enough to support any further insight, but enough to see a halo of wisdom around some cliched defence of inequality.

The neo-liberal ideologies of the market discussed in the previous chapter have risked losing this psychological advantage traditionally adhering to the politics of the right by allying themselves more with the omnipotent and narcissistic visions of a world in which radical deprivations and essential conflicts do not exist. However, to take full advantage of this an opposition needs to be able to establish possession of its own 'realism', that is of a political language informed by a sense of tragedy rather than by the wish for transcendence.

It may then be possible to give some sort of qualified answer to at least the second of the two questions posed above. While a world without illusion may be an illusion, an impossible dream, various degrees of disillusion may in many circumstances be both possible and desirable to work for. Painful feelings of guilt and loss have been successfully confronted in countless therapeutic exchanges, and where in the political sphere the only alternative is the manipulation of such feelings by destructive forces like racism and militaristic nationalism then there is a democratic responsibility to work for their clarification and containment, for insight and endurance rather than for intolerance of the other.

For such intolerance, I have repeatedly argued, is what the kinds of illusions discussed in this book can be traced to. It is a long way from analyses of the cultural vicissitudes of psychological ideas to observations on the aims of politics, but it has been one aim of the book to point to such connections. In the responses to psychoanalysis we find an ideological moment of considerable significance to modern culture and politics, fixed in a form so powerful that it appears in otherwise very different spheres of intellectual effort, and has survived through numerous replays this century. It is a moment of refusal, of rejection of the greater part of our emotional development. It marks the limits of endurance, as these are currently drawn in our culture. Freud's own life was in many ways an exemplary one of endurance, but to do full justice to the principles which he recommended to us we have to look beyond individual and private achievements, towards the complex conflict between the capacity for endurance and the wish for transcendence in the public domain of ideas and politics.

This conflict is not one between reason and feeling, although it may be that another of the ways in which our culture has chosen to understand psychoanalysis is to see it as yet another formulation of this old dichotomy. One version of the Freudian message to the polity, echoing a well established tenet of liberalism, is that we need to establish a devisceralized Reason in the seat of government. On this view, all feeling is the enemy of far-sightedness and justice. A more rounded consideration of the psychoanalytic tradition would yield a very different view, in which the category of 'feeling' or 'emotion' is seen in a more complex way. Most importantly it would make a distinction between feeling on the one hand as primitive phantasy and on the other as the activation of moral resources.[10] As phantasy, 'emotion' is fundamentally destructive of rational politics; it is the basis of both passionate dogma and its obverse of gullibility and manipulation by others who – also possessed by the phantasy – invite us to shape the outer world to

173

the demands of the inner world. As a moral resource in politics, 'emotion' is in contrast the deployment in public affairs of the reparative, reality-bound feelings which are the main achievement of a basic degree of maturity in psychic and interpersonal development.

In practice this distinction can be very hard to make consistently, especially for the project of developing an effective opposition to a leader whose appeal is heavily passionate. When for instance do defences of socialized health and welfare arrangements cease to be guided primarily by realistic assessment of their value in meeting the needs of others, and become instead expressions of the wish for an idealized parental or family object? If an obliteration of the real other can be at work in discourses which appear to be emphatic affirmations of the needs of others, as in some of the psychological ideas discussed here, then the development of a political culture in which omnipotence and illusion are minimized is a very difficult task.

Picking one's way through the various images of Freud which circulate in our intellectual culture, and trying to define the moral perspectives within which these images are drawn, is but one way of gaining access to this task. There are many other fields in which the same basic themes could be traced, in which the inexhaustible ways of illusion seek to limit the endurance of truth. Yet taking the cultural history of psychoanalytic ideas is a particularly appropriate way of doing it, in that the moral issues themselves can be so well formulated by psychoanalytic theory and its powerful model of endurance. The imagery of 'Freud' has come to represent the discredited father, the baleful authority who wants us to suffer. In seeking to reinterpret or replace Freud with an image of human nature either more prosaic or more sublime, and so to free us from suffering, the theoretical manoeuvres of psychology are playing their part in a great modern struggle. While this is often carried on as a struggle against authority, it is also a struggle against the separateness of the other.

Cultural responses have been defined here almost entirely in terms of ideas and their vicissitudes. Ideas have been considered as expressions both of states of mind, and of social forces. The relationships between intellectual culture, states of mind and social context are formidably complex, and the pattern of relationships identified here can be only a part of the story. Nonetheless, in studying the patterns of psychic and social meaning that have cohered around ideas about psychoanalysis, with its rich and difficult messages, we may hope to learn something of value about how we currently understand ourselves and our possibilities.

NOTES

Preface

1. Rieff's classic essays are *Freud: The Mind of the Moralist* (1959) and *The Triumph of the Therapeutic* (1966).

1   Introduction: Freud in Culture

1. For example in Britain there are now at least half-a-dozen expanding organizations offering training in psychoanalytic psychotherapy, most of them established in the last twenty years.
2. This influence, though, may have been overestimated – see, for example, Yelloly's (1980) critique of the view that psychoanalysis once dominated casework practice in social work. To the extent that psychoanalytic theory was influential, it was anyway often in transmuted form.
3. I am still speaking here of Britain, and elsewhere the relationship between psychoanalysis and the academic 'counter-culture' may well have been different. In France, as Turkle (1978) showed, psychoanalysis was more centrally involved in the political travails.
4. See Martin's (1981) argument that the cultural changes of the 'Sixties' (which she terms an 'Expressive Revolution') were an important stage in the process, basic to modern culture, of the working out of the principles of romanticism. See also Campbell's (1987) analysis of the roots of consumer culture in romanticism.
5. Many behaviourists have, though, tried to absorb the impact of this period by devising humanized and generally 'softened' versions of behaviourism, apparently containing a space for the human subject. See Richards (1983).
6. One of Eysenck's most recent broadsides is the *Decline and Fall of the Freudian Empire* (1985). Gellner's *The Psychoanalytic Movement* (1985) is

much more sophisticated but equally vitriolic.

7. A quick survey of books offering general discussions of Freud and published this decade in English might note, amongst others and with apologies to any omitted, Badcock (1988), Bettelheim (1983), Bocock (1983), Brome (1984), Clark (1980), Dilman (1983; 1984), Erdelyi (1985), Feffer (1982), Freeman (1980), Gabriel (1983), Peter Gay (1987), V. P. Gay (1983), Grunbaum (1983), Isbister (1985), Kline (1984), Lewis (1981), Marcus (1984), Masson (1984), Stevens (1983), and Weber (1982). A major new biography by Peter Gay has also just appeared (1988). A substantial literature had already built up during the 1970s.

8. I use this term conventionally to include both full psychoanalytic treatment (involving 4 or 5 sessions per week) and psychoanalytic psychotherapies, a range of less intensive but often still very long-term procedures involving up to 3 sessions per week, and distinguished from other forms of psychotherapy by being based on psychoanalytic theory.

9. See Dicks (1970), and Rustin (1985).

10. For some very different approaches to this theme, see Halmos (1965), North (1972), Rieff (1966), and Szasz (1971).

11. See, for example, the exchanges between Hinshelwood and Rowan in the *British Journal of Psychotherapy* (1988, 4/2), in which Rowan is at pains to reject the argument that humanistic psychology is substantially indebted to psychoanalysis.

12. See his *PsychoPolitics* (1982), a book based on critiques of Goffman, Laing, Foucault and Szasz.

13. Much of the 'radical psychology' of the early 1970s took this line. See, for example, Brooks (1973).

14. Thus this study is not comparable with the scholarly works of Hale (1971) and Burnham (1967; 1978; 1979) on the American reception of psychoanalysis, or of Decker (1977) on Germany.

15. See Witham (1985) for a discussion of this manic element in our current discourse of death.

16. In the *Guardian*, 2 May 1988.

17. The substantial literature on bereavement often highlights the irrational guilt felt by the bereaved. See, for example, Parkes (1986).

18. See Preface, note 1; and Boyers (1975) for an interesting collection of papers organized around Rieff's work.

19. 1985, p. 20.

2   The First Duty

1. Freud (1915b), p. 300.

2. See *The Minimal Self* (1984), which extended the analysis of his earlier *The Culture of Narcissism* (1979).

3. See Freud (1908b). This question is taken up again in Chapter 6.

4. In Freud's concept of sublimation, sexual energy is transformed through its deployment in the service of non-sexual aims (Freud, 1905, p. 206). In the ego there accumulate the non-sexual imperatives of the reality principle (Freud, 1911). See also Chapter 4.

5. Some interesting ones are Frosh (1987), Greenberg and Mitchell (1983), Guntrip (1961; 1968), Kernberg (1980), Kohon (1986), and Symington (1986).

6. Bion (1977) is a compendium of writings up to 1970, including his attempts at a highly abstract typology of mental processes; see also Meltzer (1978). In Bion's later writing (e.g. 1979) he eschews systematization altogether in favour of a more literary mode. For a favourable view of Bion's contribution, discussed in relation to Chasseguet-Smirgel (see note 10 below), see Colman (1988).

7. For some contributions to this debate, see Gill and Holzman (1976), Rycroft (1966; 1985), and Spence (1982).

8. For Freud on primary narcissism, see, for example, 1917b, p. 416, and 1940, p. 150.

9. See for example Winnicott (1964, Part 1; 1971, *passim*).

10. See Chasseguet-Smirgel (1985; 1986). To her clear and consistent treatment of the role of illusion, both in individual psychopathology and in cultural processes, a lot of the underlying argument of this book is indebted. (Though see also Chapter 6.)

11. Mann (1936), p. 61.

12. See Klein (1952), and Segal (e.g. 1973, Chapter 6). Kalin (1975) gives a philosopher's anti-utopian reading of Freud.

13. See Freud (1913).

14. One of these was Freud's own (1930). See also Marcuse (1955), and Meyerhoff (1957).

15. Freud (1917c), p 156.

16. Laplanche and Pontalis (1980), p. 212. See also Meissner (1981), p. 15, for a view of incorporation as an attempt to re-establish a lost unity.

17. Laplanche and Pontalis, op. cit., p. 206.

18. See Ferenczi (1909), Laplanche and Pontalis, op. cit., p. 230, and Ducat (1988), 'Appendix'.

19. Freud (1915a), p. 136. This second notion is also encompassed in Ferenczi's second paper on introjection (1912), where he defines it (p. 316) as including 'every sort of object love'. Overall, his thinking in this area is confused, and his influence has probably been less than helpful.

20. Freud (1921), p. 107.

21. A. Freud (1936), Chapter 9.

22. Here as on many other points Laplanche and Pontalis (op. cit.) provide a scrupulous overview of the theoretical choices within European traditions of psychoanalytic thought; Meissner (op. cit.) reviews the problematics of internalization in the context of debates in contemporary American psychoanalysis.

23. See Rosenfeld (1981) and Sandler (1988) for a discussion of its complexities.

24. For example Grotstein (1981). This sort of current usage is a major expansion of Klein's own original use of the term (1946), which referred to particular phantasies of attacks on others.

25. Freud (1895), p. 305.

26. Greenberg and Mitchell (op. cit., Chapter 12) offer an interesting discussion of this paradox, linking the two sides of the human condition – intersubjectivity and separateness – to relational and drive models respectively in the history of psychoanalysis. They also point to a further link between this dichotomy and that between two major traditions in political thought – those described by Isaiah Berlin as based on 'positive' and on 'negative' conceptions of liberty. In the former, personal fulfilment is achieved through community; in the latter, through individual agency.

3 Psychoanalysis in Reverse: Freud and Modernity

1. Kris (1987).

2. See, for example, Zilboorg (1952), who contrasts Freud's free association technique with the directive procedures used by Ferenczi, Jung and Rank.

3. This thesis is advanced by Bakan (1958), though it is disputed by Gay (1987) and Robert (1974).

4. See Chapter 2, note 7 for references to some contributions in this area.

5. op. cit., p. 170.

6. Bellak (1961), pp. 13ff.

7. See Jones (1954), p. 62.

8. See Decker, op. cit., p. 200; Jung (1906); and O'Neil (1982), Chapter 4.

9. By, for example, Andersson (1962). For J. S. Mill's associationism, see, for example, his *A System of Logic* (1843), Book 6, Chapter 4. Concerning British Idealism, see Bradley (1887), and also Wollheim (1975).

10. See Wyss (1966), pp. 101–2.

11. Boerne (1823), reproduced in Trosman, 1969.

12. Freud reported (Jones, 1954, Vol. 1, p. 31) that his adolescent decision to study medicine was inspired by Goethe's romantic vision of nature. The other sources on Freud and romanticism referred to here are Galdston (1956), Trosman (1973), Wittels (1931), and Whyte (1978).

13. See Chapter 8.

14. See Foucault (1976).

15. See, for example, Kovel (1976) on the 'critical origins' of psycho-analysis.

16. Gay (1978), p. 33.

17. Compare Esslin (1972) on Vienna's commitment to hedonism with

Trosman's (1973) rebuttal of the argument that a Viennese looseness of conduct helped to produce psychoanalysis.

18. Zanuso's (1986) study of Freud's Vienna stresses its complex of contradictory cultural and political tendencies.

19. Mumford (1938), Chapter 4.

20. Weber (1958), p. 70.

21. Mumford, op. cit., pp. 233 and 240 respectively.

22. Stone (1983), Chapter 5. See Marcus (1984) for an account of the nineteenth-century precursors of this 'revolution'.

23. Baudelaire (see Williams, 1973, p. 234) was an influential enthusiast for the modern 'fever'. Williams also discusses the dark and horrendous visions of the city in nineteenth-century literature, as in Gissing's 'Nether World'. Humphrey Jennings's *Pandaemonium* documents how some contemporary observers recorded their experiences of the emergent metropolitan environment. For example, in the late nineteenth-century the metaphor of a mass of molecules was used by a number of writers to capture the atomized, dissociated quality of pedestrian crowds in the cities (Jennings, 1985, pp. 347–8).

24. Freud (1900), p. 18.

25. Fromm (1947), p. 77.

26. See also Berger (1965) for an explanation of the origins of psychoanalysis in the predicament of personal identity in industrial society, in the need to bring a healing insight to frail identities surrounded by an opaque, bureaucratized public sphere.

27. A fuller discussion of this hypothesis can be found in Richards (1984).

28. See Chapter 2, note 2.

29. See, for example, Adorno (1967/8), Horkheimer (1941; 1947), Horkheimer and Adorno (1944), and Marcuse (1941; 1970).

30. The overall historical scenario sketched out by this analysis is as follows. It was during the early period of capitalism that the autonomous individual most fully emerged, in the form of the economically independent bourgeois who was free to make certain choices in life and so could act with some moral direction and coherence. Thus market relations in early, liberal capitalism were not necessarily corrosive of psychic integrity; they were on the contrary the basis, for the bourgeois class, of a strong ego and a vigorous self. Only with their development into the administered world of monopoly capitalism do they become disintegrative in their effects, and even then it is not so much the experience of market exchange as such that does the damage as the 'culture industry' (e.g. advertising, the degradation of education), the invasive technologies of welfare, and other aspects of the relentless regulation of life undertaken by the modern state.

31. Jameson (1984).

32. Sennett (1970).

33. Berman, *All That Is Solid Melts into Air* (1982); Saunders (1986).

34. This term is used by Joel Kovel (1978) to denote those features of our condition – such as early dependency – which enter into and help to determine social relations in all historical epochs.

35. Martin Jay quotes it, without reference, in his book on the Frankfurt School (Jay, 1973). I have been unable to trace the source.

36. Freud (1924), p. 163.

37. Masson (1985), pp. 314, 403, 336 and 409 respectively. Freud also said (p. 337): 'Vienna stinks to high heaven and I cannot bear the stench.'

38. Jones (1957), p. 245.

39. See Schoenwald (1973) for an interesting hypothesis about links between anality, public health and the city.

40. See Cooley (1922) and Mead (1934).

41. Bakan (1966).

42. In addition to those discussed in the text (Hyman, 1962; Ginzburg, 1980; Shepherd, 1985), there are papers by Musto (1968) and Radford (1988), and a novel by Meyer (1975). A recent radio play ('The Strange Case of Sherlock Holmes and Sigmund Freud', by Cecil Jenkins, Radio 3, 27 December 1988), compared the two projects of investigation, and also included the interesting suggestion that Holmes's vision of criminal evil was actually a paranoid delusion. Freud himself was apparently not altogether happy about the comparison between himself and Holmes, perhaps finding it rather lowbrow – see Hyman, op. cit., p. 24 footnote.

43. Marcus, op. cit., p. 248.

4 The Fate of Freud in Academic Psychology

1. Eysenck (1972), p. 25.

2. Radford and Govier (1980), p. 27.

3. Skurnik and George (1967), p. 84.

4. ibid., p. 88.

5. Atkinson *et al.* (1987), p. 475. This notion may have originated in the influential *Primer of Freudian Psychology* of Hall (1956) where (p. 92) the role of projection as a basis for rationalization is rather misleadingly discussed.

6. Laplanche and Pontalis (1973), p. 376.

7. ibid., pp. 130ff. See also Padel (1985).

8. Howarth and Gillham (1981), p. 78.

9. Bootzin *et al.* (1986), p. 458.

10. Hardy and Heyes (1987), p. 167.

11. Burns and Dobson (1984), p. 522.

12. Taylor *et al.* (1982), p. 173.

13. Bootzin *et al.* (1986), p. 457.

14. Dember *et al.* (1984), p. 651.

15. Freud (1933), p. 77.

16. Freud (1911). See Chapter 2, note 4.

17. ibid., p. 233.

18. Taylor *et al.* (1982), p. 564.

19. Thus psychoanalysis has been seen (Feuer, 1955) as providing a basis for an altruistic utilitarianism, in that it sees the individual's greatest happiness as being found in work for the happiness of others. Whether this is, as Feuer sees it, a rewritten version of utilitarianism, or whether the principle of utility has by this move been transformed into something else, may depend on how the concern for others is seen as developing.

20. See, for example, Kovel (1983).

21. Howarth and Gillham (1981), p. 87.

22. Bootzin *et al.* (1986), p. 458.

23. Mannoni (1971), pp. 190–1.

24. ibid., p. 182.

25. Gross (1987), p. 659.

26. For example Hardy and Heyes (1987), p. 166.

27. Bourne and Ekstrand (1982), p. 333. We should note that it is not only in academic psychology texts that we find the internalization of others restricted to the superego. Talcott Parsons, the sociologist whose rendering of Freud has been a major source of knowledge of psycho-analysis in social science, also presented the ego only as an adaptive cortex (Parsons, 1952). Yet he saw as well the inadequacy of such a conception, stressing that not only moral standards but 'all the components of the common culture are internalized as part of the personality structure' (1952, p. 108). Unfortunately, and significantly, this part of his position did not become as well known. Later (Parsons, 1958) he developed a more complex appraisal of the Freudian ego, seeing Freud as having moved towards an object-relations theory that located society in the ego and the id as well as the superego. See Karl Figlio's (1987) discussion of this trend in Parsons's thought.

28. Bee (1981), p. 400.

29. ibid., p. 10.

30. ibid., p. 396.

31. Taylor *et al.* (1982), pp. 563–4.

32. Freud (1933), p. 67.

33. Radford and Govier (1980), p. 565.

34. Taylor *et al.* (1982), p. 565.

35. ibid., p. 173.

36. Kristal (1979), p. 100.

37. Taylor *et al.* (1982), p. 22.

38. See Bruner (1956); Jahoda (1963; 1977).

39. See Herma *et al.* (1943), p. 331, and Shakow and Rapaport (1964), pp. 10 and 86ff.

40. Harlow *et al.* (1971), p. 371.

5   Humanistic Psychology Dispels the Freudian Gloom

1. The 'despair work' of Joanna Macy for peace movement activists, for example, is a mixture of humanistic psychology and eco-mysticism. See Macy (1983) and Childs (1986). Bull and Horncastle's (1983) review sketches the early impact upon police training of humanistic ways of thinking.

2. For example Rosen (1977).

3. Maslow (1971), p. 23.

4. ibid., p. 16. Or take Maslow (1954, p. 219): '"instinctoid" needs are good, desirable and healthy'.

5. Maslow (1971), Chapter 3.

6. ibid., Chapter 22.

7. ibid., p. 341.

8. Enright (1970), pp. 107–8.

9. The title of a classic treatise in physiology written by W. B. Cannon in 1932, and a phrase used by both Rogers and Maslow (e.g. 1971, p. 219).

10. Maslow (1971), p. 15.

11. Rogers (1961), p. 25.

12. Rogers (1981), p. vii. See Richards (1986) for some general discussion of these influences. For a more detailed and completely convincing argument, see Robert Fuller's lucid report of the influence of American Transcendentalist writers, especially Emerson, on the humanistic psychologists, and on how American protestant traditions of 'harmonial piety' dominated the reception of psychoanalysis in the United States (Fuller, 1986). Theological responses to Freud, as seen by Peter Homans in his 1970 review of them, have generally adopted the same critique of Freud (as 'reductionist') as has the humanistic tradition in psychology.

13. Kirschenbaum (1980), p. 58.

14. ibid., Chapter 8; also Rogers (1977), Chapter 1.

15. Kirschenbaum (1980), p. 84.

16. Maslow (1971), p. 51.

17. ibid., p. 180.

18. ibid., p. 181. Maslow rarely, it seems, used one word if three would do.

19. Jacoby (1975).

20. Enright (1970), pp. 111–13; see also Wallen (1957), p. 11. Perls *et al.* (1951) saw Reich's theory of the 'motoric armour' as fundamental to gestalt therapy.

21. Enright (1970), p. 112 (italics original).

22. Perls (1969), p. 1.

23. The increasing attention paid by contemporary psychoanalysis to 'containment' as a way of conceptualizing the management of disturbing affect is perhaps one sign of a move towards a formulation of how

emotional development takes place in which 'repression', though still an essential concept, is no longer the best way of describing the fundamental process of self-formation.

24. Rogers (1951), p. 440.

25. Maslow (1971), pp. 11–12.

26. Holland (1977), p. 74.

27. Williams (1961), pp. 103–4.

28. Holland (1977, Chapter 4) is reasonably sceptical that existentialism was an important influence, pointing to the great differences in temperament between the manic American and melancholic European traditions.

29. For example Maslow's reference (1971, p. 27) to 'the kind of sickness or crippling or stunting that we share with everybody else and therefore don't notice'.

30. There are of course cases of an exceptional degree of determination by the given organic material, most clearly where there is severe congenital impairment.

31. Maslow (1971), p. 48.

32. Perls (1969), p. 4. See Perls (1973, pp. 32–5) on the distinction between introjection and assimilation.

33. Some of the writings of Aldous Huxley provided a literary endorsement of psychedelics, and Huxley is appropriately excerpted in a collection co-edited by Maslow (Chiang and Maslow, 1969). Many other literary, conceptual and historical links between the 'growth' and drug cultures, at least during the 1960s, could be cited.

34. Though one was implicit in the earlier work of R. D. Laing (1959).

35. Geiger (1971), p. xiv.

36. Maslow (1971), p. 218.

37. ibid., p. 19.

38. ibid., pp. 19ff. Maslow was sublimely unaware of the irony, and likely unconscious significance, of his citing as an exemplary research programme the one which led to the production of nuclear weapons.

39. For example Rowan (1988), p. 142.

40. Maslow (1971), p. 30.

41. ibid., p. 210 (quotation from Ruth Benedict).

42. ibid., p. 326.

43. Holland (1977), p. 67.

44. See Rogers (1962, p. 188), and also Matson (1981), Raskin (1948) and Kirschenbaum (1980, pp. 90–5) on the influence on Rogers of early secessionists from the psychoanalytic movement.

45. Rowan (1976), p. 176.

46. Maslow (1971), p. 355.

47. Holland (1977), p. 76.

48. Kirschenbaum (1980), p. 84.

49. Stevens (1967).

50. Maslow (1971), p. 54.
51. Rogers (1977), p. 4.
52. ibid., p. 248.
53. ibid., *passim*.

6 Freud on His Head: Psychoanalysis and the Left

1. This chapter grew out of a short talk given at the Radical Philosophy Conference in London in 1986, as part of a workshop on psychoanalysis. An earlier version of it appeared in *Radical Philosophy* 48 (Spring 1988), 3–13.
2. My focus here is on tendencies in *British* left-political culture in the last twenty years. However, since an indigenous British body of work in this area has been emerging, rather slowly and patchily, only since the mid-1970s, many of the intellectual reference points in the following account are non-British (and most are pre-1968!). For that reason, at least some of the points to be made here will apply to other national contexts as well, in so far as debates there have been organized around the same sources and paradigms.
3. No such review seems to have appeared to date, though there are a small number of widely read articles defining important positions, e.g. Rustin, 1982a and b; Lasch, 1981; Rose, 1983. Part III of the recent book by Stephen Frosh (1987) covers some of the same ground as this paper.
4. Juliet Mitchell's 1974 book *Psychoanalysis and Feminism* was one important starting point (see Waddell *et al.*, 1978) for a 'Freud-Marx' group linked to the *Radical Science Journal* collective, which later developed into the editorial board of *Free Associations*.
5. The cruder Marxist inversion of Freud has to be distinguished from the efforts of Jacoby and others to reclaim Freud and the early spirit of psychoanalysis – humanistic, intellectually outgoing and culturally committed – from the fate of professionalization and technicization which, Jacoby argues, overtook it in the exigencies of fleeing fascism and relocating in post-war America. This historical analysis of the politics of psychoanalysis does not prescribe any particular view of the psychoanalysis of politics. For a nuanced example of the analysis of psychoanalysis as ambivalent, see Ingleby (1984).
6. Kovel (1984), p. 152.
7. See, for example, the collection of essays from the Women's Therapy Centre in London (Ernst and Maguire, 1987).
8. This meant that the present incumbents of the citadel – behaviourism and other schools of empirical psychology – had to be booted out, which could be accomplished, I hoped, with the critique of empiricism – Willer and Willer, 1973; Richards, 1977. I use the term 'scientism' loosely here,

to refer to any attempt to impose a narrow prescription of what 'science' is and to proscribe all non-'scientific' knowledge as mere ideology or speculation. Althusser (1965) is a prime example. My guides to realism were Harré (1974) and Bhaskar (1975).

9. Guntrip (1961) was particularly explicit about his philosophical influences, chief amongst whom was John Macmurray, the Scottish philosopher of the 'personal'. Macmurray was brought to the attention of the left in an interesting resumé of his thought by Conford (1977), but he remains 'a neglected philosopher'.

10. See Collier (1981), Rustin (1987), and Will (1980; 1986).

11. Young (1986; 1987).

12. For example Henriques *et al.* (1984).

13. See Habermas (1968), and McCarthy (1978); Keat (1981); Whitebook (1985).

14. Compare, for example, the Marxist usage of Freud by Schneider (1973) or Lichtman (1982) with the liberal interpretation by Badcock (1988). See p. 148.

15. Here, compare for example the use made of Guntrip's work by cultural critic David Holbrook (e.g. 1972) with that by feminist therapists Eichenbaum and Orbach (1982).

16. See Dinnerstein (1976) and Chodorow (1978).

17. Elshtain (1984); Temperley (1984).

18. The best-known and most controversial position in these debates is that of Lasch (1979; 1984). For two contrasting evaluations of his work, see Barrett and McIntosh (1982), and Richards (1985). See also the symposium on narcissism reported in *Telos* 44 (1980).

19. As in Raymond's (1986) critique of 'therapism' and the 'publicization of personal life'.

20. See Chapter 5, note 1.

21. Victor Wolfenstein's (1981) analysis of Malcolm X's autobiography, and the work of Peter Gay (e.g. 1985), give very interesting (and very different) examples of how psycho-historical work might develop.

22. It does, though, seem very appropriate to speak, as does Rose (1983), of a 'utopianism of the psyche' with reference to the call of Irigary and some other feminists for a return to a condition of psychic oneness.

23. For example my own attempt to introduce object-relational thinking into this tradition (Richards, 1984).

24. What I am saying overall at a personal level is that I now remain involved in psychoanalytically oriented intellectual work for reasons which are in some ways the opposite of those which originally led me to it. I do not assume that others will have as perverse a relationship to the subject as this, and I am not clear about the extent to which this personal movement is an age-related emotional change, a trajectory of the political times, or the outcome of psychoanalytic teachings. My hope is that these fragments of intellectual autobiography illustrate some significant

moments in the left's post-'68 relationship with psychoanalysis, and the diverse options available for engagement with it.

25. See Abramson (1984); and Kovel (1986) for his critique of Chasseguet-Smirgel and Grunberger.

26. See Alexander (1984).

27. Horowitz (1977), p. 214.

28. See Chapter 1, pp. 17–18; also Dervin (1981).

29. From the television play 'Blast from the Past', by Deborah Levin (Channel 4, 1 May 1988).

30. For example the Cultural Centre for Freudian Studies and Research in London, and the Oxford Psychoanalytic Study Group.

31. See Rustin (1982).

32. For example Gallop (1982).

33. See Lacan (1966), and Benvenuto and Kennedy (1986); also Bird (1982).

34. See Marcuse (1955).

35. This view of the self does not, though, necessarily involve a conception of an *original* whole, contrary to the implication of Mitchell's definition of humanism (1982, p. 4) as entailing the assumption that 'the subject exists from the beginning'.

36. See Keat (1986) on the similar problem of naturalism in Foucault (and Reich).

37. For example Deleuze and Guattari (1972).

38. As noted by Macey (1983).

39. Rose (1983), p. 11.

40. Some recent reports of psychotherapeutic work in Nicaragua (e.g. Pickvance, 1987) and South Africa (Straker, 1988) have introduced a very different note, far removed from the troubles of the metropolitan intellectual.

7 Psychoanalysis and Market Ideologies

1. Macpherson (1977), p. 263.

2. See Chapter 1, note 4.

3. Hindess (1987), Chapter 9.

4. Fromm (1932).

5. For example Freud (1908a); Abraham (1921). See also Bornemann (1973).

6. I have discussed Schneider's (1973) work more fully in Richards (1984).

7. See Badcock (1980), pp. 198–204.

8. Williams (1958), pp. 322ff.

9. Barber (1977) observes this to be the case, even amongst Marxist economists.

10. See, for example, the two Fabian Tracts by Plant (1984) and Forbes,

ed. (1986); the articles by Frankel (1985) and Hedman (1981), and the work of Nove (1983; 1985).

11. Winnicott (1950), p. 254.

12. See Parsons (1960), and Donzelot (1977). Such conceptual parallels probably tell us more about the influence of dominant modes of thought on different thinkers (and perhaps about the influence of everyday economic thinking upon Freud) than about actual relationships between the inner and outer worlds.

13. Hayek (1967), p. 231.

14. ibid., p. 236.

15. See Schafer (1960).

16. It might be said that Rawls's famous first principle is a classic statement of the problem that Hayek ignores – the problem of others. Rawls (1971, p. 60) proposes equal rights for all to the most extensive degree of basic liberty compatible with similar liberty for others.

17. Hayek, loc. cit.

18. His 1985 Disraeli Lecture on the legacy of permissiveness. See Tebbit (1988), p. 246.

19. The following analysis is extracted from an article in the quarterly *Changes* (Richards, 1987).

20. In a Conservative Party Political Broadcast, 15 March 1988.

21. Maslow (1971), p. 20.

22. ibid., p. 219.

8 Political Disillusionment

1. Freud (1928), quoted in Jones (1957), pp. 477–8.

2. Developed in Richards (1983), and summarized more fully in Richards (1986).

3. Gay (1987). Hyman (1956) makes a related point, seeing Freud's Darwinian secularism as the basis for his tragic view of the 'radical imperfectibility' of humankind.

4. Gay (op. cit.) argues that given Freud's self-conscious allegiance to the Enlightenment and science, we cannot agree with those who have seen the influence of Jewish outlooks in the development of his thought (see Chapter 3, note 3). This seems to me to be an unnecessary dichotomy: a philosophical commitment to rationality is open to a range of moral inflections, and it may well be in Freud's case that – as Dennis Klein (1985) has argued – his work was infused with moral ambitions stemming from Jewish culture.

5. Freud (1933).

6. By, for example, Gay (op. cit., p. 44), and Kariel (1964, p. 33).

7. Freud's later writings on religion and society are the main expression of this.

8. See Kovel (1971) and Frosh (in press) for good examples.

9. As for example in the work described by Cohen (1987).

10. A similar distinction is made by Abramson (op. cit., Chapter 1). In his use of classical Freudian theory, 'Eros' is both an ally and enemy of freedom – the former in the commitment to the public realm which it sustains, the latter in its potential as a basis for manipulation.

BIBLIOGRAPHY

Abraham, K. (1921) Contributions to the theory of the anal character. In *Selected Papers of Karl Abraham*, 370–92. London: Hogarth, 1949.

Abramson, J. (1984) *Liberation and Its Limits: The Moral and Political Thought of Freud*. New York: Free Press.

Adorno, T. (1967/8) Sociology and psychology. *New Left Review* 46, 63–80 and 47, 79–97.

Alexander, S. (1984) Women, class and sexual difference in the 1830s and 1840s: some reflections on the writing of a feminist history. *History Workshop Journal* 17, 125–49.

Althusser, L. (1965) *For Marx*. New York: Vintage, 1970.

Andersson, O. (1962) *Studies in the Prehistory of Psychoanalysis*. Stockholm: Svenska Bokforlaget/Norstedts.

Arato, A. and Gebhardt, E., eds. (1978) *The Essential Frankfurt School Reader*. Oxford: Blackwell.

Armistead, N., ed. (1974) *Reconstructing Social Psychology*. Harmondsworth: Penguin.

Atkinson, R. L., Atkinson, R. C., Smith, E. and Hilgard, E. (1987) *Introduction to Psychology*. New York: Harcourt Brace Jovanovich (9th edn).

Badcock, C. (1980) *The Psychoanalysis of Culture*. Oxford: Blackwell.

Badcock, C. (1988) *Essential Freud*. Oxford: Blackwell.

Bakan, D. (1958) *Sigmund Freud and the Jewish Mystical Tradition*. Boston: Beacon Press, 1975.

Bakan, D. (1966) Behaviorism and American urbanization. *Journal for the History of the Behavioral Sciences* 2, 5–28.

Barber, B. (1977). Absolutization of the market: some notes on how we got from there to here. In G. Dworkin *et al.*, eds., *Markets and Morals*, 15–31. Washington: Hemisphere, and New York: Wiley.

Barker, F. *et al.*, eds. (1982) *The Politics of Theory*. Colchester: University of Essex Sociology of Literature Conference.

Barrett, M. and McIntosh, M. (1982) Narcissism and the family: a critique of Lasch. *New Left Review* 135, 35–48.

Bee, H. (1981) *The Developing Child*. New York: Harper and Row (3rd edn).

Bellak, L. (1961) Free association: conceptual and clinical aspects. *International Journal of Psycho-Analysis* 42, 9–20.

Benvenuto, B. and Kennedy, R. (1986) *The Works of Jacques Lacan. An Introduction*. London: Free Association Books.

Berger, P. (1965) Towards a sociological understanding of psychoanalysis. *Social Research* 32, 26–41.

Berman, M. (1982) *All That Is Solid Melts into Air*. London: Verso, 1983.

Bernstein, R., ed. (1985) *Habermas and Modernity*. Cambridge: Polity Press.

Bettelheim, B. (1983) *Freud and Man's Soul*. London: Chatto and Windus/ Hogarth.

Bhaskar, R. (1975) *A Realist Theory of Science*. Leeds: Leeds Books.

Bion, W. (1977) *Seven Servants*. New York: Jason Aronson.

Bion, W. (1979) *The Dawn of Oblivion*. Strath Tay: Clunie Press.

Bird, J. (1982) Jacques Lacan – the French Freud? *Radical Philosophy* 30, 7–14.

Bocock, R. (1983) *Sigmund Freud*. Chichester: Ellis Horwood.

Bootzin, R., Bower, G., Zajonc, R., and Hall, E. (1986) *Psychology Today: An Introduction*. New York: Random House (6th edn).

Bornemann, E., ed. (1973) *The Psychoanalysis of Money*. New York: Urizen Books, 1976.

Bourne, L. and Ekstrand, B. (1982) *Psychology: Its Principles and Meanings*. New York: Holt, Rinehart and Winston (4th edn).

Boyers, R., ed. (1975) *Psychological Man*. New York: Harper Colophon.

Bradley, F. (1887) Association and thought. In *Collected Essays*, 205–238. Oxford: Oxford University Press, 1969.

Brooks, K. (1973) Freudianism is not a basis for a Marxist psychology. In P. Brown, ed., *Radical Psychology*, 315–74. New York: Harper and Row.

Brome, V. (1984) *Freud and His Disciples*. London: Caliban Publications.

Brown, P., ed. (1973) *Radical Psychology*. New York: Harper and Row.

Bruner, J. (1956) Freud and the image of man. In P. Roazen, ed., *Sigmund Freud*, 22–9. Englewood Cliffs, N.J.: Prentice Hall, 1973.

Bull, R. and Horncastle, P. (1983) *An Evaluation of the Metropolitan Police Recruit Training in Human Awareness Training (HAT)*. London: Police Foundation.

Burnham, J. (1967) *Psychoanalysis and American Medicine: 1894–1918*. New York: International Universities Press (Psychological Issues Monograph 20).

Burnham, J. (1978) The impact of psychoanalysis upon American culture.

In J. Quen and E. Carlson, eds., *American Psychoanalysis: Origins and Development*, 52–72. New York: Brunner/Mazel.

Burnham, J. (1979) From avant-garde to specialism: psychoanalysis in America. *Journal for the History of the Behavioral Sciences* 15, 128–34.

Burns, R. and Dobson, C. (1984) *Introductory Psychology*. Lancaster: MTP Press.

Campbell, C. (1987) *The Romantic Ethic and the Spirit of Consumerism*. Oxford: Blackwell.

Cannon, W. (1932) *The Wisdom of the Body*. London: Kegan Paul, 1947 (revised edn).

Chasseguet-Smirgel, J. (1985) *The Ego-Ideal*. London: Free Association Books.

Chasseguet-Smirgel, J. (1986) *Sexuality and Mind*. New York: New York University Press.

Chasseguet-Smirgel, J. and Grunberger, B. (1976) *Freud or Reich? Psychoanalysis and Illusion*. London: Free Association Books, 1986.

Chiang, H.-M. and Maslow, A., eds. (1969) *The Healthy Personality*. New York: Van Nostrand.

Childs, D. (1986) A deep ecology workshop with Joanna Macy. *Psychologists for Peace Newsletter* Winter 1986, 2–3.

Chodorow, N. (1978) *The Reproduction of Mothering*. Berkeley: University of California Press.

Cioffi, F., ed. (1973) *Freud*. London: Macmillan.

Clark, R. (1980) *Freud: The Man and His Cause*. London: Weidenfeld and Nicolson.

Cohen, P. (1987). *Racism and Popular Culture: A Cultural Studies Approach*. London: University of London Institute of Education Centre for Multicultural Education, Working Paper No. 9.

Collier, A. (1981) Scientific realism and the human world: the case of psychoanalysis. *Radical Philosophy* 29, 8–18.

Colman, L. (1988) The place of the parents in psychoanalytic theory. *Free Associations* 12, 92–125.

Conford, P. (1972) John Macmurray: a neglected philosopher. *Radical Philosophy* 16, 16–20.

Cooley, C. (1922) *Human Nature and the Social Order*. New York: Schocken Books.

Decker, H. (1977) *Freud in Germany: Revolution and Reaction in Science, 1893–1907*. New York: International Universities Press (Psychological Issues Monograph 41).

Deleuze, G. and Guattari, F. (1972) *Anti-Oedipus*. London: Athlone, 1984.

Dember, W., Jenkins, J. and Teyler, T. (1984) *General Psychology*. New York: Lawrence Erlbaum.

Dervin, D. (1981) Trashing the sixties: defensive reactions within psychoanalysis. *Journal of Psychohistory* 9, 185–97.

Dicks, H. (1970) *Fifty Years of the Tavistock Clinic*. London: Routledge and Kegan Paul.

Dilman, I. (1983) *Freud and Human Nature*. Oxford: Blackwell.

Dilman, I. (1984) *Freud and the Mind*. Oxford: Blackwell.

Dinnerstein, D. (1976) *The Rocking of the Cradle, and the Ruling of the World*. London: Souvenir Press, 1978.

Donzelot, J. (1977) *The Policing of Families*. London: Hutchinson, 1980.

Ducat, S. (1988) *Taken In: American Gullibility and the Reagan Mythos*. Tacoma, Wa.: Life Sciences Press.

Dworkin, G., Bermants, G. and Brown, P., eds. (1977) *Markets and Morals*. Washington: Hemisphere, and New York: Wiley.

Dyos, H. and Wolff, M., eds. (1973) *The Victorian City*, Vol. 2. London: Routledge and Kegan Paul.

Eichenbaum, L. and Orbach, S. (1982) *Outside In ... Inside Out*. Harmondsworth: Penguin.

Elshtain, J. (1984) Symmetry and soporifics: a critique of feminist accounts of gender development. In B. Richards, ed., *Capitalism and Infancy*, 55–91. London: Free Association Books.

Enright, J. (1970) An introduction to gestalt techniques. In J. Fagan and I. Shepherd, eds., *Gestalt Therapy Now*, 107–24. New York: Harper Colophon, 1971.

Erdelyi, M. (1985) *Psychoanalysis. Freud's Cognitive Psychology*. New York: Freeman.

Ernst, S. and Maguire, M., eds. (1987) *Living with the Sphinx*. London: The Women's Press.

Esslin, M. (1972) Freud's Vienna. In J. Miller, ed., *Freud: The Man, His World, His Influence*, 41–54. London: Weidenfeld and Nicolson.

Eysenck, H. (1965) *Fact and Fiction in Psychology*. Harmondsworth: Penguin.

Eysenck, H. (1972) *Psychology Is about People*. Harmondsworth: Penguin, 1977.

Eysenck, J. (1985) *Decline and Fall of the Freudian Empire*. Harmondsworth: Penguin (Viking).

Fagan, J. and Shepherd, I., eds. (1970) *Gestalt Therapy Now*. New York: Harper and Row, 1971.

Feffer, M. (1982) *The Structure of Freudian Thought*. New York: International Universities Press.

Ferenczi, S. (1909) Introjection and transference. In *First Contributions to Psycho-Analysis*, 35–93. London: Hogarth, 1952.

Ferenczi, S. (1912) On the definition of introjection. In *Final Contributions to Psycho-Analysis*, 316–18. London: Hogarth.

Feuer, L. (1955) *Psychoanalysis and Ethics*. Springfield, Illinois: Charles C. Thomas.

Figlio, K. (1987) The lost subject of medical sociology. In G. Scambler, ed., *Sociological Theory and Medical Sociology*, 77–109. London: Tavistock.

Forbes, I., ed. (1986). *Market Socialism: Whose Choice?*. London: Fabian Society (Fabian Tract no. 516).

Foucault, M. (1976) *The History of Sexuality, Volume I: An Introduction*. Harmondsworth: Penguin, 1981.

Frankel, B. (1985). The historical obsolescence of market socialism – a reply to Alec Nove. *Radical Philosophy* 39, 28–33.

Freeman, L. (1980) *Freud Rediscovered*. New York: Arbor House.

Freud, A. (1936) *The Ego and the Mechanisms of Defence*. New York: International Universities Press, 1946.

Freud, S. (1895) The psychotherapy of hysteria. In Breuer, J. and Freud, S., Studies on Hysteria. *The Standard Edition of the Complete Psychological Works of Sigmund Freud* (hereafter 'SE') Vol. II, 253–305. London: Hogarth.

Freud, S. (1900) The Interpretation of Dreams. *SE* IV and V, 339–627.

Freud. S. (1901) The Psychopathology of Everyday Life. *SE* VI.

Freud, S. (1905) Three Essays on the Theory of Sexuality. *SE* VII. 125–245.

Freud, S. (1908a) Character and anal erotism. *SE* IX, 167–75.

Freud, S. (1908b) 'Civilised' sexual morality and modern nervous illness. *SE* IX, 181–204.

Freud, S. (1911) Formulations on the two principles of mental functioning. *SE* XII, 213–26.

Freud, S. (1913) Totem and Taboo. *SE* XIII, 1–162.

Freud, S. (1915a) Instincts and their vicissitudes. *SE* XIV, 109–40.

Freud, S. (1915b) Thoughts for the times on war and death. *SE* XIV, 275–302.

Freud, S. (1917a) Mourning and melancholia. *SE* XIV, 243–58.

Freud, S. (1917b) Introductory Lectures on Psychoanalysis, XXVI: The libido theory and narcissism. *SE* XVI, 412–30.

Freud, S. (1917c) A childhood recollection from *Dichtung und Wahrheit*. *SE* XVII, 145–56.

Freud, S. (1921) Group Psychology and the Analysis of the Ego. *SE* XVIII, 65–143.

Freud, S. (1924) The economic problem of masochism. *SE* XIX, 155–170.

Freud, S. (1930) Civilisation and its discontents. *SE* XXI, 57–145.

Freud, S. (1933) New Introductory Lectures on Psychoanalysis. *SE* XXII, 1–182.

Freud, S. (1940) An Outline of Psychoanalysis. *SE* XXIII, 139–207.

Fromm, E. (1932) Psychoanalytic characterology and its relevance for social psychology. In *The Crisis of Psychoanalysis*, 163–89. London: Cape, 1971.

Fromm, E. (1947) *Man for Himself*. London: Ark, 1986.

Frosh, S. (1987) *The Politics of Psychoanalysis*. Basingstoke: Macmillan.

Frosh, S. (in press) Psychoanalysis and racism. In B. Richards, ed., *Crises of the Self*. London: Free Association Books, forthcoming.

Fuller, R. (1986) *Americans and the Unconscious*. London: Oxford University Press.

Gabriel, Y. (1983) *Freud and Society*. London: Routledge and Kegan Paul.

Galdston, I. (1956) Freud and romantic medicine. In F. Cioffi, ed., *Freud*, 103–23. London: Macmillan, 1973.

Gallop, J. (1982) The mother tongue. In F. Barker *et al.*, eds., *The Politics of Theory*, 49–56. Colchester: University of Essex Sociology of Literature Conference.

Gallop, J. (1985) *Reading Lacan*. Ithaca: Cornell University Press.

Gay, P. (1978) *Freud, Jews and Other Germans*. New York: Oxford University Press.

Gay, P. (1985) *Freud for Historians*. New York: Oxford University Press.

Gay, P. (1987) *A Godless Jew: Freud, Atheism and the Making of Psychoanalysis*. New Haven: Yale University Press.

Gay, P. (1988) *Freud: A Life for Our Time*. London: Dent.

Gay, V. (1983) *Reading Freud: Psychology, Neurosis and Religion*. Chico, Ca.: Scholars' Press.

Gedo, J. and Pollock, G., eds. (1976) *Freud: The Fusion of Science and Humanism*. New York: International Universities Press (Psychological Issues Monograph 34/35).

Geiger, H. (1971) Introduction: A. H. Maslow, in A. Maslow, *The Farther Reaches of Human Nature*, xiii–xix. Harmondsworth: Penguin, 1973.

Gellner, E. (1985) *The Psychoanalytic Movement*. London: Paladin.

Gill, M. and Holzman, P., eds. (1976) *Psychology versus Metapsychology. Psychoanalytic Essays in Memory of George S. Klein*. New York: International Universities Press (Psychological Issues Monograph 36).

Ginzburg, C. (1980) Morelli, Freud and Sherlock Holmes: clues and scientific method. *History Workshop* 9(5), 5–36.

Greenberg, J. and Mitchell, S. (1983) *Object Relations in Psychoanalytic Theory*. Cambridge, Mass.: Harvard University Press.

Gross, R. (1987) *Psychology*. London: Edward Arnold.

Grotstein, J. (1981) *Splitting and Projective Identification*. New York: Jason Aronson.

Grunbaum, A. (1983) *The Foundations of Psychoanalysis: A Philosophical Critique*. Berkeley: University of California Press.

Guntrip, H. (1961) *Personality Structure and Human Interaction*. London: Hogarth.

Guntrip, H. (1968) *Schizoid Phenomena, Object Relations and the Self*. London: Hogarth.

Habermas, J. (1968) *Knowledge and Human Interests*. London: Heinemann, 1972.

Hale, N. (1971) *Freud and the Americans*. New York: Oxford.

Hall, C. (1956) *A Primer of Freudian Psychology*. London: Allen and Unwin.

Halmos, P. (1965) *The Faith of the Counsellors*. London: Constable.

Hardy, M. and Heyes, S. (1987) *Beginning Psychology*. London: Weidenfeld and Nicolson.

Harlow, H., McGaugh, J., and Thompson, R. (1971) *Psychology*. San Francisco: Albion.

Harré, R. (1974) Blueprint for a new science. In N. Armistead, ed., *Reconstructing Social Psychology*, 240–59. Harmondsworth: Penguin.

Hayek, F. (1967). *Studies in Philosophy, Politics and Economics*. London: Routledge and Kegan Paul.

Hedman, C. (1981). Rawls' theory of justice and 'market socialism'. *Radical Philosophy* 28, 23–8.

Henriques, J., Hollway, W., Urwin, C., Venn, C., and Walkerdine, V. (1984) *Changing the Subject*. London: Methuen.

Herma, H., Kris, E. and Shor, J. (1943) Freud's theory of the dream in American textbooks. *Journal of Abnormal and Social Psychology* 38(3), 319–34.

Hindess, B. (1987). *Freedom, Equality and the Market: Arguments on Social Policy*. London: Tavistock.

Hinshelwood, R. (1988) Is psychoanalysis humanistic? A correspondence between John Rowan and Bob Hinshelwood. *British Journal of Psychotherapy* 4(2), 142–7.

Holbrook, D. (1972) *The Masks of Hate*. Oxford: Pergamon.

Holland, R. (1977) *Self and Social Context*. London: Macmillan.

Homans, P. (1970) *Theology after Freud*. Indianapolis: Bobbs-Merrill.

Horkheimer, M. (1941) The end of reason. In A. Arato and E. Gebhardt, eds., *The Essential Frankfurt School Reader*, 26–48. Oxford: Blackwell, 1978.

Horkheimer, M. (1947) Rise and decline of the individual. In *The Eclipse of Reason*, 128–61. New York: Seabury Press, 1974.

Horkheimer, M. and Adorno, T. (1944) *Dialectic of Enlightenment*. London: Allen Lane, 1973.

Horowitz, G. (1977) *Basic and Surplus Repression in Psychoanalytic Theory: Freud, Reich and Marcuse*. Toronto: University of Toronto Press.

Howarth, I. and Gillham, W. (1981) *The Structure of Psychology: An Introductory Text*. London: Allen and Unwin.

Hyman, S. (1956) Psychoanalysis and the climate of tragedy. In B. Nelson, ed., *Freud and the Twentieth Century*, 163–81. London: Allen and Unwin, 1958.

Hyman, S., (1962) On 'The Interpretation of Dreams'. In P. Meisel, ed., *Freud: A Collection of Critical Essays*, 121–44. Englewood Cliffs, N.J.: Prentice Hall, 1981.

Ingleby, D. (1984) The ambivalence of psychoanalysis. *Radical Science* 15 (*Free Associations* Pilot Issue), 39–71.

Isbister, N. (1985) *Freud: An Introduction to His Life and Work*. Cambridge: Polity Press.

Jacoby, R. (1975) *Social Amnesia*. Hassocks: Harvester, 1977.

Jacoby, R. (1983) *The Repression of Psychoanalysis*. New York: Basic Books.

Jahoda, M. (1963) Some notes on the influence of psychoanalytic ideas on American psychology. *Human Relations* 16, 111–29.

Jahoda, M. (1977) *Freud and the Dilemmas of Psychology*. London: Hogarth.

Jameson, F. (1984) Postmodernism, or the cultural logic of late capitalism. *New Left Review* 146, 53–91.

Jay, M. (1973) *The Dialectical Imagination*. London: Heinemann.

Jennings, H. (1985) *Pandaemonium*. London: Pan, 1987.

Jones, E. (1915a) War and individual psychology. In *Essays in Applied Psychoanalysis*, Vol. 1, 55–76. London: Hogarth.

Jones, E. (1915b) War and sublimation. In *Essays in Applied Psychoanalysis*, Vol. 1, 77–87.

Jones, E. (1954) *Sigmund Freud: Life and Work. Vol. 1: The Young Freud*. London: Hogarth.

Jones, E. (1957) *Sigmund Freud: Life and Work. Vol. 3: The Last Phase*. London: Hogarth.

Jung, C. (1906) Psychoanalysis and association experiments. In *Collected Works, Vol. 2: Experimental Researches*, 288–317. London: Routledge and Kegan Paul.

Kalin, M. (1975) *The Utopian Flight from Unhappiness*. Totowa, N.J.: Littlefield, Adams.

Kariel, H. (1964) *In Search of Authority*. Glencoe: Free Press.

Keat, R. (1981) *The Politics of Social Theory*. Oxford: Blackwell.

Keat, R. (1986) The human body in social theory: Reich, Foucault and the repressive hypothesis. *Radical Philosophy* 42, 24–32.

Kernberg, O. (1980) *Internal World and External Reality*. New York: Jason Aronson.

Kirschenbaum, H. (1980) *On Becoming Carl Rogers*. New York: Dell.

Klein, D. (1985) *The Jewish Basis of the Psychoanalytic Movement*. Chicago: University of Chicago Press.

Klein, M. (1952) Some theoretical conclusions regarding the emotional life of the infant. In *Envy and Gratitude*, 61–93. London: Hogarth, 1975.

Kline, P. (1984) *Psychology and Freudian Theory*. London: Methuen.

Kohon, G. (1986) *The British School of Psychoanalysis: The Independent Tradition*. London: Free Association Books.

Kovel, J. (1971) *White Racism*. London: Free Association Books, 1988.

Kovel, J. (1976) Therapy in late capitalism. In *The Radical Spirit*, 121–146. London: Free Association Books, 1988.

Kovel, J. (1978) Rationalisation and the family. In B. Richards, ed., *Capitalism and Infancy*, 102–21. London: Free Association Books, 1984.

Kovel J. (1981) *The Age of Desire*. New York: Pantheon.

Kovel, J. (1983) *Against the State of Nuclear Terror*. London: Pan.

Kovel, J. (1984) On being a Marxist psychoanalyst (and a psycho-analytic Marxist). *Radical Science* 15 (*Free Associations* Pilot Issue), 149–154.

Kovel, J. (1986) Why Freud or Reich? *Free Associations* 4, 80–99.

Kris, A. (1987) *Free Association – Method and Process*. Harvard: Yale University Press.

Kristal, L. (1979) *Understanding Psychology*. London: Harper and Row.

Lacan, J. (1966) *Ecrits: a Selection*. London: Tavistock, 1977.

Laing, R. (1960) *The Divided Self*. Harmondsworth: Penguin, 1965.

Laplanche, J. and Pontalis, J.-B. (1973) *The Language of Psycho-Analysis*. London: Hogarth.

Lasch, C. (1979) *The Culture of Narcissism*. New York: Norton.

Lasch, C. (1981) Freud and the New Left: the theory of cultural revolution. *New Left Review* 129, 23–34.

Lasch, C. (1984) *The Minimal Self*. New York: Norton.

Lewis, H. (1981) *Freud and Modern Psychology*. New York: Plenum.

Lichtman, R. (1982) *The Production of Desire*. New York: Free Press.

Lomas, P., ed. (1966) *Psychoanalysis Observed*. Harmondsworth: Penguin, 1968.

McCarthy, T. (1978) *The Critical Theory of Jurgen Habermas*. Cambridge: Polity Press.

Macpherson, C. (1962) *The Political Theory of Possessive Individualism*. Oxford: Oxford University Press.

Macey, D. (1983) Fragments of an analysis: Lacan in context. *Radical Philosophy* 35, 1–9.

Macy, J. (1983) *Despair and Personal Power in the Nuclear Age*. Philadelphia: New Society Publishers.

Mann, T. (1936) Freud and the future. In F. Cioffi, ed., *Freud*, 57–75. London: Macmillan, 1973.

Mannoni, O. (1968) *Freud: The Theory of the Unconscious*. New York: Pantheon, 1971.

Marcus, S. (1984) *Freud and the Culture of Psychoanalysis*. Boston: Allen and Unwin.

Marcuse, H. (1941) Some social implications of modern technology. In A. Arato and E. Gebhardt, eds., *The Essential Frankfurt School Reader*, 138–62. Oxford: Blackwell, 1978.

Marcuse, H. (1955) *Eros and Civilisation*. Boston: Beacon, 1974.

Marcuse, H. (1970) The obsolescence of the Freudian concept of man. In *Five Lectures*, 44–61. London: Allen Lane.

Martin, B. (1981) *A Sociology of Contemporary Cultural Change*. Oxford: Blackwell.

Maslow, A. (1954) *Motivation and Personality*. New York: Harper and Row, 1970 (2nd edn).

Maslow, A. (1965) *Eupsychian Management: A Journal*. Homewood, Illinois: Irwin and Dorsey.

Maslow, A. (1968) *Toward a Psychology of Being*. New York: Van Nostrand (2nd edn).

Maslow, A. (1971) *The Farther Reaches of Human Nature*. Harmondsworth: Penguin, 1976.

Masson, J., ed. (1985) *The Complete Letters of Sigmund Freud to Wilhelm Fliess 1887–1904*. Cambridge, Mass.: Harvard University Press.

Matson, F. (1981) Epilogue. In J. Royce and L. Mos, eds., *Humanistic Psychology: Concepts and Criticisms*, 295–304. New York: Plenum.

Mazlish, B., ed. (1963) *Psychoanalysis and History*. Englewood Cliffs, N.J.: Prentice Hall.

Mead, G. (1934) *Mind, Self and Society*. Chicago: University of Chicago Press.

Meisel, P., ed. (1981) *Freud: A Collection of Critical Essays*. Englewood Cliffs, N.J.: Prentice Hall.

Meissner, W. (1981) *Internalisation in Psychoanalysis*. New York: International Universities Press (Psychological Issues Monograph 50).

Meltzer, D. (1978). *The Kleinian Development* (3 vols.). Strath Tay: Clunie Press.

Meyer, N. (1975) *The Seven Per Cent Solution*. London: Hodder and Stoughton.

Meyerhoff, H. (1957) Freud and the ambiguity of culture. In B. Mazlish, ed., *Psychoanalysis and History*, 56–68. Englewood Cliffs, N.J.: Prentice Hall, 1963.

Mill, J. S. (1843) *A System of Logic*. London: Longmans, 1872 (8th edn).

Miller, J., ed. (1972) *Freud: The Man, His World, His Influence*. London: Weidenfeld and Nicolson.

Mitchell, J. (1974) *Psychoanalysis and Feminism*. Harmondsworth: Penguin.

Mitchell, J. (1982) Introduction. In J. Mitchell and J. Rose, *Feminine Sexuality: Jacques Lacan and the Ecole Freudienne*, 1–26. London: Macmillan.

Mumford, L. (1938) *The Culture of Cities*. London: Secker and Warburg.

Musto, D. (1968) A study in cocaine. *Journal of the American Medical Association* 204(1), 207.

Nelson, B., ed. (1958) *Freud and the Twentieth Century*. London: Allen and Unwin.

North, M. (1972) *The Secular Priests*. London: Allen and Unwin.

Nove, A. (1983) *The Economics of Feasible Socialism*. London: Allen and Unwin.

Nove, A. (1985) Debate on market socialism. *Radical Philosophy* 39, 24–7.

O'Neil, W. (1982) *The Beginnings of Modern Psychology*. Brighton: Harvester (2nd edn).

Padel, J. (1985) Ego in current thinking. In G. Kohon, ed., *The British School of Psychoanalysis*, 154–72. London: Free Association Books, 1986.

Parkes, C. (1986) *Bereavement. Studies of Grief in Adult Life*. Harmondsworth: Penguin (2nd edn).

Parsons, T. (1952) The superego and the theory of social systems. In P. Roazen, ed., *Sigmund Freud*, 103–17. Englewood Cliffs, N.J.: Prentice Hall, 1973.

Parsons, T. (1958) Social structure and the development of personality: Freud's contribution to the integration of psychology and sociology. In *Social Structure and Personality*, 78–111. London: Free Press, 1964.

Parsons, T. (1960) Some reflections on the problem of psychosomatic relationships in health and illness. In *Social Structure and Personality*, 112–126. London: Free Press, 1964.

Perls, F. *et al.* (1951) *Gestalt Therapy*. New York: Delta.

Perls, F. (1969) *Gestalt Therapy Verbatim*. Lafayette, Ca.: Real People Press.

Perls, F. (1973) *The Gestalt Approach and Eyewitness to Therapy*. Science and Behaviour Books.

Pickvance, D. (1987) Nicaraguan analysis. *Changes* 5(1), 290–93.

Plant, R. (1984). *Equality, Markets and the State*. London: Fabian Society (Fabian Tract no. 494).

Quen, J. and Carlson, E., eds. (1978) *American Psychoanalysis: Origins and Development*. New York: Brunner/Mazel.

Radford, J. (1988) Sherlock Holmes and the history of psychology. *The Psychologist* 1(4), 143–6.

Radford, J. and Govier, E. (1980) *A Textbook of Psychology*. London: Sheldon Press.

Raskin, N. (1948) The development of non-directive therapy. *Journal of Consulting and Clinical Psychology* 12, 92-110.

Rawls, J. (1971). *A Theory of Justice*. Oxford: Oxford University Press, 1973.

Raymond, J. (1986) *A Passion for Friends*. London: The Women's Press.

Richards, B. (1977) Empiricism and after. *Bulletin of the British Psychological Society* 30, 181.

Richards, B. (1983) *Clinical Psychology, the Individual and the Welfare State*. Unpublished Ph.D. dissertation, C.N.A.A.

Richards, B. (1984) Schizoid states and the market. In B. Richards, ed., *Capitalism and Infancy*, 122–66. London: Free Association Books.

Richards, B. (1985) The politics of the self. *Free Associations* 3, 42–64.

Richards, B. (1986) Psychotherapy and the public domain. *British Journal of Psychotherapy* 3(1), 42–51.

Richards, B. (1987). The mass psychology of monetarism. *Changes* 5(2), 326–8.

Richards, B. (1988). The eupsychian impulse: psychoanalysis and Left politics since 1968. *Radical Philosophy* 48, 3–13.

Rieff, P. (1959) *Freud. The Mind of the Moralist*. London: Gollancz.

Rieff, P. (1966) *The Triumph of the Therapeutic*. Harmondsworth: Penguin, 1973.

Roazen, P., ed. (1973) *Sigmund Freud*. Englewood Cliffs, N.J.: Prentice Hall.

Robert, M. (1974) *From Oedipus to Moses: Freud's Jewish Identity*. London: Routledge and Kegan Paul, 1977.

Rogers, C. (1951) *Client-Centred Therapy*. Boston: Houghton Mifflin.

Rogers, C. (1961) *On Becoming a Person*. London: Constable.

Rogers, C. (1962) Some learnings from a study of psychotherapy with schizophrenics. In C. Rogers and B. Stevens, *Person to Person: The Problem of Being Human*, 47–66. Lafayette, Ca.: Real People Press.

Rogers, C. (1977) *Carl Rogers on Personal Power*. New York: Delacorte Press.

Rogers, C. (1981) Foreword: The formative tendency. In J. Royce and P. Mos, eds., *Humanistic Psychology. Concepts and Criticisms*, v–xi. New York: Plenum.

Rose, J. (1983) Femininity and its discontents. *Feminist Review* 14, 5–19.

Rosen, R. (1977) *Psychobabble*. London: Wildwood House, 1978.

Rosenfeld, H. (1987) *Impasse and Interpretation*. London: Tavistock.

Rowan, J. (1976) *Ordinary Ecstasy: Humanistic Psychology in Action*. London: Routledge and Kegan Paul.

Rowan, J. (1988) Is psychoanalysis humanistic? A correspondence between John Rowan and Bob Hinshelwood. *British Journal of Psychotherapy* 4(2), 142–7.

Royce, J. and Mos, L., eds. (1981) *Humanistic Psychology: Concepts and Criticisms*. New York: Plenum.

Rustin, M. (1982a) A socialist consideration of Kleinian psychoanalysis. *New Left Review* 131, 71–96.

Rustin, M. (1982b) Kleinian psychoanalysis and the theory of culture. In F. Barker *et al.*, eds., *The Politics of Theory*, 57–70. Colchester: University of Essex Conference on the Sociology of Literature.

Rustin, M. (1985) The social organisation of secrets. *International Review of Psycho-Analysis* 12, 143–59.

Rustin, M. (1987) Psychoanalysis, philosophical realism and the new sociology of science. *Free Associations* 9, 102–36.

Rycroft, C. (1966) Introduction: causes and meaning. In P. Lomas, ed., *Psychoanalysis Observed*, 7–21. Harmondsworth: Penguin, 1968.

Rycroft, C. (1985) *Psychoanalysis and Beyond*. London: Chatto and Windus/Hogarth.

Sandler, J., ed. (1988) *Projection, Identification, Projective Identification*. London: Karnac.

Saunders, P. (1986) *Social Theory and the Urban Question*. London: Hutchinson (2nd edn).

Schafer, R. (1960) The loving and beloved superego in Freud's structural theory. *The Psychoanalytic Study of the Child* 15, 163–88.

Schneider, M. (1973) *Neurosis and Civilisation*. New York: Seabury Press, 1975.

Schoenwald, R. (1973) Training urban man: a hypothesis about the sanitary movement. In H. Dyos and M. Wolff, eds., *The Victorian City*, Vol. 2, 669–92. London: Routledge and Kegan Paul.

Sedgwick. P. (1982) *PsychoPolitics*. London: Pluto.

Segal, H. (1973) *Introduction to the Work of Melanie Klein*. London: Hogarth.

Sennett, R. (1970) *Uses of Disorder: Personal Identity and City Life*. London: Allen Lane, 1971.

Shakow, D. and Rapaport, D. (1964) *The Influence of Freud on American Psychology*. New York: International Universities Press (Psychological Issues Monograph 13).

Shepherd, M. (1985) *Sherlock Holmes and the Case of Dr Freud*. London: Tavistock.

Simmel, G. (1900) *The Philosophy of Money*. London: Routledge and Kegan Paul, 1978.

Simmel, G. (1903) The metropolis and mental life. In K. Wolff, ed., *The Sociology of Georg Simmel*, 409–24. Glencoe: Free Press, 1950.

Skurnik, L. and George, F. (1967) *Psychology for Everyman*. Harmondsworth: Penguin (2nd edn).

Spence, D. (1982) *Narrative Truth and Historical Truth*. New York: Norton.

Stevens, B. (1967) Curtain raiser. In C. Rogers and B. Stevens, *Person to Person: The Problem of Being Human*, 9–11. Lafayette, Ca.: Real People Press.

Stevens, R. (1983) *Freud and Psychoanalysis*. Milton Keynes: Open University Press.

Stone, N. (1983) *Europe Transformed 1878–1919*. London: Fontana.

Straker, G. (in press) Child-abuse counselling and apartheid: the work of the Sanctuary Counselling Team. *Free Associations*, forthcoming.

Symington, N. (1986) *The Analytic Experience*. London: Free Association Books.

Szasz, T. (1971) *The Manufacture of Madness*. St Albans: Paladin, 1973.

Taylor, A. *et al.* (1982) *Introducing Psychology*. Harmondsworth: Penguin (2nd edn).

Tebbit, N. (1988) *Upwardly Mobile*. London: Weidenfeld and Nicolson.

Temperley, J. (1984) Our own worst enemies: unconscious factors in female disadvantage. *Radical Science* 15 (*Free Associations* Pilot Issue), 23–38.

Trosman, H. (1969) The cryptomnesic fragment in the discovery of free association. In J. Gedo and G. Pollock, eds., *Freud: The Fusion of Science and Humanism*, 229–51. New York: International Universities Press (Psychological Issues Monograph 34/35).

Trosman, H. (1973) Freud's cultural background. In J. Gedo and G. Pollock, eds., *Freud: The Fusion of Science and Humanism*, 46–70. New York: International Universities Press (Psychological Issues Monograph 34/35).

Turkle, S. (1978) *Psychoanalytic Politics*. New York: Basic Books.

Waddell, M. *et al.* (1978) Marxism, psychoanalysis and feminism. *Radical Science Journal* 6/7, 107–17.

Wallen, R. (1957) Gestalt therapy and Gestalt psychology. In J. Fagan and I. Shepherd, eds., *Gestalt Therapy Now*, 8–13. New York: Harper and Row, 1971.

Weber, M. (1958) *The City*. London: Heinemann, 1960.

Weber, S. (1982) *The Legend of Freud*. Minneapolis: University of Minnesota Press.

Whitebook, J. (1985) Reason and happiness: some psychoanalytic themes in critical theory. In R. Bernstein, ed., *Habermas and Modernity*, 140–60. Cambridge: Polity Press.

Whyte, L. (1960) *The Unconscious before Freud*. London: Julian Friedmann, 1978.

Will, D. (1980) Psychoanalysis as a human science. *British Journal of Medical Psychology* 53, 201–11.

Will, D. (1986) Psychoanalysis and the new philosophy of science. *International Review of Psycho-Analysis* 13, 163–73.

Willer, D. and Willer, J. (1973) *Systematic Empiricism: Critique of a Pseudo-Science*. London: Prentice-Hall.

Williams, R. (1958) *The Long Revolution*. Harmondsworth: Penguin, 1965.

Williams, R. (1973) *The Country and the City*. London: Chatto and Windus.

Winnicott, D. (1950) Some thoughts on the meaning of the word 'democracy'. In *Home Is Where We Start From*, 239–59. Harmondsworth: Penguin, 1986.

Winnicott, D. (1964) *The Child, the Family and the Outside World*. Harmondsworth: Penguin.

Winnicott, D. (1971) *Playing and Reality*. London: Tavistock.

Witham, A. (1985) The idealisation of dying. *Free Associations* 3, 80–91.

Wittels, F. (1931) *Freud and His Time*. London: Peter Owen.

Wolfenstein, E. (1981) *The Victims of Democracy*. Berkeley: University of California Press.

Wollheim, R. (1975) The Good Self and the Bad Self: The moral psychology of British Idealism and the English school of psychoanalysis. *Proceedings of the British Academy* LXI, 373–98.

Wyss, D. (1966) *Depth Psychology: A Critical History*. London: Allen and Unwin.

Yelloly, M. (1980) *Social Work Theory and Psychoanalysis*. Wokingham: Van Nostrand Rheinhold.

Young, R. (1986) Freud: scientist and/or humanist? *Free Associations* 6, 7–35.

Young, R. (1987) Biography: the basic discipline for human science. *Free Associations* 11, 108–30.

Zanuso, B. (1986) *The Young Freud*. Oxford: Blackwell.

Zilboorg, G. (1952) Some sidelights on free association. *International Journal of Psycho-Analysis* 33, 489–95.

INDEX OF NAMES

SUBJECT INDEX

8184.